JOHN CORNFORTH

THE INSPIRATION OF THE PAST

COUNTRY HOUSE TASTE IN THE TWENTIETH CENTURY

WITH PHOTOGRAPHS BY
TIMOTHY BEDDOW

VIKING
in association with
COUNTRY LIFE

VIKING

Penguin Books Ltd, Harmondsworth, Middlesex, England
Viking Penguin Inc., 40 West 23rd Street, New York, New York 10010, U.S.A.
Penguin Books Australia Ltd, Ringwood, Victoria, Australia
Penguin Books Canada Ltd, 2801 John Street, Markham, Ontario, Canada
L3R 1B4
Penguin Books (N.Z.) Ltd, 182–190 Wairau Road, Auckland 10, New Zealand

First published 1985

Designed by Paul Bowden

Typeset and Printed in Great Britain by Butler & Tanner Ltd,
Frome and London

British Library Cataloguing in Publication Data
Cornforth, John
   The inspiration of the past: country house
   taste in the twentieth century.
   1. Interior decoration
   I. Title
   712'.6   SB472

ISBN 0-670-80180-1

CONTENTS

ACKNOWLEDGEMENTS

For a long time I have wanted to explore Romantic taste in the twentieth century and to show how private enthusiasms for old buildings link up with the preservation of country houses. Preparations for the exhibition of Treasures from English Country Houses, held in Washington in the autumn of 1985, provided a suitable opportunity. I also wished to attempt an analysis of John Fowler's contribution to English houses and his understanding of interiors before it was too late: inevitably much of his decoration had a short life, but he would have been saddened at the disappearance so soon of some of his most considered work. Perhaps it is a case of attempting to hit too many birds with one stone – and missing them all. If so, the misses are entirely mine.

For the first part of the book copies of *Country Life* have been invaluable, and indeed without the magazines, and without *Country Life*'s negatives, the book would have been impossible. In fact it is arguable that without the influence of *Country Life* some of those houses might never have existed in the form they appear here. I am grateful not only to my predecessors at *Country Life*, in particular H. Avray Tipping, Christopher Hussey and Arthur Oswald, who compiled a much more vivid record of their own day than I expect they realized, but also to Michael Wright, editor from 1973 to 1984, who agreed to a collaboration with Viking that made possible the inclusion of no fewer than 138 *Country Life* photographs. That was particularly important because the high reproduc-

tion fees now demanded led to the omission of a number of other significant illustrations.

As far as the second half of the book, which concentrates on John Fowler, is concerned, it has been a case of making a patchwork. I found no haul of documentary material, and so it has been a case of talking to and writing to a number of his old friends, colleagues and clients. The process of sewing the fragments together has been a laborious one, but it has also been exceedingly heartening, because of the warmth of the feeling for him that I have encountered, the affection and respect, the admiration and love, the sense of indebtedness and the delight in his company.

To all those who have helped me I am most grateful, but in particular Hardy Amies, Colin Anson, John Aspinall, Peter Atkins, Lady D'Avigdor Goldsmith, Mrs Michael Babington Smith, Nancy Lady Bagot, Christopher Beharrel, Sir Alfred Beit, Geoffrey de Bellaigue, Countess Bernstorff, Mrs D. C. Berry, Mrs Bilibin, Mrs David Bruce, Mario Buatta, Mary Duchess of Buccleuch and Queensberry, Major and Mrs J. W. Chandos-Pole, the Dowager Marchioness of Cholmondeley, Michael Colefax, Sir Terence Conran, the Duchess of Devonshire, Martin Drury, Mrs Eric Dugdale, Mr and Mrs James Dugdale, Stanley Falconer, Miss Yvonne Ffrench, Christopher Gibbs, Lady Glendevon, the Knight of Glin, St John Gore, the Hon. Desmond Guinness, Mrs Desmond Guinness, the Earl and Countess of Haddington, the Dowager Duchess of Hamilton and Brandon, Miss Elizabeth Hanley, Robert Harling,

Mrs Hayward, Colonel Roger Hesketh, David Hicks, Christopher Hobbs, Mrs Jean Hornak, Mrs Michael Hornby, Geoffrey Houghton Brown, Mrs Christopher Hussey, Peter Inskip, Keith Irvine, Gervase Jackson Stops, Philip Jebb, the Earl Jellicoe, Lady Kleinwort, Mrs C. G. Lancaster, James Lees-Milne, Stephen Long, Ian McCallum, Barry McIntyre, John Mason, Dr Mason, Mrs Paul Mellon, David Mlinaric, George Oakes, Miss Barbara Oakley, Mrs Alan Palmer, Mrs Henry Parish, Tom Parr, Michael Player, Mattei Radev, the Dowager Countess of Radnor, Lady Redgrave, Peter Reid, Anne Countess of Rosse, Anne Scott-James, Mrs Reginald Sheffield, Mrs Frank Stone, Paul Tanqueray, Miss Imogen Taylor, Richard Timewell, Michael Tree, Mrs P. A. Tritton, John Vickers, Christopher Wall, Merlin Waterson, John White, Michael White, Mrs Peggy Willis and the Earl of Wilton.

In many cases it was not just a matter of answering a letter but of writing more than one considered reply; a number of people devoted a great deal of time to talking about their connection with John Fowler, sometimes on more than one occasion; several people read sections of the draft, while others put up with my reading parts of it to them. Imogen Taylor kindly read the whole typescript.

Because of the informal nature of much of the material I decided against footnotes, and partly because of the number of *Country Life* references I have not included a bibliography. Most of the *Country Life* articles on houses can be checked though the cumulative index of those articles that is usually published once a year.

Sadly I have to record the death of Rupert Alec-Smith, whose feeling for the eighteenth century had always been a pleasure to his friends. The short section about him is based on conversations with him on a visit to Winestead a few months before he died. The other sadness has been the ill health of Nancy Lancaster. I came to know her only after John Fowler's death, but since 1977 I have had the chance to talk to her about her own interest in houses and her partnership with John; and I read her quite a lot of the draft, and while, characteristically, she said she did not wish to be mentioned in the book, Mrs Hills, who has been far more than her secretary for years, seemed to nod approval at the bits describing the world that was familiar to her.

Almost all the new photography for the book has been done by Timothy Beddow. The business of getting so many illustrations together is very time-consuming, but Susan Rose-Smith at Penguin Books did a great deal of the chasing, and Lisa Markwell at *Country Life* had the laborious task of finding the negatives and having them printed up. However, it has needed the eye of Paul Bowden to create coherence and, in my view, elegance of design out of chaos in a cardboard box.

INTRODUCTION

When in forty years' time it becomes possible to look
at the history of the country house in the twentieth
century and see it in a perspective of the previous four
centuries, it will surely seem a surprising one. Concern
for preservation and interest in decoration will both
appear as strong threads, but by then the element of
decoration will be particularly difficult to judge,
because so little will survive in good condition. So this
book attempts to do two things. First, it takes a look
at the changing enthusiasms for old country houses, as
opposed to new ones, since the early days of this century and attempts to show how out of private concerns
for repair, restoration and furnishing of castles and
manor houses and the rediscovery of the eighteenth
century have grown concepts of country house preservation. Thus this book is about people as well as
places; and links between people. But it makes no
claim to be exhaustive or comprehensive.

Second, it looks at the work of John Fowler, doyen
of English decorators for twenty-five years after the
Second World War. Again no attempt is made to list
all the places he worked in; rather it sets out to try to
explain his approach to country house decoration and
preservation and to show how that approach developed, how it slotted into the needs of a time and
why his influence has spread across the Atlantic.

The result is not a detached view, because the idea
of the book has grown partly out of my work at *Country Life* for over twenty years and becoming interested
in the world of Christopher Hussey, who had started
there forty years before I did; and partly through
knowing John Fowler in the last ten years of his life
and trying to set down his historical knowledge. I have
tried to suggest how certain enthusiasms have fitted
together in this century and influenced the way we
now look at country houses and traditional decoration.

CHAPTER ONE

DECORATION AND THE RISE OF MIDDLE-CLASS TASTE

For centuries there has been a streak in the English creative character that has been backward-looking, and it has been a remarkably fruitful one, particularly as regards the country house. It is strong in the Elizabethan and Jacobean period in the fantastic, still consciously Gothic silhouettes of houses like Burghley and in the concepts of castles like Bolsover and Lulworth, intended as revivals of the age of chivalry. A little later in the seventeenth century it is present in the churches and collegiate buildings associated with Archbishop Laud and his supporters, which fuse together classical and Gothic forms to proclaim the antiquity and continuity of the English Catholic Church; and later in the century it is to be found in the steeples of Wren's London churches. Certain country houses of the Wren period display it too, in the way their owners retained the idea of the medieval great hall, installing fittings and ornaments with medieval allusions, as at Hampton Court, Lyme Park and Canons Ashby, and hanging on their walls portraits of imaginary ancestors, as at Boughton and Drayton.

Vanbrugh was well aware of the 'castle air' that he introduced at Blenheim and Grimsthorpe as well as in his own house at Greenwich; and he anticipated the Palladian taste for large houses with a central block and four corner pavilions that could strike contemporary visitors as being built 'castle-wise'. Thus the gothick revivals of William Kent and Horace Walpole are not bolts from the blue. Then, as the movement entered the nineteenth century, it gathered pace: the leaders of aristocratic taste rediscovered the *ancien régime* as well as the world of abbeys and castles, and on occasion combined them, as at Belvoir. At the same time the gentry rediscovered the manor houses of Old England, restored them, refurnished them and recreated them. At Charlecote, for instance, antiquarianism was combined with contemporary design and the Elizabethan Revival with the eclecticism of William Beckford.

Recently the Victorian and Edwardian periods have been returning to favour, and there is a growing literature on the second Old English Revival of Norman Shaw and Nesfield, the Queen Anne Revival and the start of the Georgian Revival. Naturally the emphasis has been on new buildings, on their plans and elevations and their social background, but so far, except for some of the houses like St Fagan's Castle, near Cardiff, and Stanway in Gloucestershire, associated with The Souls, a circle of brilliant men and women with aesthetic interests and romantic inclinations who came together round A. J. Balfour and Lord Curzon in the mid-1880s, little has been written on other aspects of the last hundred years, on restorations and alterations, on decorating and collecting, on the influence of artists' houses, and the connections between the development of contemporary architecture, the changing interest in historic architecture and the growth of enthusiasm for preservation.

The Edwardian period was one when money was plentiful, building was cheap, people had confidence, and there was a ready supply of servants – it is surely no accident that the female domestic population reached its peak of half a million in 1911 – so there was a great deal of activity in the country house field, not only rebuilding or extending existing large houses but building from scratch on a considerable scale, as Clive Aslet has shown in *The Last Country Houses*. Also much of interest was being done in the field of the middling house. Indeed so active was the latter that for many years *Country Life* ran a successful regular series of articles called The Lesser Country House, mostly devoted to new houses but also covering alterations and restorations of old ones. Thus there is a massive amount of material to digest before it will be possible to work out how mid-twentieth-century attitudes and fashions have developed out of late-nineteenth- and early-twentieth-century Romanticism.

Interior decoration has played a significant role in this development, because, while its roots go back to the collaboration of architects and upholsterers in the late seventeenth and eighteenth centuries, it is a phenomenon of the present century, reflecting a different kind of time-scale from that of the eighteenth century. It is based on the acceptance of the situation in which a family rarely lives in a house for even one complete generation, and at the same time it is a response to all the uncertainties and longings that come from change, while reflecting the need for change because of the over-use of visual ideas. Moreover it has been closely related to the growth of American influence, and also of its own acceptability and that of antique dealing as occupations for artistic and educated people.

The history of restoration also needs to be considered both for its own sake and in its relation to the history of preservation. Although William Morris might not like the idea, the preservation movement has been an essentially middle-class one, and that is of significance in the growth of the National Trust. The Trust has achieved an effective alliance between owners of country houses, most of whom have inherited their property, and people of different backgrounds and enthusiasms prepared to work for the preservation of landscape, buildings and works of art; and together they have won widespread public support for their aims as well as the goodwill of government. Like so many English institutions the Trust has sought aristocratic support, but it has done so in a way that calls for an unusual degree of active work. Indeed it is interesting to find that as long ago as 1932, before the Trust's Country Houses Scheme got going, R.C. Norman, who was a banker, declined an invitation to become the chairman, because he foresaw the day when large estates might be given to the Trust and thought that the chairman should be a great landowner in touch with the potential donors of such estates. Indeed the Trust is a most interesting response to social change and a uniquely British success story based on empiricism and compromise as well as imagination – and a dash of eccentricity.

The history of country house enthusiasm in this country is a long one, going back well before the days of Celia Fiennes, and during the last century it has increased both in breadth and in depth. So perhaps not surprisingly it has had a marked influence on taste: in the last twenty-five to thirty years the so-called 'country house style' has developed from being one fashionable among a small circle of people to a popular one in decoration. In fact the enthusiasm for country houses and the general application of country house style to a variety of buildings have advanced almost hand in hand.

However, the combination of decoration and the pull of the past is not a purely British phenomenon, as can be seen from the three quotations that follow. They set the scene for much that was to happen.

The first is from Edmond de Goncourt:

I have often said to myself that if I were not a man of letters, if I had not got money, my chosen profession would have been to invent interiors for rich people. I should have loved being allowed to have my own way by some banker who would have given me carte blanche to work out the decor and furniture of a palace with just four bare walls, using what I could find from dealers, artists, modern industry, and in my own head.

The second is from Henry James, writing in 1873:

It was not specially for the pictures that I went to the Corsini Palace, however; and certainly not for the pictures that I stayed. I was under the same spell as the inveterate companion with whom I walked the other day through the beautiful apartments of the Pitti Palace and who said: '. . . I prefer a good "interior" to a good landscape. The impression has a greater intensity – the thing itself a more complex animation. I find I like fine old rooms that have been occupied in a fine old way . . .'

The third is from J.M. Whistler, in a letter to Théodore Duret written in 1885:

For you know that I attach just as much importance to my interior decorations as to my paintings.

These quotations exemplify the artistic approach to interiors that has been the inspiration for much of the decoration done in the past hundred years. None of them is directly concerned with the requirements of middle-class people, and yet their needs and tastes have been of crucial importance in the development of the trade of decoration as we see it today. In 1879 Rhoda and Agnes Garrett, the first two lady decorators in England, or at least two of the first, wrote *Suggestions for House Decoration in Painting, Woodwork and Furniture*; and it was so successful that it ran into six editions in that year. In it they said quite bluntly:

It is middle class people specially who require the aid of a cultivated and yet not extravagant decorator who may help them to blend the fittings of their now incongruous rooms into pleasant and harmonious habitations.

Lord Carlisle, a talented painter who went to Philip Webb to design his house, 1 Palace Green, Kensington, in 1867, would have agreed with them. Walter Crane, in *An Artist's Reminiscences*, wrote of Lord Carlisle, who was a friend and patron of his, bringing Henry James to see them at Beaumont Lodge in the 1870s; of James admiring English houses; and of Mr Howard, as he then was (he succeeded as 9th Earl in 1889), saying that 'he must not suppose that they were all like ours, or that artistic feeling was by any means the rule of English interiors'.

Quite suddenly in the 1870s, some twenty years before Edith Wharton and Ogden Codman's book *The Decoration of Houses*, which they claimed to be the first book on decoration as part of architecture in America, there was in England a burst of books and new magazines with articles on decoration. The titles in the series of which the Garretts' book was a part give a good idea of their character: *A Place for Art in the House* by W. J. Loftie; *The Drawing Room* by Mrs Orrinsmith; *The Dining Room* by Mrs Loftie. Mrs Haweis, the author of *Beautiful Houses* (1882), was the wife of an author and preacher (they lived in Rossetti's house in Cheyne Walk). In the 1880s J. Moyr Smith edited a magazine called *Decoration*. Most of these books and magazines do not even get a mention in footnotes now, and only Eastlake's *Hints on Household Taste* (1868) and J. J. Stevenson's *House Architecture* (1880) are still remembered.

Almost all these publications promoted the Queen Anne style, which, as Mark Girouard has shown in *Sweetness and Light*, was the first middle-class style. In that book he traced its development and the many uses to which it was put in the last three decades of the nineteenth century. There are three aspects of it that are particularly significant for twentieth-century taste: it was not only middle-class, it was eclectic and it was romantic. In the advertisement for their book the Garretts wrote:

The so-called 'Queen Anne' style, is rather a selection and refinement of the beauties in form and colour of other styles than anything clearly distinct. At the same time, it is necessary to point out that its affinities are rather classical than Gothic though it may be said to connect the two extremes of the Tudor and the Georgian periods, it sympathizes more with Wren than Wolsey, and with Inigo Jones than with John of Padua.

It drew what it wanted from the past and whatever corner of the world suited it, and the aim was to create a comfortable and harmonious whole that was at the same time stimulating and evocative. As J. J. Stevenson wrote: 'State and grandeur have become irksome to us, and are even despised, no doubt because so frequently they are the sign of power which has departed ... comfort and convenience are all that are insisted on ...'

The literature of the time concentrates on smaller houses and on town houses, and so it is particularly fortunate that an early, artistic, expression of that kind still survives in London and has been carefully preserved – 18 Stafford Terrace, Kensington. It was first occupied in 1874, the year he married, by Edward Linley Sambourne, an artist who had been contributing to *Punch* since 1867 and was a friend of Walter Crane, Luke Fildes, Charles Keene and Kate Greenaway.

If the Garretts emphasized middle-class needs, J. Moyr Smith in *Ornamental Interiors, Ancient and Modern* (1887) noted that 'While the new style received ample support from the rich middle classes, the aristocracy, with few exceptions, held themselves aloof, and gave but slight encouragement to the modern style of design.' By the late 1880s landed families were feeling the effect of the agricultural slump and the drop in rental income, but that was not the only reason. More important were the psychological effects of the two Reform Acts of 1832 and 1868, in which the aristocracy and the landed gentry accepted the passing of their political control. It was a gradual and peaceful process, and, of course, individual members of old families have continued to play an active role in national affairs, but it is significant that the great Duke of Wellington was the last duke to be Prime Minister, in 1834, and the 3rd Marquess of Salisbury was the last Prime Minister to sit in the House of

1. 18 STAFFORD TERRACE, KENSINGTON, LONDON. THE DRAWING ROOM. Linley
Sambourne, an artist and illustrator, took the house when he married in 1874. After his death its
eclectic artistic interiors were carefully preserved by his daughter, Mrs Leonard Messel, who was
largely responsible for the remodelling of Nymans [36–38] in the 1920s. It was here that her daughter,
Lady Rosse, founded the Victorian Society in 1958. The house now belongs to the GLC and is opened
to the public by the Victorian Society.

Lords, in 1902. In 1861 Matthew Arnold could write: 'The aristocracy still administers public affairs;' but after the Second Reform Act the old aristocratic families started to retreat from their great London houses, starting with the demolition of Northumberland House in 1874.

Political retirement was paralleled by aesthetic retirement. No longer were the aristocracy the key patrons and leaders of taste as they had been in the eighteenth century and early nineteenth century. That was noted at the time by, among others, Tom Taylor, who as early as 1860 wrote:

The nobleman is no longer the chief purchaser of pictures. It is mainly to our great manufacturing and trading towns that the painter has to look for the sale of his works. The class enriched by manufactures and commerce is now doing for art in England what the same class did in earlier times in Florence, Geneva, and Venice, for the art of Italy ...

The process of aesthetic withdrawal is harder to plot than that of political withdrawal, but it is doubly significant in that it developed into a cult of philistinism and of indifference, even hostility, to aesthetic matters. An interest in architecture, pictures or furniture was regarded as doubly suspect, as being both common and soft. In *The English Gentleman* (1982) Philip Mason has written of the Victorian gentleman:

As to being a poet, that was distinctly to be deprecated ... It was quite the thing to be philistine. To be a scholar and a gentleman was a matter for praise, though sometimes remarked on with a note of slight surprise, but on the whole the change is in the direction hostile to the intellect and the arts. It is a swing to the country and away from the court. The emphasis is now on character, on avoiding excess, or doing the right thing naturally.

It would be fascinating to know more about when and why this defensive attitude developed and how closely it was tied up with the development of public schools and the cult of athleticism, but in the long term its importance lies in the reaction it stimulated in the twentieth century.

Few people have commented on that reaction, but in *Another Self* (1970) James Lees-Milne wrote of his father (who in fact loved half-timbered buildings and was a good gardener):

Art ... was anathema to him. The very word had on him the effect of a red rag upon a bull. He turned puce in the face and fumed at the mere mention of it; and his deadliest, most offensive adjective was 'artistic'. It denoted decadence, disloyalty to the Crown, and unnatural vice.

That is particularly significant, because James Lees-Milne became the first Historic Buildings Secretary of the National Trust in 1936 and also he was one of the founder members of the Georgian Group in 1937; and, as with several of his contemporaries involved with the Trust and the Group, his own reaction against Edwardian philistinism has been a driving force all his life.

If aristocratic dominance was declining, there was the new element of American influence, but that too is still scarcely realized, because there had been no detailed study of social and cultural links between America and England from 1850 onwards. But it was recognized by some contemporaries. Mrs Haweis, for instance, wrote in *Beautiful Houses* of G.H. Boughton, an Anglo-American painter who lived on Campden Hill in London in a house designed for him by Norman Shaw and who was a friend of Whistler and Walter Crane:

he has brought from America a certain elegance of style in living which has not yet become common on this side of the Atlantic: less posé than French taste, more subtle than English. The prevailing impression of the house is softness, refinement, harmony. There is nothing *bizarre* or eccentric, to startle and not seldom annoy.

American influence is complicated, because the part played by money is recognized, but the cultural background is usually ignored. Yet American attitudes to the American past are significant, and, although in the late nineteenth and early twentieth century they were almost all East Coast attitudes, there are distinctions to be made between those in New England, the mid-Atlantic states and the South. In the Southern state of Virginia, for instance, there was an essentially aristocratic attitude to land and houses and a social hierarchy that had much in common with that found in England; and defeat in the Civil War led to economic decline afterwards. The world of Henry James, on the other hand, was essentially a New England world, and so was that of the Colonial Revival. National self-consciousness after the Civil War was combined with a renewed sense of American values and traditions, and both were heightened by the run up to the Centennial celebrations of 1876; all three contributed to the success of the Colonial Revival in new architecture and a greater awareness of the Colonial legacy in old buildings, and furniture and the decorative arts.

The now familiar pattern of Americans living in England first becomes apparent about 1850 with William Wetmore Storey, who arrived in London that year, as Henry James explained: 'He dines with the then little American world of London, and lays the foundation of the friendship that was to be the most valued of his life and to constitute for him, in after years, a close tie with London, with England.' Whistler first came to England in 1857, showing at the Royal Academy three years later; he took his first house in Chelsea in 1863 and built his famous White House in Tite Street in 1878. Earlier, he had helped others with their houses, perhaps the first being W.C. Alexander, a banker and connoisseur, who bought Aubrey House in Kensington in 1873. Alexander, who was born in 1840, was one of the first Victorian collectors to be interested in Chinese and Japanese art and also probably one of the first to appreciate eighteenth-century furniture. Whistler, who painted his daughter, Cicely, helped him with the colours at Aubrey House.

Henry James, who met Morris, Rossetti, Burne-Jones and Ruskin on his first visit to England in 1869, came to live in England in 1876, settling in Bolton Street off Piccadilly. He responded to country houses early on: as Leon Edel has written, he found a mellow and ancient feeling in the country and above all its houses – Montacute, Barrington, Forde and others. Henry James himself wrote: 'These delicious old houses, in the long August days, in the South of England air, on the soil over which so much has passed and out of which so much has come, rose before me like a series of visions'.

It is not clear who was the first American to buy a large English country house. Was it W.W. Astor, who acquired Cliveden in 1893?

By then a number of English men had married American wives. Among the early ones who we know had an interest in houses and decoration were the Jerome sisters, Lady Randolph Churchill and Mrs Moreton Frewen. In *Left Hand, Right Hand* Sir Osbert Sitwell described 25 Chesham Place, London, which his parents rented from Mrs Frewen in 1900:

It was 'done-up' in the height of the fashion of the moment, for interior decoration had only just started as a mode and on its present professional basis, and Lady Randolph had been almost the first person to interest herself in it and may perhaps have had a hand in these colour schemes. Before 1900, the aesthetes alone had shown an interest in the rooms in which they beautifully existed ...

Gardening, too, played a part in the Anglo-American story, and here Lawrence Johnston and his garden at Hidcote in Gloucestershire come to mind. The son

of American parents, he was born in Paris but largely educated in England; and after he came down from Cambridge, he became naturalized in 1900. His mother bought him Hidcote in 1907, and he immediately started on the garden.

It is perhaps no accident that those who have written about late-nineteenth- and early-twentieth-century architecture have been less interested in interiors and their treatment, because it is the interiors of most new houses and their furnishings that let them down. At Standen, for instance, an interesting and sympathetic house in Sussex built in the 1890s by Philip Webb that retains all its original contents, the furniture is ordinary reproduction of eighteenth-century forms. Most late-nineteenth- and early-twentieth-century plasterwork is oddly insensitive, with fat, flabby mouldings and lifeless cast ornament, whether inspired by Wren or by Adam. (Only in Scotland did Lorimer succeed in getting plasterwork of real vitality carried out in his houses.) Lutyens's Wrennaissance plaster ornament never comes alive, and, while his forecourts, halls and corridors are exciting spaces, constantly inventive in their exploration of levels, textures and light, his formal, classical reception rooms often seem lifeless, almost as if he had lost interest in them.

The dullness of new rooms must have encouraged people of sensibility to look for old furniture for them, and it is striking that the growing enthusiasm for simple old furniture went hand in hand with a simplification of the treatment of interiors. That is particularly apparent in the early Lutyens country houses like Munstead Wood in Surrey and the Deanery Garden at Sonning in Berkshire [2], which Gertrude Jekyll and Edward Hudson furnished in a romantic way with old country furniture, oak, often unpolished, and some walnut but almost no mahogany, and with generous use of pewter and brass. They were not the first to like that kind of thing, but Charles Latham's poetic photographs of the Deanery Garden published in *Country Life* in 1903 must have made more people aware of it.

It was a taste that probably started among artists some twenty-five years earlier, and William Morris may well have been responsible for it. He discovered Kelmscott in Oxfordshire [3] in 1871 and held it on a lease until his widow bought the freehold in 1913, the year before her death; their daughter, May, lived on there until her death in 1938. Certainly the taste was well established by the 1890s, as can be seen at Mathern Palace in Monmouthshire [4–6], which H. Avray Tipping acquired in 1894, about ten years

2 (above left). THE DEANERY GARDEN, SONNING, BERKSHIRE. THE HALL FIREPLACE. The house, built in 1899–1902, was the first commission Edwin Lutyens received from Edward Hudson, the founder of *Country Life* and one of his most fervent supporters. The carefully composed photograph by Charles Latham was illustrated in his first volume of *In English Homes*, edited by H. Avray Tipping and published in 1904.

3 (below left). KELMSCOTT MANOR, OXFORDSHIRE. THE GREEN ROOM. William Morris leased the house from 1871, and the photograph shows the room as it was in 1921, when the house was the home of his daughter, May. The walls were hung with his 'Kennet' chintz.

4 (above). MATHERN PALACE, MONMOUTHSHIRE. THE EAST FRONT BEFORE RESTORATION. A medieval house, formerly a residence of the Bishops of Llandaff, it was rescued by H. Avray Tipping in 1894 and remained his home until 1910.

5 (right). H. AVRAY TIPPING PHOTOGRAPHED AT MATHERN IN ABOUT 1910.

6. THE OAK PARLOUR AT MATHERN. The room, formed in 1898, was photographed for Tipping's article on the house in *Country Life* in 1910.

before he became a regular contributor to *Country Life* and collaborated with Charles Latham. Born in 1856, he read history at Oxford and for a time was on the staff of *The Dictionary of National Biography*, but, as Richard Haslam explained in *Country Life* in 1979, it was his love of plants that led to the laying-out of gardens 'and gardens led to houses', to restoring them and writing about them. Through his articles, which are signed from 1907, and his books, he must have had a considerable influence on the enthusiasm not only of his contemporaries but of the next generation.

The simplification that is apparent in those rooms seems to have developed on both sides of the Atlantic at about the same time. Edith Wharton, who wrote *The Decoration of Houses* with Ogden Codman in 1897, first met her collaborator when he helped her over the house that she and her husband had taken at Newport, Rhode Island, in 1893. Apparently she had already discovered eighteenth-century Venetian furniture on trips to Italy made after her marriage in 1885, and in *A Backward Glance* she described what she did at Newport: the exterior of the house was incurably ugly, but

within doors there were interesting possibilities. My husband talked them over with a clever Boston architect, Ogden Codman, and we asked him to alter and decorate the house – a somewhat new departure, since the architects of that day looked down on house-decoration as a branch of dress-making, and left the field to the upholsterers, who crammed every room with curtains, lambrequins, jardinieres of artificial plants, nobbly velvet covered tables littered with silver gew-gaws – and festoons of lace on mantelpieces and dressing tables.

Codman shared my dislike of these sumptuary excesses, and thought as I did that interior decoration should be simple and architectural; and finding that we have the same views we drifted, I hardly know how, toward the notion of putting them into a book.

No one seems to have written about the matter so clearly in England, and so one has to rely on descriptions of rooms in novels. There is a particularly graphic one in Vita Sackville-West's *The Edwardians* (1930) that has a ring of acute observation about it:

The very rooms in which they [Lord Roehampton's sisters] dwelt differed from Silvia's rooms or the rooms of her

friends. There, a certain fashion of expensive simplicity was beginning to make itself felt; a certain taste was arising, which tended to eliminate unnecessary objects. Here, the overcrowded rooms preserved the unhappy confusion of an earlier day. Little silver models of carriages and sedan chairs, silver vinaigrettes, and diminutive silver fans, tiny baskets in silver filigree, littered the table under the presiding rotundity of the lampshade ... Palms stood in the corner of the room, and among the branches of the palms nestled family photographs, unframed but mounted upon a cardboard of imperishable stiffness ...

Yes, certainly the room was overcrowded. There were too many chairs, too many hassocks, too many small tables, too much pampas grass in crane necked vases, too many blinds and curtains looped and festooned about the windows. The whole effect was fusty, musty, and dusty. It needed destruction, it needed air ...

It is fascinating to compare that picture with Sir Osbert Sitwell's description in *Great Morning* of Mrs George Keppel's house, 16 Grosvenor Street, where she lived from 1912 to 1924:

surely one of the most remarkable houses in London. Its high façade, dignified and unpretentious as only that of a London Georgian mansion can be, very effectively disguised its immense size. Within existed an unusual air of spaciousness and light, an atmosphere of luxury, for Mrs Keppel possessed an instinct for splendour, and not only were the rooms beautiful, with their grey walls, red lacquer cabinets, English eighteenth-century portraits of people in red coats, huge porcelain pagodas, and thick, magnificent carpets, but the hostess conducted the running of her house as a work of art in itself.

Photographs seldom record that atmosphere, and, alas, there are all too few good paintings of interiors at that period. But one that captures the spirit very well is Orpen's picture of the young Sir Philip Sassoon and his sister, Sybil, in the drawing room of 25 Park Lane [colour plate 1], painted in 1912. The house had belonged to their parents, who had installed the French *boiserie*, but the choice and arrangement of the objects was Sir Philip's and the sense of space around each one seems to look forward not only to his rooms at Trent Park in Hertfordshire, which he had designed in an eighteenth-century style in the mid-1920s, but to so many aspects of English taste during the course of the next half century.

CHAPTER TWO

THE CULT
OF THE CASTLE AND
THE MANOR HOUSE

Edwardian classicism has a marked tendency to coarseness and even vulgarity. It was a confident, even over-confident style, whether drawing its inspiration from Renaissance Italy, Versailles, or eighteenth-century England, and it reflected the mood of imperial success. But it was not the only one for new building in the years round about 1900. There was also, of course, the vernacular style, of which Lutyens was the master. However, there was yet another alternative open to those who had an urge to build and make a garden: the restoration of an old house, preferably a manor house or castle that had come down in the world. As Mark Girouard has written in *The Return to Camelot* of the circle of The Souls: 'To build a new castle was by now considered hopelessly inept; yet something was needed, with a special quality to take it out of the ordinary into the world of romance.'

Early in the new century the romantic ruin of Kirby Hall in Northamptonshire was advertised in *Country Life* as being available for restoration. When Martin Conway wanted such a house in 1905, he advertised in *The Times* on 15 May: 'Wanted to purchase, old manor-house or abbey, built in the sixteenth century or earlier, with old garden, not much land, no sporting facilities, preferably five miles or more from a railway station.' That was how he found Allington Castle near Maidstone in Kent [7]. There were a considerable number of people who felt like him, and so many castles and manor houses were restored between about 1890 and 1930 that they form a distinct group in the

history of the country house. Indeed many of the people knew each other. Philip Tilden, the architect, wrote of Martin Conway's reconstruction of Allington: 'A veritable infection of reinstatement seemed to have spread throughout the land and to have attacked such people as Lord Curzon, Claude Lowther and other wealthy connoisseurs and owners.'

The English castles that were restored to live in include Allington, Hever, Leeds, Lympne and Saltwood in Kent, Herstmonceux in Sussex [8, 9], begun by Claude Lowther in 1913 and continued after 1933 by Sir Paul Latham, and Lindisfarne in Northumberland [10], restored by Edward Hudson, the owner of *Country Life*, with the aid of Lutyens. Unlike these people, Lord Curzon preserved Bodiam and Tattershall Castles as ancient monuments, and when he died he left them to the National Trust. There were other restorations in Scotland and Wales. On the whole their owners were fairly free in the way that they approached their task. To quote Martin Conway again:

We set at naught the theories of the so-called antiscrape school [of William Morris]. According to them we ought never to have replaced old work by new of the same design. Our renovations and repairs ought to have been obviously modern and of to-day. My principle was that I must retain every existing old feature, but that I was then free to do what I liked, with a view not to an attempted re-creation of what had disappeared, but to the one controlling purpose of making a beautiful thing of the whole. Just as the Wyatts, in

7. ALLINGTON CASTLE, KENT, IN 1928. Acquired by Martin Conway in 1905, the castle was repaired and embellished over the next twenty years. At the end of his life, Conway married as his second wife the owner of Saltwood Castle in Kent, where he continued her first husband's programme of restoration.

10. LINDISFARNE CASTLE, NORTHUMBERLAND. THE SHIP ROOM. Having been discovered in an abandoned state by Edward Hudson, the castle was given its present form in 1903 by Edwin Lutyens, his first essay in a castle style.

8 (above left). HERSTMONCEUX CASTLE, SUSSEX, BEFORE RESTORATION. Work was begun in 1913 by Colonel Claude Lowther and was first described in *Country Life* by Martin Conway in 1918. The operation was finished only in 1935 by Sir Paul Latham, who had acquired it in 1933.

9 (below left). THE CASTLE IN 1935; THE DREAM REALIZED. The repair of the fabric and the refilling of the moat was completed that year.

the time of Henry VIII, had done just what they pleased to bring the old house into habitable and beautiful harmony, so could we act in our day and generation.

Among the many manor houses restored are Ightam Mote and Sissinghurst in Kent; Parham and Great Dixter in Sussex; Ockwells in Berkshire; Kelmscott and Beckley in Oxfordshire; Avebury, Great Chalfield, Hazelbury, Westwood and Woodlands in Wiltshire; Cold Ashton and Owlpen in Gloucestershire; Chantmarle, Cothay and Lytes Cary in Somerset; Athelhampton and Sandford Orcas in Dorset; Dartington in Devon; and Penheale in Cornwall. None of these were old family houses, though an exception is the restoration of Haddon Hall in Derbyshire [11] by the Marquess of Granby, later 9th Duke of Rutland.

If here they appear as just a list of houses, there are many connections between the people involved, some of which will become apparent in the course of this and the next chapter. Violet, Duchess of Rutland, the wife of the 8th Duke and the mother of the restorer of Haddon, was the sister of Colonel Harry Lindsay, an amateur house enthusiast, who restored Sutton Courtenay [12, 13]; his wife, Norah, was one of the leading gardening figures of her day and the friend of seemingly all the country house enthusiasts of her generation and the next, including Lawrence Johnston, Colonel R. A. Cooper, Sir Philip Sassoon, Lord Gerald Wellesley, later 7th Duke of Wellington, and the Ronald Trees. Norah Lindsay, in Philip Tilden's view, 'was one of the most instructive gardeners of this generation'; 'if she had written one-tenth as amusingly as she talked, she would have become a best-seller'; and, as Alvilde Lees-Milne has written, 'she was gay, witty, amusing, and indeed wonderfully stimulating'.

One of the Duchess's daughters, Marjorie, married the 6th Marquess of Anglesey, and Colonel Lindsay was involved in the restoration of Beaudesert [78, 79], the Angleseys' house in Staffordshire. Later, in the mid-1930s, Lord Anglesey did a great deal of work on Plas Newydd in Anglesey [80-83]; and Lady Anglesey was a close friend of Lady Colefax, who was also a close friend of Colonel Cooper.

There was also what might be seen as an ex-Foreign Office circle. It included not only Colonel Cooper and Harold Nicolson, who had been at school together, and Lord Gerald Wellesley, but E.G. Lister, who restored Westwood Manor; G.J. Kidstone, who acquired Hazelbury Manor in 1919; and Sir Louis Mallet, a friend of Colonel Cooper and Sir Philip Sassoon and someone whose taste may well have influenced both of them. It was a close-knit world with a great many cross-threads.

Sir Louis Mallet (1864-1936), who had been ambassador at Constantinople in 1913-14, comes to life in the memoirs of Philip Tilden (*True Remembrances*, 1954): he describes 'the red letter day' when he first met Sir Louis at Allington, 'for I was to learn of the beautiful things of this life more than I can ever acknowledge from Sir Louis, who was a man of rare taste and genius'. Of his house, Wardes in Kent [14, 15], Tilden wrote: 'That little house at Otham was probably the most perfectly chosen and arranged set of objects, circumstances and materials that England had to show. Again, there was no millionaire's purse, but only flair for collection and a perfect sense of cumulative effect, colour, form.'

Fortunately the house was illustrated in *Country Life* on 30 August 1919, soon after Sir Louis had sold it, but it seems as if the photographs show it as he had it. The author of the article confirms everything that Philip Tilden says about it: he refers to 'the seeing eye' of Sir Louis, who before the war had 'detected amid the ruin and squalor [of an L-shaped group of cottages] the possibility of restoring an exceptionally fine old timber house to something like its pristine beauty'. In the work of restoration of the late-fourteenth-century house Sir Louis was assisted by his brother Stephen, 'who may be said to have left a monument of his admirable taste and skill in handicrafts in the oak doors and their ironwork, cunningly contrived by him'; and the additions were designed by Hubert Benstead. Among Sir Louis's friends was Lady Juliet Duff, the only daughter of the 4th Earl of Lonsdale and the widow of Sir Robert Duff, who had been killed in 1914: in June 1919, she married Major Keith Trevor, and it was as Lady Juliet Trevor that she is described as the owner of the house in the article. It seems that she bought a good deal of the furniture with the house, and so it is a fascinating illustration of the development of twentieth-century taste to imagine her at Wardes about 1920 and then from 1933 at Bulbridge House at Wilton, a Georgian house to be illustrated in the next chapter [76, 77].

R. Furneaux Jordan described the new houses of the 1890s and early 1900s as 'dream houses', and so provided Roderick Gradidge with the title of his book subtitled *The Edwardian Ideal*; but really it is a phrase that suits the restoration of manor houses even better, because the best ones were remarkable visions of the past and complete works of art, with a consistency of approach to repair and alteration of fabric, to the

1. THE DRAWING ROOM AT 25 PARK LANE, LONDON, BY SIR WILLIAM ORPEN, 1912. Sir Philip Sassoon is painted with his sister, Sybil, now Dowager Marchioness of Cholmondeley.

II. LYTES CARY, SOMERSET.
THE GREAT PARLOUR. When Sir
Walter Jenner found the house in
1907, this room was in use as a farm
store and the panelling and
chimneypiece had been painted over.
Like many houses furnished at that
time, it is strong in textiles and
needlework.

III. THE GREAT CHAMBER AT
LYTES CARY. The unity and
mellowness of tone, with soft faded
colours, was characteristic of the
taste of the Jenners and their
contemporaries who restored old
houses.

IV. JULIANS, HERTFORDSHIRE. THE ENTRANCE HALL IN 1938. In about 1937 Colonel Cooper moved from the West Country to this eighteenth-century house, but his instinct was to set it back in time, as can be seen in Christopher Hussey's watercolour.

V. KNIGHTSTONE, DEVON. THE SCREENS PASSAGE IN 1942. Christopher Hussey's watercolour is of Colonel Cooper's fourth and final house, to which he had moved the previous year.

VI. PARHAM PARK, SUSSEX. THE LONG GALLERY. One of the last contributions made to the restoration of the house by Mr and Mrs Clive Pearson was to commission Oliver Messel in the late 1950s and early 1960s to replace the decayed nineteenth-century ceiling with the present one in five sections and to design the painted decoration of trailing foliage.

VII. THE WEST ROOM AT PARHAM. As part of the preparation for the opening of the house after the Second World War, Clive Pearson hung groups of portraits, of seventeenth-century Bysschops, who had owned the house, and of contemporary Derings, who were connections of the Bysschops and ancestors of Mrs Pearson. They are placed over earlier *point d'hongrie* hangings from Quenby Hall, which they had bought before they came to Parham in 1922.

VIII. LEEDS CASTLE, KENT.
THE DINING ROOM. This was
designed in about 1936 for Lady
Baillie by Boudin as a French
interpretation of a Georgian room,
but the finishing touches were added
only after the Second World War.
The chairs were made by Jansen with
covers of antique leather painted
white, giving the room a Hollywood
air; but then Boudin did not take
English styles seriously.

IX. LADY BAILLIE'S BEDROOM
AT LEEDS. Boudin was brilliant at
getting boiserie to look old and
employed skilled French painters.
Here the woodwork was probably
first worked over with a steel brush
to bring out the grain and then
painted in a series of thin glazes
before the final coat of dry colour
was rubbed into the boiserie and
waxed.

X. LUTTRELLSTOWN CASTLE,
CO. DUBLIN. THE BALLROOM.
A room formed and decorated in the
1790s, it was enriched in the 1950s by
Felix Harbord, who introduced the
superb English marble chimneypiece
by J. F. Moore and the pedimented
double door. Gradually he helped to
build up the richly varied group of
furnishings: the French commodes,
painted chairs and gilt console tables,
the Franco-Dutch decorative
canvases, the English Rococo glasses
and the Russian carpet.

XI. CHATSWORTH, DERBYSHIRE. THE BLUE DRAWING ROOM IN 1967. It is interesting to compare the approaches of two different generations at Stratfield Saye [101 and 103] and Chatsworth: a completely formal arrangement of the rooms at the first; and a skilful combination of formality and informality in the furniture and upholstery, with a changing balance of eighteenth- and twentieth-century pictures, in this room, first occupied by the Duke and Duchess of Devonshire in the late 1950s.

11. HADDON HALL, BY REX WHISTLER. Painted in 1933 for the 9th Duke of Rutland (1886–1940), the restorer of Haddon.

laying-out of gardens and the treatment of interiors that combined sound knowledge with poetic feeling. A few of the great eighteenth-century houses like Houghton, Holkham and Kedleston are entirely consistent works of art, and Beckford aimed to achieve that quality at Fonthill, but it is arguable that it was only with these restorations that a comparable degree of consistency and artistry was captured again. Of course there was an element of escapism about them that some people today find hard to accept, a sense of borrowing from history, and their owners would have been aware of that. Most of them represented the second or third generation of families who had made their money through trade and industry during the nineteenth century, or sometimes the professions, very much the same people as Lutyens's patrons. An interesting sidelight on their attitude to the past comes in a letter

from Colonel Cooper, of whose houses more will be said here, to Christopher Hussey, who told him he was about to go to Powis to stay with his cousin in order to write a series of articles for *Country Life*; he said how lucky Christopher was to have such connections, for they both responded to the romance of historical continuity.

There was another aspect too, the pleasure of building. Lady Louisa Conolly wrote in 1761: 'It is so pleasant I think to have some work going on, that one looks over oneself.' What appealed to someone like Martin Conway was, as Joan Evans pointed out, the process of rebuilding the castle at Allington rather than living in it.

A considerable number of these restorations were described in *Country Life*, and in the case of two Wiltshire houses, Woodlands in 1924 and Westwood in

12. THE MANOR HOUSE, SUTTON COURTENAY, BERKSHIRE. THE LONG GARDEN IN
1931. In *Country Life* that year Christopher Hussey wrote: 'Colonel and Mrs Lindsay have created
something exquisite, in which colour and atmosphere and romance blur the lines of objective truth.'

13 (right). THE ENTRANCE HALL AT SUTTON COURTENAY. Although it might be presumed to
be a historic room, in fact it owed its form and character to Colonel Lindsay, who enjoyed altering and
refitting houses, as could be seen at Beaudesert [78, 79].

14 (above left). WARDES, OTHAM, KENT. THE LIBRARY. Photographed when it was still the home of Sir Louis Mallet, who had begun its restoration about 1911. Sir Louis's taste was much admired by his friends, including Sir Philip Sassoon and Philip Tilden, who painted the overmantel.

15 (below left). THE DINING ROOM AT WARDES. Tilden added the plasterwork and the decorative painting.

16. PARHAM PARK, SUSSEX. THE GREAT HALL. The plate from Joseph Nash's four-volume series *The Mansions of England in Olden Time*, published between 1839 and 1849, shows the Elizabethan hall as it appeared in the 1840s. The present appearance of the hall is shown in illustration 34.

1926, their respective owners, the Reverend Meyrick Jones and E.G. Lister, were allowed to write the articles themselves. Indeed the concept of *Country Life*, with its concern for the past and the present, was as clearly bound up with them as it was with the career of Lutyens. That is apparent as early as 1904, when H. Avray Tipping wrote in the introduction to the first volume of *In English Homes* by Charles Latham: 'More than sixty years have elapsed since the publication of that renowned book, Nash's *Mansions of England in the Olden Time*. It was a book that made an instant appeal to the age in which it appeared.' The series of *In English Homes* appears to have been intended to have a similar impact on Edwardians.

Christopher Hussey must have looked at those books a good deal when he was growing up, and when in 1931 he came to write of Sutton Courtenay, which Lord Wantage had left to Colonel Harry Lindsay in 1901, he said:

There are certain houses, that, like a poet's verse, have caught the spirit of the place as well as endowed with a sense of period. In my own mental gallery there are several pictures of houses that thus crystallize a scene and a season: Cold Ashton Manor House standing for the Cotswolds in March, and Owlpen for their secret valleys in autumn; Great Wigswell ... for Sussex in Spring; Dunderave Castle ... for the Western Highlands in winter; and Sutton Courtenay for golden marshes, flickering silver of poplar and willow, old red roofs and lilac, in a word, for May in the Thames valley ...

It is remarkable how early people responded to houses that had that sense of remoteness in time. Horace Walpole was struck by that at Ham in 1770. Less well known is Edward King's comment on Haddon in *Archaeologia* in 1782: he hoped that 'this princely habitation may never come so far into favour as to be modernized, lest the traces of ancient times and manners which are now rarely preserved should be utterly lost here also'. By the early nineteenth century Cotehele in Cornwall was much admired, and in *The Three Howard Sisters* by Maud Lady Leconfield and John Gore there is an account of a visit in 1827: Lord Valletort

then took us to the house, where we found an excellent dinner prepared in that delightful dining room you must remember. One really felt transported to the times in which the house was built; every thing in such perfect keeping and character, the old pewter plates, with family arms, the tall, narrow wine glasses, the salt cellars, spoons, forks, tankards and salvers, etc., all in complete unison.

That was the kind of interior faithfully recorded by Nash in his *Mansions of Old England* [16], but,

because he added figures in period costume, it is not often realized how accurate was his depiction of architecture. The Bucklers made hundreds of drawings of old English houses and they had many imitators among antiquarians, professional and amateur; and historically-minded architects began to do careful surveys and measured drawings that were published in books of historic architecture.

Great Chalfield Manor in Wiltshire [18-20] is a perfect illustration of the growing interest, and a particularly interesting one because of its later history. In 1823, in the time of Admiral Sir Harry Burrard Neale, it was drawn by J.C. Buckler, and when in 1837 the Admiral decided to restore it, he commissioned a set of drawings from T.L. Walker, a pupil of Pugin; but nothing happened because of the Admiral's death in 1840. And, in fact, the restoration was not done until 1905-12 for R.F. Fuller by Sir Harold Brakespear. When Mr Fuller died in 1943, he left the house to the National Trust.

Most of the restored manor houses were in the South of England, in areas of stone building and of land good for gardening. Indeed gardening and

17. COTEHELE, CORNWALL. THE DINING ROOM. One of the lithographs after Nicholas Condy's watercolours in Arundell's *History of Cotehele* in about 1840.

18. GREAT CHALFIELD MANOR, WILTSHIRE. J.C. Buckler's watercolour was done in 1823, in the time of Admiral Sir Harry Burrard Neale, who in 1837 commissioned T.L. Walker to make a survey with a view to its restoration.

19. GREAT CHALFIELD AS IT WAS IN 1900. The photograph shows the house before Sir Harold Brakespear began its restoration for G.P. Fuller in 1905.

20. GREAT CHALFIELD AFTER REPAIR. From a *Country Life* photograph of 1920.

21. LYTES CARY, SOMERSET. The approach to the east front as it was restored for Sir Walter and
Lady Jenner after 1907.

22. THE GREAT HALL AT LYTES CARY. When the Jenners found the house, the fifteenth-century
hall was used as a cider store. The screen was a restoration by Sir Walter.

restoration went hand in hand, as can be seen at Athelhampton, in Dorset, where Inigo Thomas began the garden for Alfred Cart de Lafontaine as soon as he bought the place in 1891.

Three at least of these restorations survive more or less as they were left by their creators: Lytes Cary in Somerset, Westwood Manor in Wiltshire, both of which belong to the National Trust, and Beckley Park in Oxfordshire. A photograph of Lytes Cary from the east, such as that of illustration 21, taken in 1946 in the lifetime of Sir Walter Jenner, who restored the house, could be seen as a mid-twentieth-century equivalent of one of the plates in Nash's *Mansions*: the stone-flagged path leads past stumps of clipped yew to the porch that forms part of the mid-fifteenth-century hall building; on the left is the chapel, built about a hundred years before, and on the right the eighteenth-century farmhouse, seemingly turning its shoulder to the old manor house. It was a farmhouse

when the Jenners discovered it in 1907, with the hall used as a cider store and the parlour as a farm store. In the following years they carefully repaired the fabric of the house and furnished it, created the garden that frames it, and, with the aid of C.E. Ponting, built on a new range, rather larger in scale than the medieval house, so as to have a library and a Wren-style dining room that would take their full-length portraits of Charles II and Monmouth. Like many houses furnished at that time it is strong in textiles, and in this the Jenners were almost certainly influenced by Colonel L.C.W. and Mrs Jenner, who was an outstanding needlewoman. Lady Jenner and Mrs Jenner were sisters who married the two brothers in 1893 and 1899. Earlier in the new century Colonel and Mrs Jenner leased Avebury Manor, which also had become a farmhouse, and they bought it together with much of its traditional contents in 1907. When Sir Walter died in 1948, he bequeathed Lytes Cary to the Trust, and

so the main rooms in the old house are still much as he knew them, with the particular character of a frozen house.

On the other hand, at Westwood [23], where restoration was begun a few years later and which came to the Trust in 1956, the feeling is rather different, because the house has been let to tenants. In essence, however, it has changed remarkably little, as can be seen if the rooms today are compared with photographs of them taken for E.G. Lister's articles of 1926. It is a fifteenth-century manor house, somewhat reduced and altered in the early seventeenth century and considerably refitted at that time; in the early nineteenth century it became a farmhouse and it was still occupied in that way when it was acquired in 1911 by E.G. Lister who was then in the Diplomatic Service. He was a man of great sensibility, with a talent for early music and needlework as well as a remarkable feeling for old houses; and he was a friend of several

people mentioned in this chapter, not only Colonel Cooper and Lord Gerald Wellesley, but Thomas Gough, the expert on early musical instruments, Colonel and Mrs Jenner and Evelyn, Duchess of Devonshire. As Denys Sutton wrote of him in the National Trust guidebook: 'He was, in fact, faced with an exciting and exacting task; for instance, much of the original panelling in the Great Parlour was covered by wallpaper and this fine room was divided in two, one section being used as an apple store. The so-called King's Room served as a kitchen. With fine taste, he made a number of sensible and restrained restorations;' and, as the photographs show, by 1926 Westwood had completely settled down as a mellow evocation of a long vanished world.

As E.G. Lister grew older he naturally began to think of what would happen to the house after his death, and in the early 1940s, equally naturally, his thoughts turned to the National Trust's still new

23. WESTWOOD MANOR, WILTSHIRE. THE CORNER BEDROOM IN 1928. Like a number of his contemporaries, E. G. Lister had an eye for old materials and needlework.

24. BECKLEY PARK, OXFORDSHIRE. THE HALL IN 1929. This romantic house has continued to inspire and influence painters and those concerned with houses and decoration.

Country Houses Scheme. Therefore it is not surprising to find references to the house in *Ancestral Voices* by James Lees-Milne, who met him soon after he joined the Trust through Michael Peto, who had inherited Iford Manor. Clearly it made a deep impression on him: 'Ted has given me the North Room next to the Parlour, the room with a double bed and original blue-green and white crewel-work William and Mary hangings ... I lay in bed and with one candle guttering behind a glass hurricane globe (for there is no electric light in the house) and the logs flickering thin flames, seen rather than felt through the half-drawn bed curtains ...' (3 April 1942).

He returned on 15 August, to settle the restrictive covenants which he had persuaded E. G. Lister to give to the Trust:

Each time I come here I am overwhelmed by the perfection of this house. Everything Ted has done to it is in the best possible taste and proves his astonishing, instinctive understanding of the late medieval and Jacobean periods. He has restored the interior porches, the late Gothic mullions and glazing bars, the stucco and stonework, with a restraint and sensitivity which I have never experienced in any English country house of these early dates. Even the patchy rendering of the outside walls, washed over with a primrose to russet harl, rough and broken, with an occasional rambler rose lolloping over the upper windows, is contrived to perfection.

In contrast to the picturesque growth of Lytes Cary and Westwood, Beckley [24] is a Tudor house of strongly formal character set within a moat, but today it has a more naturally romantic quality than either of them. That is partly because it has continued to be lived in by the Feildings, who restored it over sixty years ago and laid out the garden, but it is also because Basil Feilding is a painter who has been inspired by the surroundings in which he grew up. At the same time its romantic appeal has been heightened because its magic cannot be taken for granted: for some years its sense of remoteness on Otmoor has been threatened by road-building plans; and also there is a sense of fragility about the place. That vulnerability in turn strengthens its impact on those who have seen it, in particular painters and those with a special enthusiasm for houses. Among them are two people whose names will recur later in the book, Mrs Lancaster and David Mlinaric. Mrs Lancaster, who lives near by and has a particular love of the place that she always wants other people to share, tells the story against herself that once when she took her aunt, Lady Astor, to see the house, Lady Astor asked Mrs Feilding whether they opened the house. 'No,' was the answer, 'but Mrs Lancaster does.' David Mlinaric went there first when he was a student and remembers it as the first country house that made a deep impression on him.

It was bought in 1920 by Percy Feilding, who had been taken to see it by Lady Ottoline Morrell, with whom he was staying at Garsington. He had been trained as an architect in the office of Sir Reginald Blomfield and he not only restored the house but laid out the garden as well. However, there is a rather freer and bolder approach to the furnishing and arrangement of the house than was usual at that time, with a good deal of German, Dutch and Italian furniture that looks perfectly at home in the rather austere early Tudor rooms. Some of this was inherited by his wife, who was the daughter of Henry Brewster, an American who had been educated in Paris, had married a German wife and lived much of his life in Italy. He was a figure from the world of Henry James, and, indeed, they were friends and correspondents. Mrs Feilding first came to live in England when she went up to Cambridge. After a year of reading mathematics, she was sent down for smoking; so she switched to architecture, meeting her future husband in Sir Reginald's office, and for a time they both practised. She remained a cosmopolitan figure, and it is probably her background and inclination that give a special character to Beckley as she and her husband created it. Now sixty years later their creation has been overlaid with an added mellowness, as can be seen by comparing the *Country Life* photographs published in 1929 with those in *Interiors* in the issue for December 1982/January 1983: the rooms have not been frozen, but the character that they gave them has been retained because it has appealed so much to their son and daughter-in-law, Mr and Mrs Basil Feilding, who have added more things in a similar spirit.

Of the many people who restored old houses and created gardens round them in the first thirty years of this century one of the most intriguing is Colonel Reginald Cooper [25]. Before the First World War he was in the Diplomatic Service and in Istanbul with Sir Louis Mallet, Lord Gerald Wellesley and Harold Nicolson. After serving in the war, he retired and developed a new life devoted to the rescuing of houses and the making of gardens. None of his papers apparently survives, but from a scattering of facts and memories and a few surviving letters to Christopher Hussey, who became a close friend in the mid-1920s, an appealing impression of him emerges. Some time in 1923 he bought Cold Ashton Manor [26–28] in Gloucestershire, and in February 1925 Christopher

Hussey wrote of it in *Country Life*: 'Now you would not know of their long tenancy [for two hundred years it had been the home of yeoman farmers] nor do you notice that the dark furniture and hangings have not aged together in their places for that period' ... 'Everything has that natural and untouched appearance that only the most sympathetic restoration can give.'

Colonel Cooper did not stay there long. In 1925 he found Cothay in Somerset [29-31] and called in Harold Brakespear, who specialized in early houses, also working at Great Chalfield and Hazelbury, to help with the restoration of the gate tower. By 1927 the house was ready to be photographed for Christopher Hussey, and he, being a talented amateur painter, was particularly struck by the colours in the Solar, analysing it at length to show 'how well a simple colour scheme of full colours fits a medieval interior without the introduction of hangings or wainscotting. Nor has any attempt been made to restrict the furniture to a period – an artificial restriction in any case, and impossible for this period.'

Colonel Cooper remained at Cothay for about twelve years and then he bought Julians, an eighteenth-century house in Hertfordshire. He did not stay long enough for *Country Life* to photograph it and the best record is Christopher Hussey's water-colour of the Hall [32]. Although Colonel Cooper admired eighteenth-century architecture and recommended Ditchley to the Trees, it seems that he himself did not feel completely at home in a house of that period, and in 1941, with a sense of relief, he moved back to the West Country, to a fourteenth-century manor house, Knightstone [33]. It was only in 1950 that Knightstone was ready for photography, and evidently its feeling was very similar to Cothay. Indeed the tapestries, pictures and furniture can be followed from house to house, the only real difference over the years being that they increased in number; but there were still 'the deep soft harmonies of old stuffs and mellowed woodwork, against clear white wash'.

Most of these manor houses were of a moderate size by country house standards of their day, but one of the larger houses that found sympathetic new owners between the wars was Parham in Sussex [VI, VII, 34, 35], which was bought in 1922 by the Hon. Clive Pearson, the second son of the 1st Viscount Cowdray. It

29. COTHAY MANOR, SOMERSET. The fifteenth-century house seen across the valley before
Colonel Cooper restored the gatehouse in 1927.

30. THE GATEHOUSE AT COTHAY RESTORED. The restoration was done by Harold Brakespear,
who worked on a number of early houses in the region, including Great Chalfield and Hazelbury.

31 (right). THE SOLAR AT COTHAY. Christopher Hussey described how this was painted an apricot
colour, made out of ochre and rennet, that harmonized well with the upholstery, 'the prevailing colour
of which is wool green, ranging from dark figured velvet curtains through the blue velvet of the chairs,
to the dry-grass greens of the needlework settee, and the mingled faded hues of the rugs, in which green
and dark tints predominate'.

32. JULIANS, HERTFORDSHIRE. THE ENTRANCE HALL IN 1947. After the Second World War, Stéphane Boudin redecorated the house for Mrs Pleydell-Bouverie. Its appearance in Colonel Cooper's day is seen in illustration IV.

33 (right). KNIGHTSTONE, DEVON. THE GREAT HALL IN 1950. It was with evident relief that in 1941 Colonel Cooper returned to an early house in the West Country and set about its restoration.

was then in a poor state and completely unmodernized, but the Pearsons were able to buy some of its historic contents; and over the years they restored the fabric of the building with infinite care, as they were also to do at Castle Fraser in Aberdeenshire. They had been looking for a country house for some time before they found Parham and, as their eldest daughter, Mrs P. A. Tritton, has written to me,

They must have already known that they were searching for an Elizabethan or Jacobean house. I never heard them talk fondly of any other date of house, and in my childhood grown-up conversations were filled with words like Littlecote, Loseley, Blickling, Danny, Wiston and many more ... they were looking for a house that needed help – an orphan child.

They also wanted a house on which Clive Pearson could exercise his engineering skill. He soon grew to love all the processes of repair and restoration, working out how the building had evolved, finding the physical evidence for it buried in the fabric and then taking it as evidence for restoration, or, if he decided not to go so far, leaving it so that others could see it without great difficulty. In all this he was helped by his architect, Victor Heal, but it was a long-drawn-out process, because the Pearsons were often away for months on end on business in South America, and, if anything came to light at such a time, work had to stop while Clive Pearson and Victor Heal exchanged cables. However, Clive Pearson was in no hurry to see it finished and he enjoyed the process of working away

34 (left). THE GREAT HALL AT PARHAM IN THE EARLY 1950S. Whereas Lord Zouche had
filled the Great Hall with armour [16] Mr and Mrs Clive Pearson enriched it with sixteenth- and
seventeenth-century portraits that they had acquired with the house in 1922.

35. THE SOLAR BEDROOM AT PARHAM IN 1951. The bed, with its seventeenth-century hangings,
came from Wroxton Abbey and was given to the Pearsons by Clive Pearson's mother, Lady Cowdray,
when they went to live at Parham. They placed it here when they opened the house to the public in 1948.

with his own estate staff. Gradually he removed most
of the traces of the rather cheap Georgian and Victorian alterations and reinstated the early panelling that
had been found in the house and he had carefully
repaired, so that slowly the Elizabethan character of
the house was revealed once more; and other rooms
were remodelled to be in tune with that character,
among them the Great Parlour, where the plasterwork
was done in the early 1930s but the panelling not until
the early 1950s. Moreover, as a result of country house
sales in the 1920s and 1930s he was able to extend the
group of Elizabethan and Jacobean portraits in the
house with appropriate historical additions from Ruf-
ford Abbey, East Knoyle and Surrenden Dering.

Mr Pearson was a rather isolated figure as well as
an individualist in his tastes and he and his wife do

not seem to have had many close friends who shared
their enthusiasm for restoration and collecting. Apart
from Victor Heal, with whom he kept up a volumi-
nous correspondence, one of their close friends in later
years was Rupert Gunnis, who persuaded them to
open the house to the public after the war and helped
them to rearrange it for the benefit of visitors. They
continued to make purchases that filled gaps and made
more sense of the house. One of their last contributions was to commission Oliver Messel to paint the
ceiling of the Long Gallery [VI].

It is mainly through the collection of portraits that
one senses the Pearsons' feeling for history, and above
all for the history of Parham, but, like a number of
contemporary collectors, they had a great appreciation
for textures in a house, particularly textiles, and there

36. NYMANS, SUSSEX. The south front as it was in 1932, with the 'fourteenth-century' Great Hall and the 'Tudor wing'. The house was remodelled as a West Country manor house in the 1920s by Colonel and Mrs Leonard Messel. The conception was Mrs Messel's, and from her sketches Norman Evill and Walter Tapper developed their designs. This range was burnt in 1947 and is now a ruin.

37 (above right). THE LONG DRAWING ROOM AT NYMANS. There was a deliberate contrast between the style and contents of this house and the Messels' London house in Lancaster Gate.

38 (below right). MRS MESSEL'S BEDROOM AT NYMANS. The fireplace came from Gloucester and was not stripped of its old paint; as Christopher Hussey said, 'A less discerning hand would have scraped it off, and with it the patina of Time.'

are fine carpets and a good deal of needlework. However, what is particularly fascinating is the part the house itself played in the process of refurnishing: Mrs Tritton has written that while her parents chose what they thought 'it liked and needed', 'Strangely the house was very selective and quite rejected various things that had been most carefully chosen for it.' In the end the sequence of rooms reflected the history of Parham not only through their form but through their furnishing and pictures, but without any forced sense of period; and everything came together so that Parham became a complete work of art in its own right.

One of the last of these romantic restorations, and now certainly the most famous, is that of Sissinghurst Castle in Kent, to which the Harold Nicolsons went to live in 1930. Knole was never far from V.

Sackville-West's mind, and what she wrote of that magical place in the first chapter of *Knole and the Sackvilles* (1922) seems to encapsulate the essence of that period:

... the house lies below one in the hollow, lovely in its colour and serenity. It has all the quality of peace and permanence; of mellow age; of stateliness and tradition. It is gentle and venerable. Yet it is, as I have said, gay. It has the deep inward gaiety of some very old woman who has always been beautiful, who has had many lovers and seen many generations come and go, smiled wisely over their sorrows and joys, and learnt an imperishable secret of tolerance and humour. It is, above all, an English house. It has the tone of England; it melts into the green of the garden turf, into the tawnier green of the park beyond; into the blue of the pale

1890. He was loath to leave it, because it was in such admirable gardening country, ideal for growing all the kind of plants that interested him most, and the garden started by his father was maturing well. So, instead of moving, he and his wife transformed the ugly house that they inherited into what Christopher Hussey in 1932 described as 'so clever a reproduction' of a fourteenth-century house 'added to intermittently till Tudor times, that some antiquary may well be deceived by it, even if not inspired to elaborate a correspondingly convincing history'. He continued: 'From the beginning Mrs Messel has been able to visualize her house complete – indeed her sketches exist for many of the rooms;' and it was from these that Norman Evill and Walter Tapper developed their detailed plans, the former working on the west range, which was found to incorporate a late-sixteenth- or early-seventeenth-century house, and the latter on the Great Hall and south range.

One of the last figures who shared the enthusiasms of that group of people was Evelyn, Duchess of Devonshire [39], the wife of the 9th Duke, who succeeded in 1908. During the Duke's lifetime she does not seem to have made a strongly positive impression on the appearance of Chatsworth, except in the alterations in the Painted Hall in 1911, but she was always deeply interested in the history of the collections. After the Duke's death in 1938, however, she went to live at Hardwick, probably the first person to make it her home since the seventeenth century. During the remaining twenty-two years of her life, except during the war, she lived there all the time and devoted herself to the preservation of its interior and contents, repairing tapestries and needlework and bringing back the rush matting that is such a feature of the house. Indeed, as the present Duchess of Devonshire records in *The House*, her portrait of Chatsworth, Duchess Evelyn 'was delighted when, at work on her favourite task of mending tapestry, she was watched by an expert on the subject, who told her she was wasting her time being a Duchess and should go and work for him'. She was greatly loved by younger people, particularly those who appreciated Hardwick, and Mark Girouard, who spent the first part of the war with her at Edensor – she was his great aunt – and afterwards used to stay with her at Hardwick, owes his introduction to Elizabethan architecture to those visits. Today she is still a presence in the house, and that is as it should be, because through her contribution to Hardwick she was one of the people who made the conscious preservation of country houses possible.

39. EVELYN, DUCHESS OF DEVONSHIRE, BY EDWARD HALLIDAY. The Duchess is painted repairing tapestry in the High Great Chamber at Hardwick, where she lived after the death of the 8th Duke in 1938.

English sky; it settles down into its hollow amongst the cushioned tops of the trees; the brown-red of those roofs is the brown-red of the roofs of the humble farms and pointed oast-houses, such as stain over a wide landscape of England the quilt-like pattern of the fields.

In addition to these restorations there is one creation of a manor house that also should be included, Nymans in Sussex [36–38]. Nymans is now only a fragment of the house that Colonel and Mrs Messel altered in the 1920s, because most of it was gutted in a fire in 1947, but what seemed of little account and not really worth preserving after the fire has already developed its own romantic appeal and in a surprising, even disconcerting, way it has come to be regarded as worthy of preservation for its own sake. What the Messels would have really liked to have done was to have taken a manor house in the West Country, restore it and fill it with their collection of oak furniture and tapestry. However, in 1915 Colonel Messel inherited the Nymans estate, which his father had acquired in

CHAPTER THREE

AUGUSTAN NOSTALGIA AND NEO-GEORGIAN SCHOLARSHIP

It is seldom satisfactory to define a period by giving firm dates, because they invariably prove to be inaccurate, and certainly it is hard to suggest a precise date for the start of the enthusiasm for Georgian art, architecture and decoration. If one suggests 1900, one soon has to retreat to 1890, and even into the 1870s. Indeed, as with the Gothic style, Gothic Survival and Gothick Revival, it turns out that Georgian and Georgian Revival run into one another. And a date for the end is equally impossible to give, because the enthusiasm continues. Arguably, however, the outbreak of the Second World War in 1939 marks the end of one phase of it and the start of another, as will be shown in the next chapter; and the mid-1970s strike me as marking the end of that second phase. Also that decade saw the deaths of several architects or people closely involved with architecture whose careers spanned both phases and who made a significant contribution to the classical tastes of their generation, among them Christopher Hussey (1970), the 7th Duke of Wellington (1972), Raymond Erith (1973), John Fowler (1977), and Clough Williams-Ellis (1978).

What is striking about these people is that they combined an aesthetic appreciation and a romantic feeling for the eighteenth century with a positive belief in the continuing validity of the classical tradition. At the beginning of the century there had been a new confidence in the revival of English classical architecture which found expression in books such as Albert Richardson's *Monumental Classic Architecture in Eng-*

land (1914); and it continued after the First World War in books on smaller houses like Ramsay's *Small Houses of the Later Georgian Period*, Richardson and Gill's *London Houses from 1660 to 1820* (1911), Margaret Jourdain's *English Interiors in Smaller Houses* (1923), and Richardson and Eberlein's *The Smaller English House of the Later Renaissance 1660-1830* (1925), books that combined historical recording with a sense of contemporary relevance. The sense of optimism about English classical architecture lasted until the early to mid-1930s, when well-established architects like Lord Gerald Wellesley, the future Duke of Wellington, young up-and-coming ones like Raymond Erith and people with a historical and intellectual approach to architecture like Christopher Hussey were exploring links, or at least a sense of parallelism, between the Regency style and the Modern Movement.

Only in about 1933-4 did those people become disenchanted with the Modern Movement and change direction, becoming more backward-looking and preservationist in their thinking. The intellectual–architectural crisis of those years, which has not been fully explored as yet, also relates to the Slump, to a romantic revival that started in the mid-1920s, to a crisis in patronage and to a growing concern for the preservation of historic buildings. That is obviously significant for the balance of architecture and decoration in the years ahead, and it is apparent in the difference between the post-war careers of, let us say, John Fowler as a decorator and Raymond Erith and

Francis Johnson as architects. Raymond Erith was a man of relatively secure background who never had to compromise, and after the war a small circle of people of quiet discretion and fairly ample means sought him out in Dedham in Essex, though he remained an isolated figure. So too is Francis Johnson, who has worked all his life in the North of England, mainly in his own county of Yorkshire. It was a slow process restarting his practice after the war, but in the mid-1950s he began to receive commissions to restore and alter country houses and a little later to design new ones; and because of the survival of so many landed estates in Yorkshire he has developed a unique practice and position. John Fowler had no backing of his own, but, as we shall see, he had an immense practice through a combination of his own talents and his partnership with Mrs Ronald Tree, or Mrs Lancaster as she was soon to become.

The Slump left few people in England with the confidence to build, but rather more people were willing to decorate. Edwardian philistinism left a sense of visual nervousness hanging over the period.

If the mid-1970s are seen as ending one phase, the previous seventy or eighty years are divided by the two wars. The First World War destroyed one social and political world; and both disrupted the careers of those who survived. To cite only a few examples, Lutyens's career as a country house architect never recovered from the First World War; nor did Oliver Hill's develop as it should have done, because he was just getting going in 1914 and the Second came at what should have been the peak of his career; similarly both Raymond Erith and John Fowler were just starting in the late 1930s.

As far as fashionable taste in classical interiors is concerned, among the most influential forces in the first phase were the firms of antique dealers cum architectural decorators, in particular Lenygon. In 1909 Francis Lenygon acquired 31 Old Burlington Street [41], using its handsome interior for the display of English furniture. The choice of a fine house of the early Palladian period was deliberate, because that was the masculine style those involved liked best; and it was equally typical of Francis Lenygon to take on as adviser Margaret Jourdain, who was developing her reputation as an expert on furniture and the decorative arts at a time when the study of such subjects was only just starting to outgrow a purely amateur approach and Percy Macquoid's four volumes *Age of Oak, of Walnut, of Mahogany and of Satinwood* were still new. Margaret Jourdain subsequently wrote two ex-

cellent books, *Furniture in England* and *Decoration in England*, that were published under his name. As well as selling fine furniture and decorative pictures Lenygons could supply complete rooms and fittings, such as doorcases and chimneypieces, and carry out all kinds of painting and upholstery. Whether it was the first firm to take a period house as showrooms I do not know, but Andrew Russell took 8 Clifford Street in 1914 and Thornton Smith 32 Soho Square in 1915.

There are parallels between the taste of Lenygons and that of contemporary architects apparent in Lutyens's coining of the word 'Wrennaissance' about 1905. Architectural decoration of that time was immensely thorough, with panelling and *boiserie*, genuine, fake, and reproduction, and plasterwork to match; and the range and quality of it in London houses is clearly brought out in the *Survey of London: The Grosvenor Estate in Mayfair*, Volume XL. As far as country houses are concerned that taste was well expressed at Hursley Park in Hampshire [42–44], an early-eighteenth-century house by John James bought in 1905 by Sir George Cooper – his wife had an American fortune – and promptly enlarged in a matching English Baroque style and decorated in an eclectic manner. The drawing room was early Georgian; there was late-sixteenth-century panelling in the boudoir, late-seventeenth-century panelling from the chapel at Winchester College in the Hall, and Louis XV *boiserie* in the ballroom; and there were excellent eighteenth-century English portraits in the grand manner. Polesden Lacey in Surrey [45, 46] is another and complete surviving example of that kind of taste, with Wren woodwork, continental *boiserie* and watered-down Georgian Revival rooms.

It was an increasingly serious taste, with a growing emphasis on accuracy of detail. Architects were still taught to draw fine detail, and patrons not confident about their ability to read drawings could rely on photographs, which were very well printed in large sizes. The *Architectural Review*, for instance, started the *Practical Exemplar of Architecture* as a series in 1906 and Richardson brought out *Monumental Classic Architecture* in 1914. It was also the age of museum period rooms. The Victoria and Albert Museum acquired its first six English rooms between 1891 and 1912, those from Sizergh Castle and the Old Palace at Bromley in 1891 and 1894 – the ceiling of the latter was much reproduced as a result – the late-seventeenth-century Cliffords Inn room in 1903 and the Hatton Garden room in 1912 (it was shown pickled).

40 (left). CHRISTOPHER HUSSEY AND SIR CLOUGH WILLIAMS-ELLIS. Photographed at Plas Brondanw by Mrs Hussey on the fortieth anniversary of Sir Clough's foundation of Portmeirion.

41 (below). 31 OLD BURLINGTON STREET, LONDON, IN 1949. In 1909 the house had been taken as a showroom for antique furniture by Francis Lenygon. His firm, which became Lenygon & Morant in 1915, continued to occupy it until 1953.

42 (opposite top). HURSLEY PARK, HAMPSHIRE. THE DRAWING ROOM IN 1909. When this room was illustrated, the author of the article in *Country Life* wrote: 'It carefully preserves the spirit of the English designers of George I's reign.'

43 (opposite below left). THE JACOBEAN BOUDOIR AT HURSLEY. 'It takes us back to the close of the sixteenth century. It has been lined with wainscotting from an old Yorkshire house.'

44 (opposite below right). LOUIS DECORATION IN THE BALLROOM AT HURSLEY.

45 (right). POLESDEN LACEY, SURREY. THE ENTRANCE HALL. A year after Mrs Greville acquired the house, she installed the reredos and related woodwork from St Matthew Street, buying them after the Victoria and Albert Museum reluctantly had to turn them down for lack of funds.

46 (below right). THE LIBRARY AT POLESDEN LACEY. The house, which was remodelled for Mrs Greville by Mewes and Davis, is one of the most complete expressions of fashionable country house taste in the reign of Edward VII: eclectic in style, rich in furnishing and luxurious in mood, but also aiming at a certain element of understatement.

49 (above). SUDBURY HALL, DERBYSHIRE. THE DRAWING ROOM IN 1935. About 1830 two rooms were joined to form a larger drawing room, which was effectively decorated soon after 1922 in the rich dark tones associated at that time with Hampton Court Palace and the late seventeenth century. The rooms were separated once more by the National Trust.

47 (top left). WATLINGTON PARK, OXFORDSHIRE. THE ENTRANCE HALL, PAINTED BY PHILIP TILDEN IN 1921. The painting was done for the 2nd Viscount Esher, who became one of the leaders of the preservation movement.

48 (below left). BENINGBROUGH HALL, YORK. THE DRAWING ROOM IN 1927. One of the richly carved rooms in the house that were stripped and evidently altered in about 1920. Like the drawing room at Sudbury [49] it had been first joined to its neighbour in about 1830.

The war did not end that kind of taste, and photographs of a number of big houses rearranged in the 1920s show its impact, among them Beningbrough, Sudbury and rooms done at Grimsthorpe. It can be seen in the hall at Watlington Park in Oxfordshire [47], which Philip Tilden painted for the 2nd Viscount Esher soon after he bought the house in 1921. It was through the Conways at Allington that Tilden met a number of people who were to help him with his career, among them Sir Louis Mallet, who introduced him to Sir Philip Sassoon and V. Sackville-West; and during the 1920s and 1930s he had a successful country house practice, altering and extending houses and gardens in a variety of styles as he explains in his *True Remembrances*.

In the case of Beningbrough near York [48] the house was bought in 1917 by the 10th Earl of Chesterfield, whose family had lived at Holme Lacy in Herefordshire and whose wife came from Yorkshire; and so they were able to take from a slightly earlier house pictures, furniture and some of the fittings, including much fine Gibbons carving. Beningbrough was redecorated to take them, and to that end the panelling and elaborately carved cornices in several rooms were stripped after the fashion of the day; the dining room was grained and picked out in gold; and the saloon was painted in a dense bluey-green also picked out in gold. Who was in charge of the work is not recorded, but the result as seen in the photographs taken for the 1927 articles in *Country Life* was in the manner associated with Lenygons.

At Sudbury in Derbyshire [49, 50] a somewhat similar feeling was achieved largely by rearrangement of the contents rather than by extensive decoration. The house had been let for a number of years and some of the contents had been sold, but in 1922 the 9th Lord Vernon and his wife decided to return to live there. It was at that time that the drawing room was painted in a dark Hampton Court grey-blue of somewhat similar weight to the colour in the saloon at Beningbrough.

At Grimsthorpe in Lincolnshire [51] several rooms were redecorated in the mid-1920s by Keebles for the wife of the 2nd Earl of Ancaster. Lady Ancaster was an American, and perhaps as a result the rooms were correspondingly more elaborate in their conception and execution. Her bedroom, for instance, was given a ceiling in the Charles II style and a chimneypiece and overmantel of eighteenth-century Dutch origin. The boudoir was simpler, with a late-seventeenth-century-style corner chimneypiece and an eighteenth-

century-style doorcase, but it had formal, gilt furniture.

In all three houses there was a respect for formal architecture and the relationship of the furniture to its setting. At Sudbury the results were sympathetic to the house, still seeming elegant, if out-of-date rather than truly period in feeling when the house passed to the Trust in 1967. In the case of the other two houses the seriousness was combined with a deadness of touch, and it was against that combination that the next generation was to react.

But even before 1914 a few people had discovered the Regency style. Sir Albert Richardson moved to a house of that period in 1909, Cavendish House, London Road, St Albans, and into another in 1914, 41 Russell Square, London. Finally, in 1919, he moved to Avenue House, Ampthill, in Bedfordshire [52], where he lived for the rest of his life. Through a sequence of photographs, it is possible to follow the growth of his collection from the first modest purchases made about 1909-10.

Another protagonist of the style was Edward Knoblock, an American by birth, who spent a good deal of time in Paris but made his home in England. All three elements were important in the development of his taste. He was born in 1874 and arrived in London in 1897, and, as Henry James said of him later: 'You first discovered yourself in England, just as I first did myself.' However, it was in Paris that he first had his own apartment. In 1912 he took one in the Palais Royal, then not a fashionable place to live, and he furnished it with pictures and furniture of the late Directoire and Retour d'Égypte period, which was then not sought after at all; for the dining room he commissioned William Nicholson to do painted decorations on mirror glass panels. The precise sense of period seems to derive from his American background and the evident chic of the apartment from his Parisian experience.

Shortly before 1914 he took chambers in Albany and, with the aid of Maxwell Ayrton, he decorated them as an English counterpart of his French rooms: the sitting room had marbled walls, the curtains made in Lyon were of deep purple with a formalized palm-leaf border and the furniture was 'solemn Regency'. It was towards the end of the war that he discovered the Beach House [53-55] at Worthing, which he restored and decorated in the years after 1918. Again assisted by Maxwell Ayrton, he fused together the French and Regency elements of his existing collection, which had been strengthened by his purchases at the Deepdene sale in 1917, when he bought some of the

50. THE GALLERY AT SUDBURY IN 1935. The Charles II gallery was fitted with nineteenth-century bookshelves to take the 5th Lord Vernon's library. The furniture is shown as it was arranged after the 9th Lord Vernon returned to the house in 1922. In 1967 the National Trust removed the bookshelves at the suggestion of John Fowler [L X X V I]. It is interesting to see how the idea of the room influenced his treatment of the gallery at Chequers [X L I V].

52 (above). AVENUE HOUSE, AMPTHILL, BEDFORDSHIRE. THE SALOON IN 1934. This shows the fruits of twenty years of collecting by Professor A. E. Richardson, one of the first admirers of the style of the late eighteenth and early nineteenth centuries, as well as one of the principal promoters of the continuity of the classical tradition.

51 (left). GRIMSTHORPE CASTLE, LINCOLNSHIRE. LADY ANCASTER'S BEDROOM. An elaborate scheme of eclectic historical decoration carried out by Keebles and photographed in 1924.

53. THE BEACH HOUSE, WORTHING, SUSSEX. THE LIBRARY IN 1921. The studied perfection of the house that made it the first major statement of the Regency Revival was almost certainly due to Edward Knoblock being an American who had lived in Paris before he came to live in England. The walls of the room were painted with 'hangings' of camel-hair brown with Wedgwood blue above.

54. THE ANTE-ROOM AT THE BEACH HOUSE. Sir William Nicholson originally painted the glass panels for Knoblock's apartment in the Palais Royal in Paris.

55. THE PRINCIPAL BEDROOM AT THE BEACH HOUSE. The *Country Life* article of 1921 said of the bedroom: 'Everything, down to the water-jugs in the bathrooms, is faithfully of the period.'

finest pieces of Thomas Hope's furniture. The *Country Life* photographs taken in 1921 bring out the fusion of elements: as well as the library shown in Fig. 53, there was a drawing room decorated with panels of French pictorial wallpaper, which Knoblock had found in Paris, a form of decoration always more popular with Americans than the English; the dining room he fitted up round a series of late-eighteenth-century French painted *toiles*; and in the ante-room he installed the Nicholson panels painted in 1912 for his apartment in the Palais Royal in Paris. Later he lived at 11 Montagu Place, to which reference will be made shortly. In 1939, in his memoirs *Round the Room*, he wrote about his attitude to furniture and decoration. He described his room as 'a reconstruction of other days', and said:

For at any rate the modern decorator is trying to produce something in harmony with the life about him, while my attitude is a coward's confession of the inability to march with the times ... and space, colour, balance is everything in furnishing and decorating a room.

I spent far too much time and energy and money on putting the place in order, not resisting till every moulding and door-knob in the house was of the correct period and not a thing in the place was lacking to make it completely perfect and easy to live in.

Among the people who knew him was Lord Gerald Wellesley, one of the most interesting figures of his generation, who explained in his *Collected Works* (1970) that he had always wanted to be an architect, but his parents had considered it a hazardous and uncertain career for a younger son who had his own way to make; and it was only after the First World War that he was able to fulfil his ambition. By nature a scholar and possessing a finely tuned, fastidious taste, he became involved in many projects relating to the improvement of the arts of design, public taste and later preservation, particularly of country houses, and through his friendships and his houses he had an influence on a considerable number of people. Indeed Mrs Lancaster says that he and Lady Juliet Duff were the people in England who understood the arrangement of furniture and works of art best.

In the late 1920s and early 1930s he lived at 11 Titchfield Terrace [56, 57], and in 1931 Christopher Hussey, who shared a house in the country with him, included it in an article in *Country Life* on four Regency houses in London: the others were Knoblock's house at 11 Montagu Place, H.S. Goodhart-Rendel's at 13 Crawford Street [58], and a house designed by Lord Gerald, 17 Park Square East [59]. Quotations from that article give an insight into the attitudes of the time:

There is felt to be something 'daring' about having a taste for the Regency period, something that makes friends murmur 'how exciting' or raise their eyebrows slightly. It is not simply that the word has sinister associations with 'bucks' and the wicked goings-on of the Regent's cronies. For so we were taught to regard all applied art later than the time of Robert Adam as 'heavy and tasteless' ... Even now after fifteen years of its vogue, voices are heard stigmatizing Regency design as 'ugly' ...

And he continues:

It is this kinship between Regency and modern taste (the product of similar social conditions) that is the real cause of the importation of audacity to modern 'Regency bucks' ... In this article a frankly modern room, which is at the same time a development from the Regency style, is illustrated as showing the essential similarity of the two techniques ... It must always be remembered that Regency was the last recognizable style that furniture designers employed before the great debacle of Victorianism. It is thus one of the natural points of departure into the future, and quite the best.

Lord Gerald Wellesley was drawn to that period both for aesthetic reasons and for personal ones too, because it was the period of his ancestor, the Great Duke of Wellington; but as an architect he was concerned with the present and the future, and it is interesting to see in his work and in a great deal of what Christopher Hussey wrote in the late 1920s and early 1930s that they were concerned with the future of classicism. Roger Hesketh, also a friend of Christopher Hussey and of whom I write later, shared that view. So did Raymond Erith, who wrote of his desire to create a 'new architecture out of the shambles of all the dead architectures, ancient and modern' and of his belief 'in the general classic tradition' rather than the classical style. Raymond Erith was particularly drawn to the architecture of Soane, whom he saw as 'a pro-

gressive classicist'. That interpretation is related not only to architecture but to design in general, as can be seen in a letter to Christopher Hussey in late 1933 or early 1934:

May I beg you for advice? (I regard you as a criterion of good taste and an encyclopedia of all the nicest sorts of knowledge.) Who makes good modern furniture in London? Is there, outside one's imagination, any neo-Empire or neo-Biedermeyer? Or Regency; – I feel that pure modern is happier in London if flavoured with Regency and urns.

If the Beach House at Worthing stands out as one landmark, it is apparent that round about that time several other threads started to develop. To some extent they can be followed in books, exhibitions and articles, not all in *Country Life*, and there is evidence of a growing enthusiasm, albeit confined to a small circle of people. An example was the decision of Lord and Lady Rocksavage to live at Houghton, Sir Robert Walpole's great house in Norfolk. (It had been inherited in 1797 by Lord Rocksavage's ancestor, the 4th Earl and subsequently 1st Marquess of Cholmondeley, on the death of Horace Walpole, 4th and last Earl of Orford, the 3rd Earl of Cholmondeley having married Sir Robert's daughter, Mary.) The 1st Marquess of Cholmondeley had made certain changes in the late 1790s to make up for the loss of Sir Robert Walpole's pictures, but Houghton had never become a permanent home for the head of the family and, indeed, at the end of the last century and beginning of the present one it was let. In 1913 Lord Rocksavage married Sybil Sassoon and Lord Cholmondeley made Houghton over to them. Their decision to live there was not altered when he succeeded his father as 5th Marquess in 1923, since his mother continued to live at Cholmondeley until her death in 1938.

The dedication of the 5th Marquess and his wife to Houghton, which was mentioned first in the *Country Life* articles in 1921, is one of the great country house stories of the twentieth century; indeed, theirs has been the most important period there since Sir Robert's, as well as much the longest. Lord Cholmondeley died in 1968, and his widow continues to live there. To this, the greatest of eighteenth-century houses, Lady Cholmondeley has brought not only knowledge, understanding and resources but also contact with a wider world, embracing the arts and letters as well as politics. Visually that is expressed above all in the pictures by Sargent, whom she knew well and who painted her on several occasions, and it is also apparent in the pictures and works of art that she inherited from her

56. 11 TITCHFIELD TERRACE, LONDON. THE DRAWING ROOM IN 1931. Lord Gerald Wellesley's rooms were arguably the most scholarly examples of the Regency Revival at that time. The walls had a yellow satin paper with a key paper in red, both printed from old blocks; the upright figures were cut from an old paper frieze and the gryphon motif was executed by Lord Gerald himself.

57. BAROQUE PICTURES IN A BEDROOM AT 11 TITCHFIELD TERRACE. Lord Gerald was president of the Magnasco Society, founded to encourage the revival of interest in seventeenth- and eighteenth-century Italian art.

58. 13 CRAWFORD STREET, LONDON. H. L.
GOODHART-RENDEL'S DRAWING ROOM IN
1931. The walls were painted with coffee-coloured
drapery, with bluish-grey pilasters.

59. 17 PARK SQUARE EAST, LONDON. THE
DRAWING ROOM IN 1931. The room was
designed by Lord Gerald Wellesley, who was
interested in the Regency style for his own day and
the parallel it offered to the Modern Movement.

brother Sir Philip Sassoon. In 1973, as a memorial to her husband, she reconstructed the steps on the West Front removed by the 3rd Lord Orford, and perhaps posterity will interpret them as a memorial to her too. But what cannot be preserved is the continuing pleasure and stimulation that Houghton has given her.

Of the contribution of her brother, Sir Philip Sassoon, as a patron, collector and supporter of the arts, something – though too little – will be said later in this chapter, but before that there are other aspects of taste to consider. Early in the 1920s there was a revival of interest in Baroque art and the painters who had appealed to eighteenth-century British collectors. Following an exhibition at the Pitti Palace in Florence in 1922, the first exhibition of seventeenth-century Italian painting was held at the Burlington Fine Arts Club in 1924. The same year the Magnasco Society was formed under the presidency of Lord Gerald Wellesley, 'to restore,' as Sir Osbert Sitwell wrote in *Apollo* in May 1964, 'Italian seventeenth- and eighteenth-century painting and sculpture to the position which they had formerly occupied for so long in the mind of western man'. Among the founder members were Colin Agnew, Tancred Borenius, F.D. Lycett Green, whose pictures are now in York City Art Gallery, William King, Osbert and Sacheverell Sitwell and Lord Ivor Spencer-Churchill; Christopher Hussey became a member in 1925. In its first exhibition held at Agnews in the autumn of 1924 Caravaggio, Crespi, Giordano, Feti, Magnasco and the Tiepolos were all represented.

The same year Sacheverell Sitwell published *Southern Baroque Art* as part of his personal discovery of Baroque and Rococo art and architecture in Europe. He had first encountered the Austrian Baroque and Rococo periods on a visit to Salzburg in 1922, and other people followed in the course of the decade, among them Roger Hesketh, of whom I write later. Then in the mid-1930s there was a handful of architectural and decorative manifestations of the enthusiasm, in some of Clough Williams-Ellis's work at Portmeirion, in the library that Sir Alfred Beit formed at 15 Kensington Palace Gardens [60] and in the dining room in Mr Henry and Lady Honor Channon's house, 5 Belgrave Square [62]. Lord Gerald Wellesley and Trenwith Wills were Sir Alfred's architects. The idea of the room came from a picture by Lajoue that Sir Alfred had bought, while the chimneypiece was copied from one photographed by *Country Life* at Russborough, the Irish house that by strange coincidence Sir Alfred was to acquire in the early 1950s.

The Channons' dining room was created in 1935–6 by Stéphane Boudin of Jansen, the outstanding traditional decorator of his day, who had a number of clients in England. Writing in *Country Life* on 26 February 1938, Christopher Hussey referred to Mr Channon's book *The Ludwigs of Bavaria*, published in 1933, and called the Channons 'well-known Müncheners'; and he went on to describe how 'on a ground of soft greyish blue like the sea, many mirrors reflect the brilliantly burnished silver decoration, as exquisitely modelled as Cuvilliés originals'. The room gave intense satisfaction to Henry Channon, who made many references to it in his diary. At the time of the coronation of King George VI and Queen Elizabeth in May 1937, for instance, he described dinner before the Duchess of Sutherland's ball, when Lady Honor had a dress of blue brocade to match the room: it was 'a gorgeous, glittering sight of jewels shimmering in the candlelight, of Meissen china, of decorations and splendour'. Although the form of the room had to be altered from the original at the Amalienburg 'every *motif* is to be found in Cuvilliés' executed or published work'. Jansen had an excellent library of books on architecture and the decorative arts and employed Monsieur Cazes to study historic decoration throughout Europe and build up an archive filling 120 large volumes of drawings, photographs, and prints that could be used as a quarry by Boudin and his colleagues. In contrast to this the other rooms were English in style, as can be seen from the Regency Revival library [61].

Naturally Cecil Beaton responded to the enthusiasm for the Baroque and Rococo. He met Edith Sitwell first at the end of 1926 and then her brothers; and in the *Wandering Years* he wrote: 'As for the Sitwell brothers, both of whom had established a mode of aesthetic existence that completely satisfied my own taste, no detail of their way of life was ugly or humdrum.' In 1931 he took Ashcombe and also he started to travel abroad and saw 'the pink and silver churches of Bavaria, the exquisite decoration of Cuvilliés in the Nymphenburg Palace, and the luxurious frivolities of stucco cherubs frisking among garlands of flowers and arabesques designed by the Assam brothers. Thenceforth I only thought in terms of the Rococo ... Now a clean sweep must be made of all Sheraton, Hepplewhite or in fact any English furniture.' And he describes going to Vienna: 'Here antiquaries were ransacked for cheap baroque chairs and consoles for my new home. Oliver Messel joined us.'

Soon after Sacheverell Sitwell's *Southern Baroque Art* came Christopher Hussey's *The Picturesque* (1927)

62 (above). 5 BELGRAVE SQUARE, LONDON. THE DINING ROOM. Inspired by a room by
Cuvilliés at the Amalienburg, Munich, the room was designed in 1935 by Stéphane Boudin and decorated
in blue and silver. The silver side table, the stove and the parquet floor came from the Hotel Parr in
Vienna, where Jansen had bought many complete rooms. The set of chairs were made by Jansen from
one original.

60 (top left). 15 KENSINGTON PALACE GARDENS, LONDON. THE ROCOCO REVIVAL
LIBRARY. This was designed for Sir Alfred Beit by Trenwith Wills and Lord Gerald Wellesley round
the painting of *A Cabinet of Scientific Curiosities* by Jacques de Lajoue, which Sir Alfred bought in
1936. The chimneypiece was copied from one photographed by *Country Life* at Russborough, Co.
Wicklow, the house later acquired by Sir Alfred. The pattern of the floor was taken from the picture,
and the walls were marbled in pink, dove grey, white and verde antico. See also illustrations XXII,
XXIII, 153, 154.

61 (below left). THE LIBRARY AT 5 BELGRAVE SQUARE. The bookcases were designed by Lord
Gerald Wellesley and Trenwith Wills and the black and gold paintings were by Michael Gibbon.

63 (above) and 64 (opposite). TRENT PARK, HERTFORDSHIRE. THE SOUTH FRONT AS IT WAS
IN 1903 AND 1926. This shows the effect of Sir Philip Sassoon's remodelling, using stone window
surrounds, string courses and cornice acquired when Devonshire House was demolished.

and Kenneth Clark's *The Gothic Revival* (1928). Taken together those three books broadened the appreciation of a whole generation to an extraordinary degree, and while they were about ideas and moods, there also was a growing literature concentrating on the facts of the eighteenth-century achievement. In architecture A. T. Bolton's two volumes on Robert Adam appeared in 1922 – and have never been superseded – his *Works of Sir John Soane* in 1924, and in 1928 H. A. Tipping and Christopher Hussey published the penultimate volume of *English Homes*, on Vanbrugh. In the field of furniture Percy Macquoid and Ralph Edwards produced *The Dictionary of English Furniture* in 1925 and the same year Oliver Brackett brought out the first book on Chippendale. And in America the young W. S. Lewis discovered Horace Walpole and embarked on a lifetime of collecting, editing and publishing Walpoliana.

English painting of the eighteenth century did not fare so well, as Professor Waterhouse pointed out in a lecture on British Art and Art Studies that he gave at the inauguration of the Yale Center in April 1977. In 1919, 200 of the older British pictures were transferred from the National Gallery to the Tate Gallery, but until 1929 there was no government grant to the Tate; there was no serious policy for the development of a historic collection of British painting; there was practically no library at the Tate and in 1929 it played 'absolutely no role at all in the study of British art'; and the director of the National Gallery actually disliked eighteenth-century British painting. Moreover in the 1920s little of value was published on British painting. In 1932 the Burlington Fine Arts Club held an exhibition devoted to *Some Neglected British Painters*, who included Wright of Derby, and the first big exhibition devoted to British art was held in the winter of 1934/5 at Burlington House. The one convinced supporter of eighteenth-century British painting was Sir Philip Sassoon: he organized the first exhibition of conversation pictures in his house in Park Lane in 1930

(Sacheverell Sitwell's book appeared in 1936) and in 1936 and 1937 he devoted exhibitions to Gainsborough and Reynolds.

When exactly Sir Philip began to buy eighteenth-century pictures is unclear, but the difference in character between Port Lympne, the house in Kent that Sir Herbert Baker began for him before the First World War and Philip Tilden extended afterwards, and Trent Park in Hertfordshire [63, 64], which he bought in 1923 and began to reconstruct in the classical style in 1926, suggests that it was after the war.

Christopher Hussey's comments on the design of Trent are probably as revealing of Sir Philip's intentions as his own feelings:

Though the style is traditional, the house is essentially modern in its simplicity of form and fitness for the purposes of country life. It would have been easy ... to re-face the old walls with a pastiche of Queen Anne or Georgian style ... But by disciplining his imagination to use none but the simplest elements of design ... Sir Philip has produced a building

... that can be regarded as an ideal example of English domestic architecture un-alloyed by fashion or fantasy.

Within, there were echoes of eighteenth-century houses and rooms, but the detail was so understated that there was no sense of quotation: rather were the rooms a cool setting for superb but equally under-stated pictures and furniture that were given plenty of space in which to breathe and yet were placed with a feeling for striking effect. There were, for instance, a series of pairs of late-seventeenth- and early-eighteenth-century pier glasses with the least showy of frames, and, instead of gilded furniture, there were lacquer cabinets and chests. Sir Philip particularly liked chinoiserie and oriental things made for the European market, so in the Blue Room there was red lacquer furniture, in the drawing room Delft tulip vases and black lacquer cabinets, and in the saloon a copy of a Chinese wallpaper in the Victoria and Albert Museum (the kind of thing that John Fowler began his

67. PORT LYMPNE, KENT. THE PAINTED ROOM. This was decorated in 1932 by Rex Whistler after Sert worked in the drawing room and Glyn Philpot painted the frieze in the dining room.

65 (top left). THE DRAWING ROOM AT TRENT IN 1931. Christopher Hussey praised Sir Philip for the way in which he had caught 'the essence of cool, flowery, chintz, elegant, unobtrusive rooms that rises in the mind when we think of country houses ... distilling it at Trent by virtue of having supervised the process himself and possessing chemist's skill beyond the ordinary'. Over the chimneypiece hangs Zoffany's *Colmore Family*.

66 (below left). CONVERSATION PICTURES IN THE LIBRARY AT TRENT. Over the chimneypiece hung Danckert's picture of *Charles II Being Presented with the First Pineapple Grown in England*.

68. BUXTED PARK, SUSSEX. THE LIBRARY AS IT WAS IN 1934. In 1931 the house had been acquired by Mr and Mrs Basil Ionides, who were both notable collectors in several fields, including English furniture and conversation pictures.

69. THE YELLOW DRAWING ROOM AT BUXTED IN 1934. The gilt frame over the chimneypiece came from Hamilton Palace, and the walls were hung with flock wallpaper made specially from old blocks.

70. THE YELLOW BEDROOM AT BUXTED IN 1934. The walls were hung with a yellow paper sprigged with gold.

career by painting). Also great attention was given to all the details of upholstery, with quilting of cotton, contrast piping and pleating of frills and valances. Apparently the upholstery was done by E. G. Lehmann of Welbeck Street, who carried out all Jansen's work in England.

As Sir Osbert Sitwell wrote, 'No picture of life between the wars is complete without some account of one of those houses filled always with politicians, painters, writers, professional golfers, and airmen.' So it is sad that there is no memoir of Sir Philip, for he was not only a politician and connoisseur, but a patron on his own account and supporter of the arts in the public sphere as well. At Lympne, Sert, Glynn Philpot and later Rex Whistler [67] all worked for him, and as well as organizing his annual exhibitions, he was Chairman of the Trustees of the National Gallery from 1932 to 1936 and first Commissioner of Works from 1937 until his death in 1939.

Philip Tilden, who knew him well, wrote:

I do not think that a more brilliant man of his age existed than Philip. I do not mean necessarily brilliant in scholarship, but brilliant in effect; intensely amusing and amused, full of knowledge concerning many things that others care not two pence for; imaginative, curious, and above all intelligent to the last degree.

The economic situation in the 1920s and early 1930s must also be borne in mind, for it must have clipped the wings of many Georgian enthusiasts. Money was very tight for most people, as emerges in Frank Hermann's history of Sothebys. The turnover of that firm declined every year between 1921 and 1924, though profits picked up again, reaching a new peak of £63,000 in 1927-8 and £70,000 in 1928-9. With the crash of October 1929, profits for the year halved. Then they slumped to £12,000 in 1930-31 and to £4,000 in 1931-2. With Christies there was a peak of £147,000 in 1920; then a sharp drop to £32,500 in 1921, followed by a climb back to £70,000 in 1923; another big drop, to £29,000 in 1929 turned into small losses in 1931 and 1932 and one of £8,000 in 1933.

It is interesting to compare these figures with what Christopher Hussey wrote of Buxted Park, Sussex

71. THE BOUDOIR AT BUXTED IN 1950. A chimneypiece from 30 Old Burlington Street, hangings of old damask from Belhus in Essex and Batoni's portrait of Lord Eardley.

72 (top right). ONE OF THE VISITORS' BEDROOMS AT BUXTED IN 1950. A comparison of this room with the Yellow Bedroom [70] shows the increased confidence and relaxation in the handling of eighteenth-century furniture and of upholstery in eighteenth-century rooms.

73 (below right). A WHITE BATHROOM AT BUXTED IN 1950. Despite the influence of bathrooms like that at Ditchley [126] Christopher Hussey wrote that its 'marked Georgian character is notably different from the clinical character usually thought appropriate to bathrooms'.

[68-70], in 1934, three years after it had been bought by Mr and Mrs Basil Ionides: 'The number of houses of any pretensions to beauty that have come into the market, even during the past two or three years, and have failed to find a purchaser is extraordinarily small. In fact, I cannot think of any ...' He continued: 'And these are houses that demand fine period furniture. Indeed they seem to have been in demand *because* people possessed or wished to acquire beautiful things to put in them ... The point is that people have not given up wishing to be housed amply and with dignity, or wholly lost the means with which to see to it that they are ...'

There were excellent opportunities to buy well at modest prices, as Mr Hermann suggests, but almost all the outstanding houses arranged in that period were backed by exceptional resources that were not wholly British in origin, or, if they were, involved developments abroad. Three houses in particular stand out: Ditchley in Oxfordshire, which Mr and Mrs Ronald Tree bought in 1933 and of which more will be said later; Buxted Park; and Godmersham Park in Kent, bought by Mr and Mrs Robert Tritton in 1935.

In 1903, Mrs Ionides, the daughter of the 1st Viscount Bearsted, married W.H. Levy, who died in 1923. She then married Basil Ionides, who was an architect and designer (he did the Savoy Theatre), in 1930. How early she began to collect eighteenth-century English things is not clear to me, but Hilary Spurling has discovered that in 1922 she began to be advised on a regular basis by Margaret Jourdain, who thereafter was a regular visitor to her London house. Her brother was also a great collector, and as soon as he succeeded his father in 1927 he bought Upton House in Warwickshire and called in Morley Horder to remodel it so as to take his pictures and porcelain. He gave both the house and its collections to the National Trust in 1948.

As arranged in the 1930s Buxted contained only part of the Ionides' varied and specialized collections – her Battersea enamels, for instance, were kept in London – and it was notable for the combination of fine objects, often with notable provenances, and close attention to the details of decoration, patterns of wallpaper, some specially copied from old designs, the treatment of curtains and so on.

In 1940, by which time the contents of the London house were there too, the house was gutted by fire, but the specialist collections and some of the finest pieces of furniture were saved. Immediately Mr and Mrs Ionides got permission to restore the house provided that they did not use new materials that were in short supply or rationed. By the time the house was photographed again by *Country Life* in 1950 [71-73] it was all complete, with a famous staircase from 30 Old Burlington Street, numerous fine eighteenth-century chimneypieces and conversation pictures and English furniture complemented by Chinese porcelain in the European style and Battersea enamels. Looking at the photographs thirty-five years later, it is amazing how many opportunities had presented themselves to Mrs Ionides, and how many objects that are now prized possessions of museums and private collections were to be found at Buxted.

The story behind Godmersham [74, 75] was somewhat similar. Mrs Tritton, an American, was married first to Sir Louis Baron, who collected fine seventeenth- and eighteenth-century furniture and needlework. After he died, she married Robert Tritton, a decorator and dealer. In 1935 they bought Godmersham, a house with a particularly fine hall and drawing room, but externally considerably altered. So with the aid of Walter Sarel they restored the entrance front and remodelled the garden front, forming within it a new saloon and library in eighteenth-century styles. Norah Lindsay laid out the flower garden, and the young Felix Harbord decorated the new orangery with Rococo plaster trophies symbolizing horticultural interests. The house survived intact until after Mrs Tritton's death, when its contents were dispersed in a series of sales in 1983, but while the prices for many of the things were high, there was also a sense of disappointment and the house was not considered a period piece of enough significance to have been worthy of preservation. All the good elements of the time were present, but it lacked the distinction and vitality of Ditchley, and did not display the passionate concern for objects that was the mainspring at Buxted.

One other person needs to be introduced at this point, Lady Juliet Duff, who, as was explained in the previous chapter, had gone to live at Wardes in Kent in 1919. In 1933 she moved to Bulbridge House at Wilton. Consequently it is interesting to be able to compare photographs [76, 77] taken for *Vogue* in 1935 with the *Country Life* photographs showing the house as it was in 1962, three years before her death. Although, naturally, she had made some changes over the years, they bear out Mrs Lancaster's contention that she and the Duke of Wellington were unrivalled in their talent for arranging rooms and works of art. Christopher Hussey wrote of the satisfactory combination of her personal taste and possessions and

74. GODMERSHAM PARK, KENT. THE
DRAWING ROOM. Fine original decoration of
about 1735 and notable early-eighteenth-century
needlework on the chairs and firescreen. The total
effect is like a period room in a museum.

75. THE INSPIRATION OF UPPARK. The new
staircase at Godmersham, hung with portraits and
groups by Benjamin Wilson, arranged in imitation of
the Devises at Uppark.

76 and 77. BULBRIDGE HOUSE, WILTON, WILTSHIRE. LADY JULIET DUFF'S DRAWING ROOM AS IT WAS IN 1936 AND 1963. Lady Juliet had an excellent eye for a range of works of art and furniture and also an exceptional gift for arrangement. The two illustrations bring out the increasing sophistication and elaboration of decoration after the mid-1930s. The decoration of this room in 1963 showed how ideas associated with the pre-war Regency Revival continued in use after 1945. The wallpaper was an Empire design of gold rosettes on a pink ground. The Jacob chairs were covered in a rose and white material relating in pattern to the wallpaper and in colour to the curtains draped in an Empire-Regency manner.

Wyatt's 'slight yet discerning touch', because 'both are seen to be based on the same aesthetic values'.

Moreover in this little house he is seen in an easy, relaxed mood that all too readily with him lapsed into indolence, and which is excellently suited to Lady Juliet's flair for informal *ensemblement*: for bringing together, as if carelessly, things with a certain relationship to one another and to their setting – works of art whether of the period or recent, flowers, books or products of friendship. It is this unselfconscious, catholic, but ultimately classical, certainty of taste both in design and decoration that gives the house today a distinctive and delightful coherence.

It is interesting to be able to compare what Christopher Hussey wrote with an extract from R. M.'s obituary in *The Times* on 29 September 1965:

Nobody had more close friends with contrasting interests, belonging to every generation and several nationalities. They included many little-known persons as well as stage celebrities and such distinguished figures as Maurice Baring, Hilaire Belloc (who addressed to her some of his best poems), Diaghilev, Poulenc, Vita and Eddy Sackville-West, Rose Macaulay, Mr Somerset Maugham, Lady Diana Cooper, Lady Churchill and Sir Winston, whom she went to see every week until his death.

Ditchley [XII, 123–126], Buxted and Godmersham as they were in the 1930s survive only in photographs, and Lady Juliet's rooms have gone too, but among the rare survivors of that time are the rooms at Leeds Castle in Kent [VIII, IX] which Boudin decorated for Lady Baillie. Again it is not a wholly English story: Lady Baillie was English by birth, but her mother was a Whitney, and she herself spent much of her early life in France; and, although she loved Leeds Castle, which she bought in 1926 and devoted many years to restoring and decorating, first with Rateau, a French decorator, her eye was always more international than English. So it was natural to her to turn in 1936 to Boudin for the dining room, the library and her bedroom. They are brilliant rooms, thought out and researched with infinite care, and executed with remarkable attention to the smallest details of texture, but somehow in their very perfection they strike most English people as too studied and so unsympathetic and unnatural. Also Boudin never fully saw the point of English historical styles nor the English way of life. It is for that reason that Plas Newydd in Anglesey [80–83] is the best representative of country house taste of the time. Indeed that house is doubly interesting if

it is compared with Beaudesert in Staffordshire ([78–79]; now demolished), which was also transformed by the 6th Marquess of Anglesey. Born in 1885, he succeeded in 1905, and married in 1912 Lady Marjorie Manners, one of the daughters of the 8th Duke of Rutland; he died in 1947, the year after his wife. In 1909 there was a fire at Beaudesert, and Lord Anglesey entrusted part of the restoration to Captain Harry Lindsay, the brother of his future mother-in-law, the Duchess of Rutland. When it was illustrated in *Country Life* in 1919, H. A. Tipping wrote that the house 'had suffered excessively from an outburst of neo-Gothicism a hundred years ago [at the same time as Plas Newydd], and the object was to give back to it, in very large measure, but with some later features and much modern convenience, the character it possessed towards the close of Queen Elizabeth's reign'. And he continued, '[it] is a remarkably complete and extensive example of the tendency of our age to re-create the past in all matters of architecture and the decorative arts'. Thus the design of the Yellow Drawing Room was based on rooms at Thorpe Hall and Forde Abbey, and the details of Lord Anglesey's sitting room were copied from Plas Mawr in Conway.

Lord Anglesey never grew to appreciate the late, sub-Wyatt gothick elements at Plas Newydd and, when in the mid-1930s he did a great deal of work there, he trimmed the exterior of as much gothick detail as he could and played up the Georgian classical character of the principal rooms. But the whole feeling of the house is quite different from Beaudesert – much lighter, less historicist and more consistent, more relaxed. To compare the two is a revealing demonstration of one man's reaction to changing fashion in the twentieth century.

The climax to Lord Anglesey's alterations at Plas Newydd is, of course, the dining room, looking across the Menai Straits to Snowdonia. It was painted by Rex Whistler between 1936 and 1938. That wonderful room transcends interior decoration as it is usually understood, and it conveys more vividly than anything else the mood of a time that found expression in other ways, among them Clough Williams-Ellis's development at Portmeirion (within easy reach of Plas Newydd), and the foundation of the Georgian Group.

Also it serves as an introduction not only to Rex Whistler but to two other contemporaries of his at the Slade, Oliver Messel and Felix Harbord. Oliver Messel was born in 1904, Rex Whistler in 1905 and Felix Harbord in 1906; Rex Whistler and Felix Harbord went to Haileybury and then on to the Slade. Oliver

78 (top left). BEAUDESERT, STAFFORDSHIRE. THE LONG GALLERY. When the Elizabethan house was restored after a fire in 1909, all traces of its early-nineteenth-century gothick interior were removed and it reverted to the sixteenth and seventeenth centuries.

79 (below left). THE YELLOW DRAWING ROOM AT BEAUDESERT. This was based on the famous mid-seventeenth-century room then at Thorpe Hall and now at Leeds Castle.

80 (right). PLAS NEWYDD, ANGLESEY. Rex Whistler's unfinished conversation piece of Lord Anglesey and his family begun in 1939.

81 (below). THE DINING ROOM AT PLAS NEWYDD, PAINTED BY REX WHISTLER. For a detail, see illustration XX.

82. THE DRAWING ROOM AT PLAS NEWYDD IN 1955. The set of four large landscapes by Ommerganck were installed in the mid-1930s. The room appears less fully furnished than it is today, but the *Country Life* photographer may have removed some of the furniture.

83. LADY ANGLESEY'S BEDROOM AT PLAS NEWYDD. This was decorated in the mid-1930s, apparently by Lady Colefax, who was a friend of Lady Anglesey, but the year is not recorded. It is hung with a Mauny lace-pattern wallpaper.

Messel, who was there from 1922 until 1924, began to work in the theatre in 1925; and Rex Whistler began to paint murals in 1924, at Shadwell; the decoration of the restaurant of the Tate Gallery followed in 1925–7, and after that came the halls at Dorneywood and 19 Hill Street in 1928–9, and Port Lympne in 1930 [67].

Laurence Whistler has written of how his brother discovered the painting of Poussin and Claude, Watteau and Boucher, Salvator Rosa and Canaletto and also Georgian architecture while he was at the Slade, and of the impact that Rome made on him on his first brief visit there in 1925; and of how he discovered that he wanted to draw architecture through seeing Stowe in 1926: 'He then lived in two worlds with equal pleasure: visually in the classical, poetically in the romantic.' His feeling for country houses emerges in two particular paintings, of Weston Hall, for the Sacheverell Sitwells in 1929, and of Haddon Hall, for the Duke of Rutland in 1933 [11].

It was about that time that he met the Pagets, and although it is not absolutely certain how the commission from Lord Anglesey came about in 1936, it was, as Gervase Jackson-Stops has written, in many ways a summing-up of all his previous experiences and influences, of favourite places, of Rome, Venice, and the coast of Italy, of Brighton, Dublin and London and of favourite painters, in particular Claude and Vernet.

At least one detail of its architecture shows his delight in the gothick revival, and in 1938 he painted the drawing room at Mottisfont Abbey in Hampshire [85] in the gothick style.

Rex Whistler and Oliver Messel both got established quickly. It took Felix Harbord rather longer, and for a variety of reasons he never achieved the same heights of success, but all the same he is a tantalizing figure in the world of houses who deserves to be remembered alongside them; and certainly, as will be seen in the next chapter, he had more feeling for country house decoration than Oliver Messel. However, of his pre-war work only two commissions appear to have been photographed: the orangery at Godmersham Park in Kent; and his redecoration of Kingston Russell House in Dorset, carried out immediately after Mr and Mrs William Vestey bought the house in 1939 (and illustrated in *Country Life* in 1951 [84]). Two rooms there stand out, the entrance hall and the dining room. The former was fitted out in a style that Arthur Oswald described as inspired by William Kent originals, but it seems a little later and lighter, with its swan-necked pediments to the main doorcase and overmantel, and its trophies that are his counterparts in plaster of those

in paint by Rex Whistler. The dining room he decorated round a particularly fine Rococo chimneypiece and a landscape wallpaper that came from Felix Hall in Essex.

Alongside these houses, there is one inherited house other than Houghton that stands out, Uppark in Sussex [LXXIII, 183–185], not only for itself but for the response to it of the people who inherited it in 1931. The Hon. Herbert Meade, the son of the 4th Earl of Clanwilliam, had been chosen as her ultimate heir by Miss Fetherstonhaugh (who died in 1895). She in her turn had inherited Uppark from her sister, the widow of the last Sir Harry Fetherstonhaugh, who had died in 1842 at the age of ninety-two. Admiral Sir Herbert Meade-Fetherstonhaugh, as he became, followed his father into the Navy and in 1911 he married Margaret Glyn, a daughter of the Bishop of Peterborough. They knew that they would inherit Uppark after the death of the tenant for life, and Lady Meade-Fetherstonhaugh always looked forward to the day when she would become its chatelaine and bring it to life once more. She had a strong sense of her family's position and great feeling for the romance of Uppark's history and its atmosphere of Georgian Survival. That is apparent in her Epilogue to *Uppark and Its People*, written with Oliver Warner in 1964: ' . . . Harry Fetherstonhaugh looked down from over the Saloon door in the hall and laughed. Did we hear the rustle of Emma Hamilton's muslin skirts as she caught the look in the rogue's eye, or the song of a milk maid in a chequered dairy . . . ?'

The Admiral used to say that his wife was in love with the house. Although it was she who organized the muniment room, she was neither a scholar nor an antiquarian but an informally educated Edwardian, with some talent and training as a painter. She was immensely attractive to men and excellent company, and also had an ability to get other people to do what she wanted, particularly if it concerned Uppark. Among those who helped her, for instance, was Nattie Davidson, a bachelor friend of leisure and taste who devoted a great deal of time to the rearrangement of furniture. The Admiral, too, had a fine sense of responsibility towards his inheritance and a good eye as well; it was he who gathered all the Lethieullier portraits by Devis together and hung them on the staircase. All this meant that, although they thought that they were badly off, Lady Meade-Fetherstonhaugh felt that she was reviving the old way of life at Uppark, which depended on an indoor staff of twelve until 1939.

84. KINGSTON RUSSELL HOUSE, DORSET. THE ENTRANCE HALL IN 1951. Felix Harbord
reconstituted some of the principal rooms in this eighteenth-century house in 1939. Although the
qualities of eighteenth-century decorative plasterwork were being rediscovered and Rex Whistler was
influenced by it in some of his decorative painting, Felix Harbord appears to have been the only
artist–designer to make a close study of it and recapture its spirit.

Thus, when she started on her great work of what is now called 'textile conservation' at Uppark, she was inspired as much by the economy and the financial impossibility of replacing the damask festoon curtains as by her feeling for the 'patina of age', as she always called it. She picked up snippets of information about the house and its contents from the many people who came to see what had become a legendary place that had been asleep for a hundred years; and it was through two of her husband's aunts that she met Mrs Antrobus, who ran a shop selling tapestry and needlework supplies and also did textile repairs for the Victoria and Albert Museum. It was Mrs Antrobus who introduced her to the herb *Saponaria officinalis*, the

washing of the exhausted silks at Uppark in a soap made from it by the chef, and the process of sewing the broken material to a new ground. Her methods are no longer approved by textile conservators, but as far as country houses are concerned she was a pioneer: by the outbreak of war she had revived twenty-eight curtains as well as bed hangings and chair seats. After the war she ran her workroom as an amateur business with three helpers, doing a great deal of work for other owners, and for the Royal Collection; and above all she opened many peoples' eyes to the possibility and importance of preserving textiles, just as Uppark made people aware of the special quality of the 'patina of age'. Among those on whom Uppark made a great

85. MOTTISFONT ABBEY, HAMPSHIRE. THE GOTHICK DRAWING ROOM. This room was decorated in 1938-9 for Mr and Mrs Gilbert Russell, who had bought the house in 1934. Even as late as 1954 Mrs Russell did not regard the room as complete in its furnishing. This photograph, taken in 1950, shows deep-buttoned sofas with elaborate fringes, presumably ordered in the late 1930s, which had been removed by 1954.

impression were Mrs Ronald Tree and John Fowler, but of that more anon.

Christopher Hussey's remark about the country house situation in his articles on Buxted helps to explain why hardly any thought was given to the future of country houses at that time, a situation confirmed by James Lees-Milne in *The National Trust Year Book 1976-77*: 'Strange as it may seem to-day there was little concern about the impending fate of England's country houses in the early 1930s: that is to say, little concern among preservation bodies, and absolutely none in government departments even when the Tories were in power.' Of course there was no listing of historic buildings at that time, and the brief of the Royal Com-

mission on Historical Monuments ran out in 1714, which remained the terminal date until 1962, when it was extended to 1855.

Nevertheless there were individuals in the early 1930s who foresaw the dangers ahead, among them the 11th Marquess of Lothian, of whom James Lees-Milne has written:

He was a country house product, of course, but not a typical one. He was a man who looked to the future who appreciated the artistic importance to the nation of its finest architecture. He was a man of radical views. He implicitly believed that when the families were driven from their houses, and driven they ultimately would be, the public must be enabled to use, appreciate and enjoy them.

It was his speech to the Annual Meeting of the National Trust in 1934 that led to the formulation of the Trust's Country Houses Scheme.

The Trust's report for 1935/6 remarked: 'Probably a number of these houses with their parks and gardens and contents will one day be held by the Trust for the benefit of the nation ...'; and on 12 March 1936 the first meeting was held of the Country Houses Committee, the precursor of the Historic Buildings Committee and of the present Properties Committee. (Lord Lothian became a member of it in 1936–7 and in 1939–40 agreed to become Vice-President of the Trust when he returned from the USA.) The Committee's first secretary was James Lees-Milne, who wrote in *Another Self*:

Suddenly the very job of which I had dreamt when at Oxford and did not believe existed, presented itself. The National Trust was launching a new scheme to save some of the historic houses of England, and needed a secretary. Vita Sackville-West, whose memory I bless on this account as well as a hundred others, recommended me to the Trust ...

Here it is impossible to go into the details of the Trust's negotiations with owners and the government. A number of owners began to consider offers of their property, among them Charlecote, Stourhead, which went to the Trust in 1937, Corsham and Knole; but, partly because of the way property was held, it was often a difficult and slow process for owners to make the gift or devise, and some places were in the pipeline for several years. Indeed Charlecote and Knole passed to the Trust only after the war, and the late Lord Methuen was never able to make the transfer.

The start was slow, but as the Trust's report for 1939/40 said: 'The Council remain confident that the Trust's scheme for the preservation of historic and beautiful country houses was well founded. It was never expected, for various reasons, to have rapid and spectacular results; and it has not done so ...' Of those early years James Lees-Milne has written that they 'were about the happiest, because the most fulfilled of my life. The National Trust was then truly a vocation, not a profession. The male staff – it numbered four amateurs – received very low salaries.'

The growing concern for country houses was paralleled by another for the fate of Georgian buildings and planning, which fell outside the sphere of interest of the Society for the Protection of Ancient Buildings, at that time the only national preservation society. Hence the Georgian Group was formed and it is fascinating to see how the membership of the Group overlapped with that of the Trust. The idea of the Group was that of Douglas Goldring, the novelist, poet and biographer, as Gavin Stamp explained in the *Architects Journal* for 31 March 1982; and it came into being on 2 April 1937. Lord Derwent became chairman, but it was more significant that Robert Byron became deputy chairman. The Committee included Professor Richardson, James Lees-Milne and John Summerson; and at the second meeting it was decided to invite Lord Gerald Wellesley, Margaret Jourdain, Lord Rosse and John Betjeman. Subsequently Christopher Hussey was also invited to join the Committee.

Robert Byron, who was born in 1905, had been at school with Oliver Messel and at Oxford with Harold Acton, Evelyn Waugh and Desmond Parsons, the younger brother of Lord Rosse. As Colin Amery wrote of him, he was a traveller, historian and critic and the author of some of the most stimulating architectural writing of the thirties; he was a man of passionate views. However, it was only in the mid-1930s that he underwent a kind of personal conversion as far as Georgian architecture was concerned, and it was typical of him that he should have become the most forceful spirit in the Georgian Group as well as a driving force among his friends, several of whom were on the Committee. There is an insight into his personality in Christopher Sykes's essay in memory of him – he was drowned when his ship was torpedoed in 1941 – in *Four Studies in Loyalty*. Looking back to the autumn of 1936 when they were both staying with the latter's elder brother at Sledmere in Yorkshire, Christopher Sykes recalled:

He remained a fighter to the end, but he had acquired the calm of conscious inner strength. Many prejudices were falling away, many of the bees which had buzzed so furiously in his bonnet had flown away through discovered outlets. There was now, for example, no trace of the anti-classical bee; on the contrary, he had become a champion of our English classical heritage, and had already, with his friend Lord Rosse, begun the formation of the Georgian Group, whose aim was to preserve the eighteenth century of England against English philistinism. The 'Patriot in our age' had fused into a fine and more rational loyalty; into a patriotism in our civilization.

CHAPTER FOUR

COUNTRY HOUSES AND HOUSES IN THE COUNTRY 1945-74

It is not often that taste and fashion can be seen to be so clearly related to an economic and social situation, but the influence of country houses, that is to say houses that are or were part of landed estates, and attitudes to them since the Second World War can be considered in that kind of way. Ever since the First World War the country house situation has been a very fluid one, with many changes of ownership, sales of contents and demolitions as well as restorations; and in the fifteen years after the Second World War the losses were particularly heavy. Even so it is already possible to see the years 1945 to 1974 as a distinct and constructive period in the history of the country house.

The first fifteen years after the end of the war were marked by a great determination on the part of many owners who had inherited their houses to bring them to life again and to find a new role for them; and, fortunately, a surprising number of people were prepared to buy country houses and devote their energies to their restoration. At the same time, from 1948 successive governments began to realize that they had a role to play in their survival, even if they have never played it sufficiently hard; and in the 1950s historical and artistic arguments for government aid coincided with an unprecedented degree of mobility and a new demand for recreation from a growing number of people. But those strands on their own would not have been enough to achieve success; alongside them lie the greater confidence in the years of Conservative government (from 1951 to 1964), growth on the stock ex-

change, the revival of agriculture and so the recovery of the landed estate as an economic unit. The start was slow, painfully slow, and many owners gave up, either because they could not soldier on or because they could not see a future. By the mid-1950s, however, a recovery was fairly clearly underway; and the achievement of the 1950s and 1960s that extended into the early 1970s was a most remarkable one.

Then in the autumn of 1974 came the proposal to introduce a Wealth Tax as well as replace Estate Duty by Capital Transfer Tax, and although the Wealth Tax proposal was defeated, the autumn and winter of 1974/5 seems to have marked the end of that period of recovery. As the wife of one owner wrote on 15 October 1974, to thank me for a copy of *Country Houses of Britain: Can They Survive?*, 'It is food for thought, of a bitter kind. I am afraid the game is up, and that's all there is to it. Nothing can supplant the use for which the houses were built, however imaginative. We have been incredibly lucky to catch the tag end of it all, and struggle as we may there is no going back.' Ten years later confidence has still not been restored.

It is worth going into this economic, political and social history in more detail in order to see how it related to the reaction against the years of austerity that lasted until the early 1950s and how it ran parallel to the enthusiasm of those interested in the history of English art and architecture as well as country houses and to fashionable taste in houses and decoration; and to see how and where these different threads interlocked. However, the situation is complicated by the fact that more than one generation was involved: in the 1950s most of the owners responsible for the recovery had been established before the war, or at least ready to leave school in 1939; but by the early 1960s a younger generation of owners was coming forward, new enthusiasms were developing and so was a new approach to the past.

George Howard, the late Lord Howard of Henderskelfe, who inherited Castle Howard in 1944 after his elder brother had been killed in the war, wrote of his own experiences in *The Destruction of the Country House* in 1974: 'My Trustees, many years older than myself, could not envisage my family living at Castle Howard after the war, and would have sold it to the school which occupied it from 1940 to 1949 if terms could have been agreed ...'

As far as the recovery of country houses was concerned, the most important element was the determination of owners to move back into them. That was very deep-seated, but it was part of a spirit not just confined to owners. During the war most of the larger houses had been adapted as schools or hospitals or for a great variety of military purposes, while the smaller ones had battened down their hatches. As Lady Meade-Fetherstonhaugh wrote of Uppark: 'When war came again, and the family dispersed to fight, I remained as a watch-keeper, and the house of Uppark settled down to its own remote solitude. When daylight died on warm summer evenings, and the noise of the coastal guns had lessened to an occasional muttering, the search lights would cross each other in the sky ...'

Perhaps as a result of the threat to them, country houses came to be seen in a much clearer way as part of that British tradition that was such a source of strength in a time of peril. That is to be seen in the publication of books like V. Sackville-West's *English Country Houses* and Evelyn Waugh's *Brideshead Revisited*, both of which appeared in 1944, and it is apparent in some of the pictures of John Piper. He had discovered romantic classicism for himself, first at Stowe, about the time that Rex Whistler first saw it, and then shortly before the war in his paintings of Stourhead; a little later he was drawn to the gothick style at Hafod, in 1939, and at Lacock [87], in 1940. In 1942 he received commissions from the Queen to do a series of watercolours of Windsor Castle and from Sir Osbert Sitwell to paint Renishaw and the neighbouring houses, Hardwick, Bolsover, Barlborough, and Sutton Scarsdale to illustrate the autobiography on which he was working.

Of those pictures Sir Osbert wrote in his introduction to the exhibition *The Sitwell Country* at the Leicester Galleries in January 1945:

At the very moment when the great English houses, the chief architectural expression of their country, are passing, being wrecked by happy and eager planners, or becoming sterilized and scionless possessions of the National Trust, a painter has appeared, to hand them on to future ages, as Canaletto or Guardi handed on the dying Venice of their day, and with an equally inimitable art.

Christopher Hussey, reviewing the exhibition in *Country Life* on 26 January 1945, headed his article 'The Twilight of the Great House' and referred to 'these great houses' and their 'aura of boding tragedy'.

During the war *Country Life* had played a part in the revaluation of country houses by its emphasis on tradition and by continuing its series of articles on country houses. It was an amazing achievement on Christopher Hussey's part that he was able to sustain that series virtually single-handed. The link between peace and war is well brought out in two letters to him. The first is from Lady Meade-Fetherstonhaugh describing the progress of photography by A.E. Henson at Uppark for articles published in 1941:

When photographing my Bedroom a splendid Air Battle took place in front of the House which ended in the Hun crashing and bursting into flames and I really held onto the little man's coat tails. He hung out of the window. Or again when complete with bowler hat on a lovely summer morning he stood in the Park waving a handkerchief – a signal to me that Lady Wolverton was to pull up the window blinds ...

The second is from the Hon. Mrs Lyell and is dated 16 May 1943:

Dear Christopher. Ever since Anthony was k. in N. Africa, I've been meaning to write and tell you that the last I had from him there – he said that he found a copy of Country Life in a wood and that it was so lovely to read of what one was fighting for.

It was that kind of spirit that lies behind a remark of Lady Radnor, talking of her experiences at Longford Castle to a group of American students in 1972: 'We had won the war and we would win again.' Later, in *The Destruction of the Country House*, she wrote: 'I remember standing beside our beacon fire on VE night in 1945. We were telling ourselves that the

86. CHATSWORTH, DERBYSHIRE. THE STATE DRAWING ROOM IN 1939. Edward Halliday's
painting of November 1939 shows the room in use as a dormitory by Penros College, who were
evacuated there from 1939 until 1946.

87. LACOCK ABBEY, WILTSHIRE, BY JOHN PIPER, 1940. One of a group of paintings of
country houses painted by John Piper in the early part of the Second World War.

miracle had happened: we were all alive, the house had not been bombed, the troops in it were British and not German, we had won the war. Nevertheless in all the rejoicing my husband, speaking as the owner of a country house, said to me, "Now our personal problems begin." '

That spirit is forgotten now. Also we have forgotten how long it took for the recovery to get going. The National Trust soon began to open its handful of houses and the late Duke of Devonshire re-opened Chatsworth in 1949 (although deciding not to move back there himself). Longleat opened in 1949 (George Howard only regained control of Castle Howard that year, when the school evacuated there in the war finally left); Lord Montagu of Beaulieu opened Beaulieu in 1952, the year after he came into the estate; the Duke of Bedford opened Woburn in 1955 and Lord Hertford Ragley in 1958. Thus evidence of real progress did not begin to become apparent until the mid-1950s.

The general situation is illustrated in the report of the Historic Buildings Council for 1963, reviewing the first ten years of its work.

In 1953 it is no exaggeration to say that the prevalent attitude, at any rate among owners of large houses, was one almost of despair. Staffing problems, caused by full employment and high taxation, linked with high maintenance costs, seemed to indicate that even the prospect of grants towards the cost of major structural repairs opened up by the Historic Buildings and Ancient Monuments Act of that year, would be insufficient to stem the flight from the big house and the sale of its contents ... In 1963 the position is very different, and, while there is no room for complacency, the dominant note is no longer one of despair ...'

It is interesting to compare that with Evelyn Waugh's preface to the second edition of *Brideshead Revisited* in 1959:

It was impossible to foresee, in the spring of 1944, the present cult of the English country house. It seemed then that the ancestral seats which were our chief national artistic achievement were doomed to decay and spoliation like the monasteries in the sixteenth century. So I piled it on rather, with passionate sincerity. Brideshead today would be open to trippers, its treasures rearranged by expert hands and the fabric better maintained than it was by Lord Marchmain.

The enthusiasm for country houses, however, was surely more fundamental than a combination of growing aesthetic and historical interest, the desire for recreation and romantic curiosity. One of the best explanations of it is in a thoughtful 'advertisement' for *Country Life* included in the back of the National Trust guidebooks published in about 1950:

In a famous phrase Canning spoke of calling the New World into existence to redress the balance of the old. It is not mere play on words to claim that one of the constant endeavours of *Country Life*, in these restless and changeable times, is to recall the Old World to redress the balance of the New.

In other words, *Country Life* believes that the present cannot dispense with the cumulative wisdom of the past; that unless progress and tradition go hand in hand, and good taste is preserved, there is a grave danger of destroying the good with the bad in our efforts to rebuild Britain.

When did the recovery get under way? Clothes rationing was abolished in March 1949. A Conservative government was returned in 1951. In 1954, the first full year of government repair grants for historic buildings, there were 150-200 places open to the public. By 1963 the total was about 600. By 1958 the total amount of grant aid offered had gone up from £254,304 a year to £548,597; and no less than forty of the 102 new offers made were to country houses. Obviously recovery on the stock market was one element, but by no means all owners had investment income, and it is necessary to look at agriculture and land. The depression that had started in the mid-1870s meant that the price of land (in 1871 the average price was £53 an acre) more than halved in the next twenty years. It started to recover only in 1940, but it was not until the late 1950s that it reached the 1875 figure. (That makes no allowance for the change in the value of money and, as Sir Michael Culme Seymour has pointed out, £53 in 1871 was somewhere close to £450-£500 in 1973, when the average price was £500-£600.) In the late 1950s the value of land began to increase more sharply, going up from about £58 in 1960 to £200 in 1970, and then, after a slight drop, soaring towards £450 by the beginning of 1974. With rents for agricultural land in England and Wales the mid-1870s figure was not reached until 1950, and then in the following twenty years the average figure increased from £1.50 an acre to £6.50. At the same time more and more owners were trying to take land in hand.

All that might seem far removed from the world of taste and decoration, but the general recovery is brought to life in the history of a number of houses. In the case of Sezincote in Gloucestershire, Mr and Mrs Cyril Kleinwort (as they then were) knew of the house from reading Osbert Sitwell and Margaret Bar-

XII. DITCHLEY, OXFORDSHIRE. THE HALL, PAINTED BY SERABRIAKOFF IN ABOUT 1948.

XIII. HASELEY COURT, OXFORDSHIRE.
A SECTION OF THE WALLPAPER IN THE
PALLADIAN ROOM. Starting with a
fragment of eighteenth-century wallpaper, John
Fowler and George Oakes developed the
design for a complete eighteenth-century
chinoiserie wallpaper and painted it themselves
in 1958.

XIV. PART OF THE CEILING OF THE
GOTHICK ROOM AT HASELEY. Apart
from the gothick cornice and the central rose,
all the rest of the decoration, including the
garland on the end wall, was painted in
trompe l'œil by John Fowler and George
Oakes in 1958.

XV. THE *TROMPE L'ŒIL* RELIEF OF
DIANA OVER THE CHIMNEYPIECE IN THE
GOTHICK ROOM AT HASELEY. Mrs
Lancaster's only criticism of the painting was
that John Fowler did not understand female
anatomy.

XVI. 22 AVERY ROW, LONDON.
THE YELLOW DRAWING ROOM.
Mrs Lancaster and John Fowler
transformed this room in 1958. The
curtains to the end windows,
although elaborately headed, did not
stand out from the walls, because
they were of yellow taffeta that lived
with the glossy yellow of the walls.

XVII. BIRR CASTLE, CO.
OFFALY. THE DINING ROOM IN
1970. Its early-nineteenth-century
character was reinforced in the late
1940s when Lady Rosse hung the
flock paper that she had ordered
before the war; at the same time the
panelled dado was added and the
chandelier made for the saloon was
restored.

XVIII. THE SALOON AT BIRR IN
1970. The early-nineteenth-century
room with a green and gold
Victorian wallpaper as arranged by
Lady Rosse, who introduced the set
of Chippendale furniture and
subsequently things from her parents'
house in London. She always filled
the room with spectacular
arrangements of flowers.

XIX. WOMERSLEY PARK, YORKSHIRE. THE DRAWING ROOM IN 1983. An excellent example of John Fowler's painting in the late 1950s of an architectural interior of the Georgian period.

XX. PLAS NEWYDD, NORTH WALES. PART OF REX WHISTLER'S PAINTING OF THE DINING ROOM.

XXI. A LONDON DRAWING ROOM DECORATED BY JOHN FOWLER ABOUT 1936, AS IT
APPEARED IN 1984. The Regency Revival curtains are of champagne-coloured satin panelled with pink
taffeta ribbon. The contrasting draped valances trimmed with crimson fringe are of satin and pink taffeta
with an answering satin ribbon, and the tails reverse. The early Victorian armchairs are upholstered in
yellow satin and deep-buttoned with double bows of aubergine-coloured silk ribbon.

ton's book on Brighton, and when they saw it advertised for sale in *Country Life* in the middle of the war, they went to see it and bought it. It was only in 1946, however, when Mr Kleinwort came out of the Navy, that it became possible to think of going to live there. When his wife was asked in 1968 how she got the house in order, she replied: 'Sheer perseverance, persistence, energy. And we were lucky in that our staff from the old house came with us. But it was uphill work, complicated by the fact that in those first post-war years any building work could only be carried out by government licence with a limit of something like a hundred pounds ... But gradually, as things improved we were able to press on.'

When it came to the main rooms Mrs Kleinwort sought the advice of John Fowler, and, like a number of people who did so, what lay in the back of her mind was Ditchley, which she saw for the first time about 1950, after Ronald Tree had remarried. No one could revive pre-war Ditchley life, but in its approach to furnishing and decoration it still represented an ideal.

Basildon [88-90] in Berkshire offers a parallel to Sezincote and, as the years pass, it will seem increasingly interesting as representing both the mood and the connoisseurship of the time. In the Foreword to the guidebook produced by the National Trust in 1979, after her husband had given the house, Lady Iliffe told the story:

It was in 1938, the year of our marriage, that I first saw Basildon - we just drove past it, as it was empty and there was no sign of life, the park and trees looked abandoned, but I remembered how lovely it looked in the afternoon sun. Then the war engulfed us for six years, after which came the difficult post-war period, with rationing still enforced. But our mutual interest in the eighteenth century was by then becoming evident, and we began to think of a house in Berkshire - an old rectory, for instance.

One day, in 1952, I went to look at Basildon, not thinking of it in that context, but out of sheer curiosity and interest, wondering how it had survived the war. It was just about to be derequisitioned by the Ministry of Works ... To say it was derelict is hardly good enough ... And yet, there was still an atmosphere of former elegance, and a feeling of great solidity. Carr's house was still there, damaged but basically unchanged ... We looked around in amazement, then on leaving I remember saying to a friend 'How sad, what a waste - and it could still be saved,' and he said 'Why don't you?'

That is how it started. My husband agreed and we set to work. Rationing of building materials was still in force; permits had to be obtained; we had to keep the restoration to essential repairs ... It was only later that we gradually re-

paired the whole house. But first we had to learn more about Carr's architecture, so we made a pilgrimage to Yorkshire where most of his houses are, and looked at Harewood House, Farnley Hall, any Carr house we could find, and finally Panton Hall, in Lincolnshire, which was going to be used for storing crops, and has since been pulled down. There we found just what we needed to repair our house, including the two marble chimneypieces now in the Dining Room and Library. The owner was delighted to do a deal and we returned in great excitement, followed by two loaded lorries.

Carr was such a precise architect that his mahogany doors from Panton fitted exactly in the sockets of the missing Basildon ones ... The whole of the restoration of the centre block was over in a year and a half, with the local builder, Mr Smallbone, doing a wonderful job with his skilled craftsmen. The repair to the two pavilions were to follow much later.

We were both determined not to overdo the restoration, and thus curtains and colour schemes had to be kept in control, so as to blend with ceilings where original colours had survived but faded. Hence the silk curtains in the Dining Room, the Octagon Room and the Hall, all date from the eighteenth or nineteenth centuries. Where new ones were unavoidable, we copied old shapes, taking them to pieces and realizing how much fuller they were than modern 'drapes'. The whole household helped; the butler held the ladder while the cook and I nailed the red felt on the wall. It was fascinating and exhausting, but we were all twenty-five years younger ...

Pictures were the main problem, and gradually we found ourselves exchanging early purchases, such as small French canvases, for larger Italian ones; they seemed to suit the house, and this explains why the Italian school of the seventeenth and eighteenth centuries dominates. It was a continuous process, and even the Mentmore sale yielded one or two items, but due to present prices we came back with coal scuttles instead of marble topped console tables ...

Basildon is one of the houses where the owners took advantage of sales at other houses, and thus many of the individual fittings and objects have an evocative provenance, coming as they do from Eaton Hall, Fawley Court, Brockenhurst Park and Ashburnham Place. From Ashburnham and Blenheim came curtains and their cornices and from Ditchley one of the beds redressed by Sybil Colefax. The furniture is complemented by Italian pictures, some of them by artists admired in England in the eighteenth century, but the pictures do not represent Grand Tour taste as much as the enthusiasm for Italian painting that has grown up in England since the early 1920s and initially promoted by the Magnasco Society. In the saloon, for instance, there are a set of Batonis that represent *God the Father* and some of the Apostles, not the kind of subjects that

88. BASILDON PARK, BERKSHIRE. THE SALOON. Carr's room, enriched about 1840, as furnished by Lord and Lady Iliffe in the 1950s and 1960s. The curtains came from the Grand Cabinet at Blenheim, the pelmet cornices from Ashburnham Place, the gothic chairs from Eaton Hall. The Pittoni over the door is flanked by four pictures from a set of *God the Father and the Apostles* by Batoni.

89. THE CRIMSON BEDROOM AT BASILDON. The room is furnished with a William IV bed and curtains from Ashburnham Place. Purchases made at the sale of that house in 1953 appear in many of the interesting rooms furnished in the mid-1950s [see also 160, 133].

90. THE GREEN CHINTZ ROOM AT BASILDON. The polonaise bed was originally made for
Ditchley in about 1790 and was rehung with a painted chintz, either by Boudin or Lady Colefax, for
Mr and Mrs Ronald Tree in about 1935.

would have appealed to an eighteenth-century English
collector; and in fact they only arrived in England from
Italy shortly before Lord Iliffe bought them.

Parallel to this determination of country house owners came a new development in the National Trust
situation. During the war it became clear to it that its
responsibilities were bound to increase; its report for
1942/3 noted that:

On all sides increasing interest is being shown in the Country Houses Scheme. The Trust already owns twenty-three
houses of the type intended to be preserved under this
scheme and its records show that at least a further forty
historic country houses and estates may be expected to come
to it either by gift in the near future, or by will. Preliminary
discussions are taking place with the owners of many houses.

In 1939 the Trust had 410 properties and 58,900 acres.
In 1943/4 seven country houses came to it. Thus by

1945 it had no less than ninety-three historic buildings
and 112,000 acres, with Wallington, Blickling, left to
the Trust by Lord Lothian in 1941, Cliveden and Great
Chalfield, Packwood, West Wycombe, Lindisfarne,
Polesden Lacey, Speke, Gunby, Lacock and Hatch-
lands and Charlecote all having come since 1939. In
1946 Knole, Lyme, Cotehele, Horton Court and
Osterley were accepted.

For some of those whose old family houses survived
only through being given to the National Trust, the
transfer could be painful and take many years to
accept. That comes out particularly vividly in the
'Epilogue 1946' to *Treasure on Earth* (1952), Phyllis
Sandeman's evocation of an Edwardian Christmas:

Then they rounded the bend, and there was the house
confronting them across the valley ...
All this was just as in the old days, and yet there was

91. MONTACUTE, SOMERSET. THE DINING ROOM IN 1950. An early example of a room
furnished by the National Trust and partly dependent on loan, including the Pinturicchio *Madonna and
Child*, the ribband back chairs and the tapestry. When the Trust re-opened the house after the war, it
was a novel idea in England to show a furnished country house.

surely something strange about the appearance of the house, a subtle difference – but what it was Phyllis could not at once discover. Then as they drew near she saw what it was.

The windows were no longer bright and gleaming, but shuttered and opaque; no longer looking out across the valley, they were blind eyes or eyes closed in sleep ... the place had always seemed to her to be alive, tearing with the spirit poured into it by those who had created it, loved it, lived and died in it. But now it was dead, just as they were dead; it had died when it ceased to be a home.

If the Trust was growing fast, it was still a tiny organization, with all the historic buildings work falling on James Lees-Milne and Eardley Knollys, who became the Trust's first Historic Buildings Representative dealing with 'aesthetic, architectural matters'. The latter had joined the Trust as a land agent in 1941 and at the end of 1944 he proposed that when Montacute [91] was derequisitioned the Trust should re-

open it as a furnished house, then a new idea. In April 1945, an appeal was launched for suitable furniture and a special committee appointed to supervise the task, but there was virtually no money: at one stage funds were so low that a van bringing things over from Stourhead had to be cancelled because it would have cost £3 10s. Even so the house was re-opened in July 1946.

The growth in the Trust's responsibilities is reflected in the expansion of interests represented on its Country Houses Committee. In 1942/3 Lord Esher asked Lord Methuen, Lord Rosse and G.M. Trevelyan to join it; the following year Lord Gerald Wellesley returned as Duke of Wellington. In 1944/5 Harold Nicolson became a member; in 1946/7 Sir Leigh Ashton, the Director of the Victoria and Albert Museum; in 1947/8 Anthony Blunt; and in 1949/50 Christopher Hussey.

In 1951 James Lees-Milne retired from being Historic Buildings Secretary and handed over to Robin Fedden, a man of a diversity of talents and interests as well as great determination, who, much to James Lees-Milne's surprise, had applied for the job of looking after Polesden Lacey in 1946. Robin Fedden had a certain unsentimental detachment in his approach to houses that was quite different from James Lees-Milne's and seems to have been in part a reflection of his non-English streak: brought up largely in France, after Cambridge he had lectured at Cairo University and travelled extensively in the Middle East.

Looking at the number of houses held by the Trust today and the size of the budget, it is very hard to picture the situations described by James Lees-Milne in his three volumes of extracts from his diaries, *Ancestral Voices* (1975), *Prophesying Peace* (1977) and *Caves of Ice* (1983). Indeed his acute, entertaining, and self-deprecating style disguises the nature of what was largely his creation in the early years of the Country Houses Scheme.

It is difficult to have a balanced view of the achievement of both private owners and the Trust, because their priorities are not exactly the same and there must be differences in their approaches. Yet if one is to consider the influence of the country house on attitudes and taste in the post-war period, it is surely the complementary nature of the ownership of houses that has played a part in that influence.

If Basildon represents the enthusiasm for Georgian classicism and Italian painting, there was also a growing taste for the gothick that is probably best represented at Donnington Grove [92], also in Berkshire, which the Hon. Mrs Reginald Fellowes bought in 1946 and restored with the aid of H.S. Goodhart-Rendel. The house is not well known, but it was illustrated in *Country Life* by Christopher Hussey in 1958. The photographs suggest a very thorough approach to both furnishing and decoration, with a feeling for fantasy and the exotic, and, if it does not look completely English, that is explained by Mrs Fellowes having been the daughter of the Duc Decase and the widow of Prince Jean de Broglie.

It is interesting to compare the photographs of that house with the work of Felix Harbord, after John Fowler the most talented decorator of his generation. Thanks to his training at the Slade and in Sir Albert Richardson's office, Felix Harbord had both a painter's and an architect's eye for houses and decoration, with a highly developed feeling for scale and tone. Also, as Christopher Gibbs said at his memorial service, he had:

an enviable and lightly worn knowledge of European architecture, painting and craftsmanship; and of myth and legend; that rare and real feeling for history that enabled him to recount some far off saga and make it seem new; a fascination for the ways things were made and a graceful facility as a painter and modeller that made him eager to restore the missing top of a towering seventeenth-century Delft tulipiere or paint gilded walls with tortoiseshell arabesques like Boulle marquetry.

As we saw in the last chapter, he loved eighteenth-century plasterwork; also he had a penchant for eighteenth-century Dutch decorative art and objects that is unusual in an Englishman. That is apparent in what he did at Farley Hall, near Reading [93], soon after the war for his brother-in-law and sister, Mr and Mrs Alan Palmer. Not only did he put back Georgian detail that had been removed from rooms – chimney-pieces, doorcases, cornices, chair rails and so on – but he created a new dining room, in which he combined a scheme of English decorative plasterwork that included an eighteenth-century Dutch marble urn in the overmantel with an eighteenth-century Dutch painted ceiling.

In approach that room followed on from what he had done at Kingston Russell in 1939, and in its turn it was to be followed at Oving House [94, 95], a medium-sized seventeenth- and eighteenth-century manor house in Buckinghamshire, where he worked for the Hon. Michael and Lady Pamela Berry (subsequently Lord and Lady Hartwell) in 1954 and 1955. Rex Whistler had painted Lady Pamela before the war, and so it was appropriate that they should go to Felix Harbord to elaborate the eighteenth-century decoration in the house. All the plasterwork in the Hall, except for the overmantel, is his, and it is fascinating to compare that with the *trompe l'œil* painting which John Fowler and George Oakes were to do for Mrs Lancaster in the Gothick Room at Haseley two or three years later [XIV, XV, 128].

Felix Harbord's most ambitious scheme of decoration was at Luttrellstown Castle, near Dublin [X, 96, 97], where he not only embellished existing decorations but designed whole rooms for the Hon. Mrs Aileen Plunket, finding fittings and much of the furniture for them. He first went there in 1946, and over the next twenty-five years he and Mrs Plunket tackled the house room by room, but apparently without a master plan. The Grisaille Room, for instance, was designed round a series of canvases by de Gree, a Dutch decorative painter who had a considerable practice in Ireland in the 1770s and 1780s. For the ballroom he found what

92. DONNINGTON GROVE,
BERKSHIRE. GOTHICK
FURNITURE IN THE HALL. In
1946 the mid-eighteenth-century
gothick villa was acquired, restored
and elaborately furnished by Mrs
Reginald Fellowes, who was of
French and American descent.

93. FARLEY HALL, BERKSHIRE.
THE NEW DINING ROOM IN
1952. This was completely designed
about 1948 by Felix Harbord to fit
into the early-eighteenth-century
house, which he restored after the
war for Mr and Mrs Alan Palmer,
his brother-in-law and sister.

94 (top right). OVING HOUSE,
BUCKINGHAMSHIRE. THE HALL.
Apart from the relief over the
chimneypiece, all the rest of the
plasterwork and the carpet were
designed by Felix Harbord in 1954-5.

95 (below right). THE DRAWING
ROOM AT OVING. The ceiling, the
frieze, the doorcases and the
chimneypiece up to the level of the
top of the consoles are original mid-
eighteenth-century work; the rest of
the decoration is by Felix Harbord.
The plaster trophies are copied from
those at Harleyford Manor, also in
Buckinghamshire.

96. LUTTRELLSTOWN CASTLE, CO. DUBLIN. THE GRISAILLE ROOM. Felix Harbord
transformed most of the principal rooms of this gothick house for Mrs Plunket between 1948 and 1960.
Among the earlier rooms was this one decorated round a series of grisaille paintings from Oriel
Temple, Co. Louth, by de Gree, a Dutch painter who worked in Ireland in the 1770s and 1780s.

97. THE DINING ROOM AT LUTTRELLSTOWN. Within the shell of a Victorian great hall Felix
Harbord formed a classical room with a Dutch painted ceiling similar in outline to the one in the
dining room at Farley Hall, a set of tapestries found in Ireland, and an English marble chimneypiece;
the late-Victorian doors were found in the house and he designed all the
elaborate plasterwork.

is one of the finest of all eighteenth-century English chimneypieces, probably carved by J.F. Moore for Fonthill Splendens; for the staircase hall he found a painted ceiling from Ufford Place in Suffolk. He was always intrigued by architectural fragments and making compositions out of them, as he did with the chimneypiece and overmantel in the hall.

His real *tour de force* at Luttrellstown was the dining room: within the shell of what had been a Victorian baronial hall he created a sparkling classical interior that is a brilliant evocation of the Georgian period. It is impossible to discover in what order he assembled the key elements, but the remarkable expanding circular table had been found at Luttrellstown when Mrs Plunket first went to live there in 1930; and he seems to have re-used doorcases already in the house, Georgian at first glance but, at a second, more Georgian Revival of the late nineteenth or early twentieth century. The eighteenth-century marble chimneypiece was his importation, as were the set of tapestries and the painted ceiling of *The Triumph of Bacchus and Ceres* by de Wet dated 1753. However, it is the plaster trophies that are the most remarkable feature, and, while the natural presumption might be that they were cast from eighteenth-century originals, they were in fact made by Jacksons from Felix Harbord's own drawings based on his close study of eighteenth-century plasterwork illustrated in books like *Decorative Plasterwork in Great Britain* by Turner. He absorbed the detail so fully that I find it impossible to identify the quotations.

Felix Harbord had a number of clients in England, but, although his work was occasionally illustrated in magazines, his name was not widely known here and he did not have a general influence on the style of houses and rooms. On the other hand he was someone who had an influence on a circle of younger friends, among them Christopher Gibbs, who recognizes how much he learned about objects and their disposition from him.

Most of the post-war restorations by new owners were of Georgian houses or earlier houses Georgianized, and that makes the story of Flaxley Abbey [98–100] interesting for the future. In 1960 Sir Launcelot Crawley-Boevey had to sell the house after 300 years of family occupation, and, after a period of doubt as to its future, it was saved by Mr and Mrs F.B. Watkins with the active support of Oliver Messel, whose work, in particular his Raynes shop in Bond Street, had captivated Mrs Watkins. In fact it was the only large country house that he remodelled and redecorated, and

it probably appealed to him because of its diversity of character and perhaps also because of the parallels it offered to his parents' house, Nymans in Sussex. At Flaxley Abbey, in Gloucestershire, however, the refectory and the Abbots Room were genuinely medieval. Also there were handsome neo-classical rooms by Anthony Keck. However, what had virtually disappeared was evidence of the seventeenth-century interior to match the exterior. So he suggested that period by forming a Stuart bedroom, with a new bed and genuine furniture, much of which he had inherited from his parents. Perhaps not surprisingly the house had something of the quality of a set waiting for actors to come on and bring it to life, but it seems to anticipate the broadening out of taste from the eighteenth century that was becoming stronger in the late 1960s and 1970s. That had been anticipated as early as 1954 by Cecil Beaton, a natural weathercock of fashion, who had written of the Regency style: 'It is still enjoying such a high popularity that continued over-use will surely begin to pall before long.'

Intentionally only the briefest mention of John Fowler's name has been made so far, because his work is discussed in greater detail in later chapters. However, in 1968, the year before he retired from full-time involvement with Colefax & Fowler, Robert Harling, in his introduction to *Historic Houses. Conversations in Stately Houses* (1969), put him into perspective in a remarkable way:

The Dukes of Northumberland, Beaufort, Norfolk and Atholl were amongst the subscribers to Chippendale's *Director* issued in 1754. Could any furniture designer to-day interest such a ducal quartet in his designs?

Yet there is one designer-decorator to-day who does exercise what is virtually a monopoly of patronage and practice in the decoration, restoration, furnishing and refurbishing of almost any great house in England, or, for that matter, Scotland or Ireland. That is John Fowler ...

No other designer or decorator of our time has imaginative authority comparable with that of John Fowler, who has managed the vastly tricky job of decorating eighteenth-century houses in a manner that is authentic yet never pompous and – rarest gift of all – is never pastiche ...

If the main achievement of the post-war period lay in the re-opening and restoration of country houses, there is a second one to consider: the perfection of houses in the country, that is to say houses that are not part of landed estates, smaller manor houses, granges and old rectories, for the most part houses of lesser architectural interest but possessing a certain dignity and charm and combining that with comfort

98. FLAXLEY ABBEY, GLOUCESTERSHIRE. THE REFECTORY.

and convenience. The most interesting ones owe an obvious debt to country houses in their combinations of furniture and pictures while avoiding their formality and grandeur. Obviously houses of a somewhat similar character have always existed, but perhaps only since the Second World War have they had such a deliberate romantic character, looking back not only to the eighteenth century but to the pre-war world as well. It was the kind of house in which John Fowler excelled, as can be seen at Ivy Lodge, Radway [XLV, XLVI]; a surprising number of the best ones belonged to people who knew him. Sadly many of them have gone already, among them Countess Paul Munster's arrangement of Bampton Manor, Cecil Beaton's arrangement of Reddish House at Broad Chalke, and Mr and Mrs Lees-Milne's arrangement of Alderley Grange. Not only did these houses reflect country houses, but the most successfully arranged country houses surely also owe a debt to them in terms of intimacy and informal comfort. Moreover the influence of what has come to be thought of as the English style or the country house style has come partly through them, or at least photographs of them, as well as from country houses.

In part the response of owners of country houses and houses in the country came from the heart, but also there was an intellectual back-up in some of the books of the post-war period. After 1945 there was a spate of books on the classical style and the Georgian period that were more detailed than most of those published before the war. Among them were John Summerson's *Georgian London* in 1945, Francis Thompson's *Chatsworth* (1949), David Green's *Blenheim* in 1951, the first edition of John Summerson's *Architecture in Britain* (1953) and H.M. Colvin's *Biographical Dictionary of British Architects* (1954); Christopher Hussey's trilogy on Georgian country

99. THE STUART BEDROOM AT FLAXLEY. All trace of the seventeenth-century decoration of the interior had disappeared, so Oliver Messel suggested it through this re-creation, which included the bed designed by him. Much of the furniture had belonged to his parents.

100. THE MORNING ROOM AT FLAXLEY. The cornice and chimneypiece are part of the original eighteenth-century design, but the rest of the decoration, including the hangings, the alcoves and the Spanish carpet, were designed by Oliver Messel.

houses came out between 1955 and 1958. Architectural history was developing very fast, but not all the best books were academic: probably the most influential and certainly the most inspiring was Sacheverell Sitwell's *British Architects and Craftsmen*, published in 1945, a deeply felt and richly written personal account that gave form to the mood of the time as well as influencing a younger generation.

However, interests were also moving forward. In his diary on 8 May 1946 James Lees-Milne noted: 'Roger Fulford says that he and John Summerson are both turning their interests from Regency to mid-Victorian. In some measure they have both set a fashion.' By 1958 the time was ripe for the foundation of the Victorian Society, although most of the moving spirits belonged to the generation grown up before 1939 and some had been involved with the establishment of the Georgian Group twenty years earlier. Indeed the changing taste was anticipated by Evelyn Waugh, writing in *A Handful of Dust* in 1934 of Hetton Abbey, rebuilt in the English Gothic style in 1864:

They were not in the fashion, he fully realized. Twenty years ago people had liked half timber and old pewter; now it was urns and colonnades; but the time would come, perhaps in John Andrew's day, when opinion would re-instate Hetton in its proper place. Already it was referred to as 'amusing', and a very civil young man had asked permission to photograph it for an architectural review.

By the 1950s Christopher Hussey was interested in the transition from Late Georgian to Early Victorian, as is apparent from his articles on Tregothnan, Mamhead, Charlecote and Harlaxton and the Late Georgian (third) volume of his Country House trilogy; and in the late 1950s Mark Girouard began to write regularly about High Victorian country houses in *Country Life*, in the process causing eyebrows to be raised at what still seemed the ugliness of some of them. Christopher Hussey's interest was partly a natural development of his taste, but it was also encouraged by his inheritance of Scotney Castle in Kent, where he had to think out how to treat the rooms fitted out by Salvin for his grandfather a little more than a hundred years earlier. That new appreciation of the period of William IV and the early years of Queen Victoria in its turn encouraged a less purist approach to the eighteenth century, and Regency Revival interiors of the late 1920s and early 1930s began to look rather self-conscious and stiff.

Here it is revealing to compare the Duke of Wellington's re-arrangement of Stratfield Saye in Hampshire [101, 103] immediately after the war with the Duke and Duchess of Devonshire's rearrangement of Chatsworth ten years later. The Duke of Wellington combined a marvellous gift for the arrangement of pictures and furniture with a remarkable historical sense and a connoisseur's eye, but he was sixty in 1945, and his eye and his taste with its main interest in the Baroque and Empire periods had been completely formed about 1930.

The spirit of Chatsworth [XI] is different, and while that is obviously partly a matter of the personalities involved, there is surely a difference of generation too, with the deliberate combination of periods and of the fine and grand with the simple and the comfortable; and what is fascinating is that the private rooms have gone on evolving, with pictures changing in response to the Duke and Duchess's enthusiasms. The Blue Drawing Room, for instance, was first hung with mainly eighteenth-century pictures, but gradually over the years more modern pictures have come in and Reynolds's portrait of the Duke of Cumberland has given way to Sargent's huge group of *The Acheson Sisters*.

Alongside Stratfield Saye and Chatsworth, Boughton in Northamptonshire [105-110] and Drumlanrig in Dumfriesshire [104] must surely have their place, because of the understanding of them shown by the late Duke of Buccleuch and his wife, Mary, Duchess of Buccleuch. It was an amazing achievement on their part that they steered not just two but three great houses and their collections from 1935, when the Duke inherited, through the war, and for twenty-eight years after – no museum director could have coped so well – and kept them as private houses. In neither does the word 'decorate' come to mind, because it appears quite unnecessary in those two magical houses that combine grandeur and simplicity so harmoniously. They demonstrate an appreciation of scale and tone as well as a feeling for history in the arrangement of pictures and furniture and the care of individual objects. However, if photographs of Boughton taken by *Country Life* in 1970 are compared with an earlier set taken in 1932 and another set taken for *Vogue* in 1938, it is interesting to see how much had been achieved through judicious alterations before the war and how little in essence the character of the house changed after, although an immense amount had to be done when the house was re-opened after the war. They give an impression of an unobtrusive taste guiding its arrangement.

The 1970 photographs of the Great Hall and drawing room at Boughton and the dining room at Drumlanrig

101. STRATFIELD SAYE, HAMPSHIRE. THE HALL IN 1948. After the war the Duke of
Wellington brought his architectural experience, historical knowledge, connoisseurship and gift for
arrangement to bear on the house.

102. THE 7TH DUKE OF WELLINGTON, BY PETER GREENHAM. Lord Gerald Wellesley
succeeded as Duke in 1943.

taken in 1960 record an experience even then hardly
found anywhere else in the British Isles. As Mark
Girouard wrote:

Above all, Drumlanrig is that rarity, a great house still
fully lived in, with no hint of the museum atmosphere that,
sadly, but perhaps inevitably, envelops so many country
houses to-day; the public are not regularly admitted. The
depressing panoply of red cords and drugget carpets is
absent; the great drawing room is in daily use; the glittering
table is laid for a real dinner, not as a show for visiting
tourists.

In any decade there are bound to be a variety of
threads, not necessarily all pointing in the same direction, and certainly that was so in the 1950s and 1960s.
One that needs to be borne in mind is that the opening
of houses to the public and the need to restore them

103. THE GALLERY AT STRATFIELD SAYE IN 1948. It was the Duke who arranged the large bronze busts on buhl pedestals and the Louis XVI cabinets. Later, in 1951, he had a special carpet woven in Madrid.

and redecorate them for visitors came by the middle to late 1960s to give a particular appeal to the houses that had kept their mystery and to rooms that remained unsorted by 'experts', untouched by restorers and decorators. 'Pleasing decay' was seen to have another layer, and Irish houses in their melancholy state to have a special magic, as did those few houses with a similar feeling in Britain. Erdigg, near Wrexham, had that quality because of the characters of the last two Yorkes and the way in which objects of the greatest rarity and interest somehow survived in bewildering and not always picturesque disorder: the appeal of the eccentric, the secret and the romantic was combined with the fascination of a vivid historical and social document. The enthusiasm Erdigg aroused in the 1970s has had a considerable influence not only on attitudes to preservation but on how people hope to see houses

and rooms handled if they are formally preserved; and also on decisions about what should be preserved.

The growing taste for Baroque and Mannerist pictures and works of art encouraged a taste for much bolder objects, among dealers as well as collectors, as is particularly apparent in the taste of the late Geoffrey Bennison and Christopher Gibbs.

Christopher Gibbs, who had started to deal at school, opened his first shop in Camden Passage in 1956, when he was eighteen; he moved to Elystan Street in 1960/61 and later to Bond Street. His shops and Geoffrey Bennison's have been consistently much the most exciting to visit throughout the past twenty-five years.

In decoration one of the key influences is that of David Hicks, who, as soon as he set up on his own in 1954, began to make his mark on style and fashion.

104. DRUMLANRIG CASTLE, DUMFRIESSHIRE. THE DINING ROOM IN 1960. Mark Girouard wrote in *Country Life* that it seemed remarkable that Drumlanrig was 'a great house still fully lived in, with no hint of the museum atmosphere'.

105 (right). BOUGHTON HOUSE, NORTHAMPTONSHIRE. THE GREAT HALL IN 1970. Both Drumlanrig and Boughton demonstrate a rare appreciation of scale and tone, as well as a feeling for history, in the arrangement of pictures and furniture on the part of the late Duke of Buccleuch and Mary Duchess of Buccleuch.

106 (top left), 107 (below left), 108 (above). THE DRAWING ROOM AT BOUGHTON IN 1932, 1938 AND 1970. The photographs show the effect of the re-opening of blocked windows, the tactful repainting of the wainscot and the rehanging of pictures by the Duke and Duchess of Buccleuch between 1936 and 1938.

109 and 110. THE LIBRARY AT BOUGHTON AS IT WAS IN 1932 AND 1970. When the Duke and
Duchess of Buccleuch re-opened the house after the war, John Fowler helped the Duchess with the
sorting of furniture and problems of painting and upholstery. While he did little decoration for her, it
is possible to detect his discreet influence in this room.

III. BRITWELL SALOME, OXFORDSHIRE. THE ENTRANCE HALL IN 1972. David Hicks's characteristically striking, clear, crisp decoration and arrangement, bringing history up to date, with stone-coloured joinery and chocolate-brown walls based on historical evidence.

However, although he has had a number of commissions to work in British country houses, he has had less influence in that direction than might be supposed. His approach to them in the 1960s was best represented at Britwell Salome, which he and his wife bought in 1960. There he set out to make a bridge between the past and the present by combining abstract pictures with seventeenth- and eighteenth-century portraits that his wife had inherited and furniture of modern design with eighteenth-century French and English pieces; and great play was made with careful compositions of objects and also dried flowers. The result was dramatic and exciting, particularly in the dining room, with its series of clashing reds; but there was also a certain feeling that people intruded on the composition of the rooms.

Four years after David Hicks began work, Mr and Mrs Desmond Guinness acquired Leixlip Castle [112-

114] in Co. Kildare, which soon became a rather different source of inspiration. Already it is clear that it was the key country house in the British Isles in the late 1950s and 1960s, the equivalent of Kelmarsh and Ditchley before the war but in the vastly different world of post-war Ireland, among a different circle of people and having a quite different kind of point. Earlier, in 1958, on the fiftieth anniversary of the foundation of the Georgian Society, which had produced a pioneer series of volumes on eighteenth-century Irish architecture, the Guinnesses refounded it as the Irish Georgian Society; and it was the conjunction of the look of the house, the Guinnesses' approach to life and the aims of the Society that made Leixlip such a stimulating place as well as a remarkable visual experience for the diverse circle of people who flowed in and out through the seemingly ever-open doors.

The process of restoring, decorating and furnishing

112. LEIXLIP CASTLE, CO. KILDARE. THE HALL IN 1971. When first decorated in 1958–9, the
house made an immediate impression because of the simplicity of its decoration, its strong colours and
brilliant whites, its bold sense of scale and its rejection of elaborate upholstery.

the house was very much a shared enthusiasm, with complementary contributions from two remarkable people; but it always seemed to me that the overall look of the house owed more to Mrs Guinness, who has a rare gift for composing objects and rooms in a stimulating way and combining unlikely, and occasionally unpromising, objects to create memorable effects. Comparisons with Mrs Lancaster naturally come to mind, and that was vividly summed up by Christopher Gibbs, who once described to me the taste of Mrs Lancaster as 'patrician' and that of Mrs Guinness as 'princely'.

Somewhat surprisingly the story starts in Japan, because Mrs Guinness, who before her marriage was Princess Marie-Gabrielle von Urach, regards her first experience of architecture as having taken place before she was five, when she was taken to see the temples at Kamakura, near Tokyo. Indeed her earliest memories

are of life in Japan, where her father was on the staff of the German Embassy. What struck her particularly was the great importance attached by the Japanese to the visual aspects of life. Thus it was memories of flower arrangements in Japanese taxis that led her on a flight from Sweden to England in 1940, when she was seven, to wonder how she could make the interior of the aeroplane pretty. Most of the war she spent in Sussex with her adopted aunt, Miss Hermione Ramsden, who had reacted strongly against conventional upper-class values in the 1890s, becoming a socialist and living most of the time in Norway; she also stayed a good deal in Berwickshire with her maternal grandmother, Mrs Blackadder, a Norwegian by descent but born and brought up in Darmstadt in Germany, who had met her Scottish husband while he was at a German university. Mrs Blackadder, who had been interested in the Jugendstil, had fine things of that kind as

113. THE GOTHICK ROOM AT LEIXLIP. By the mid-1960s the house contained some notable eighteenth-century Irish furniture and pictures, including a set of views of Carton by Roberts, one of which is seen over the chimneypiece. The windows in several of the rooms were left uncurtained.

114. THE DINING ROOM AT LEIXLIP. Pale-yellow wainscotting with white mouldings and part of Robert Healey's set of pastels in grisaille of the Conolly family and the Castletown hunt.

well as from the Glasgow School, and these she combined with eighteenth-century Blackadder furniture and pieces from Norway. The combination was an amazing one, particularly to an only child whose natural visual sense she did much to encourage.

After the war Miss Ramsden sent her abroad, to the Loire, to Italy and to Germany to meet members of her father's family, who lived in houses, castles and palaces of varied character ranging from the Baroque to Wagnerian Gothic, with touches of Turkish as well. Not only the individual colours but their combinations and successions made a great impression on her there, in particular crimson and dark green with brilliant white and gold, and the long white-washed corridors. After her aunt's death in 1950 she lived mainly with Mr and Mrs Brinsley Ford and so was introduced to yet another set of visual experiences essentially eighteenth-century in inspiration. She also stayed a good deal in Oxford, and nothing gave her greater pleasure than to find a friend with a motor car who could be persuaded to drive her and her friends to look at country houses round about, including Ditchley and Rousham.

It was at Oxford that Desmond Guinness became seriously interested in architecture and began to look at country houses in a conscious way, having already unconsciously absorbed the atmosphere of Biddesden in Wiltshire, where he was brought up. However, at that stage he had no thought that the cause of preservation in Ireland would become a main thread in his life. Indeed he intended to be a farmer, and after a course at Cirencester he went to Ireland to complete his training as a farmer. He had married immediately after he came down from Oxford in 1954, and, since his wife had fallen in love with Ireland on a visit two years earlier, she was delighted when the opportunity came to leave England and live there. A little later they began to look for a permanent home and at Dublin architecture, so becoming aware of the pace of destruction in the city. It was the demolition in Kildare Place that stirred Desmond Guinness to action, and in 1957 he began to sound people out about the formation of a preservation body in the shape of a revived Georgian Society, which took place formally early in 1958, with sixteen founder members.

In 1956 he had tried to buy Castletown when it was put on the market after the death of Major Conolly, but that was impossible. (It was put up for sale again in 1965 by Lord Carew, who had inherited it, but at that stage, while Desmond Guinness bought some of the key contents with a view to saving them for the house, he was still not able to acquire it; finally, in much more difficult circumstances, in 1967 he was able to buy the house with a little land in order to preserve it, and in 1979, on the twenty-first anniversary of the Society, he gave the house to the Castletown Foundation.) However, although they could not buy Castletown, Mariga Guinness was reading the remarkable eighteenth-century correspondence of the Conollys that was then being published in Ireland, and it was because of those letters that she went to look at Leixlip, a romantic house with sturdy towers and elegant Georgian gothick windows standing above the Liffey.

They did not have much money to spend on its repair or furnishing, but they set to with a will. The upper rooms contain a good deal of their own work. Mariga Guinness describes buying quantities of Walpamur in strong colours inspired by her memories of Germany and Norway to counteract the greens and greys of Ireland and seeking out good furniture that was cheap because it had had a hard life and, what was then considered unusual, leaving it unrestored. The origin of her thinking about colour is particularly interesting, because it coincided with David Hicks's quite independent use of strong, dark colours.

Her emphasis on economy needs to be borne in mind too, because the Guinnesses never spent a great deal on comfortable armchairs or sofas or on elaborate curtains which are the usual hallmark of a 'decorated' house. On the other hand Desmond Guinness was able to buy, mainly between 1960 and 1965, a number of good pictures relating to the locality in the eighteenth century, starting with the set of large views of Carton by Roberts, some fine eighteenth-century Irish furniture and a great many Irish architectural drawings. Ultimately it was the feeling for scale in the house and the combination of the Irish pictures and furniture with the simple decoration supported by prints, piles of books and quantities of shells that made it such a complete and convincing Irish country house, very carefully thought out but achieved with such brio and confidence that it seemed natural and not contrived. It managed to be stylish and unfussy; quite grand and yet informal and cut-back; and everywhere there was both a vivid historical air and a sense of fantasy.

In the early 1960s such Irish pictures did not seem important to many people in Ireland or anywhere else, and there was little commercial or academic interest in them, so the Guinnesses' enthusiasm was a new stimulus. In turn it derived strength from their circle of friends, in particular from Mark Girouard, an Oxford contemporary, Maurice Craig, originally a friend of

Lord Moyne (Desmond Guinness's father), and Desmond Fitzgerald, Knight of Glin, who appeared in their lives in 1959.

Thus the serious interest in eighteenth-century Ireland joined forces with an interest in the look of the houses, and many people were influenced by this combination, among them the Knight of Glin. Not only did it inspire many people to be bolder, but it gave heart to a number of younger people who had inherited daunting, decaying country houses in Ireland and saw for the first time how they could cope with them; and the Guinnesses not only gave them advice and moral support but turned up with Walpamur and brushes as well. Also right from the beginning American groups came to see Leixlip – the first one in 1959 – which meant that shoals of American decorators proceeded to try to copy some of the ideas, notably the Red Room. Of the British decorators who went to Leixlip, the most significant proved to be David Mlinaric.

He first went there in about 1960-61. He had recently completed three years at the Bartlett School of Architecture, where after his first term he switched from architecture to interior design and decoration. Unlike almost all his contemporaries there, he was interested in the history of architecture and classicism as well as the Modern Movement; also he was excited by what David Hicks was doing, particularly in his use of colour, his sense of display, with its concentration on objects, and the cut-back simplicity of his work. However, the first country house to make a great impression on him was Beckley, which he saw about 1958. In 1963, after two years with Michael Inchbald and six months in Rome, he returned full of enthusiasm for things English, and he set up on his own in Tite Street.

What David Hicks, Beckley and Leixlip did in different ways for him was to provide alternatives to the boredom of the look of polite Belgravia Georgian Revival, while Leixlip also provided an alternative to the life that went with that look. Yet with David Mlinaric there is the additional point that he is not wholly English, although born and brought up here; his father was Jugoslav, and so he has always looked at the English tradition with the appreciation of detachment.

His first country house commission was to furnish Lord Lichfield's rooms at Shugborough in Staffordshire, which, by coincidence, were being done at the same time as the Trust was consulting John Fowler about the main rooms (and needless to say John went to see 'what those children were up to' and recognized

that a new talent was at work). However, his first scheme of serious architectural decoration was at Millichope Park [115, 116] in Shropshire. On both occasions he was working on a much tighter budget than John Fowler would have accepted at that time, and at Millichope there was no question of restoring a historic paint scheme but of achieving an intelligent effect in emulsion paint. When I saw it for the first time about 1971 I knew David Mlinaric's name but nothing about his work, and I felt immediately that here was someone who had understood the principles of decoration as I was learning them from John Fowler but who had rethought them for new circumstances.

In England in the 1960s there was no single house that was the counterpart of Leixlip, but what was apparent was the growing enthusiasm and seriousness of the cause of country house preservation, with more houses being opened to the public, more government money for repairs, the National Trust continuing to expand its Country Houses Scheme, and more and deeper research being carried out. As far as decoration was concerned that particularly affected the National Trust. The increase in the number of visitors, the rising expectations about what they would see and the standard of facilities that they wanted for their reception exerted a much greater collective pressure on a large body such as the Trust than it did on individual owners; and as a result round about 1963-5 the Trust began to spend considerably more money on the restoration and decoration of interiors in its houses. It is that situation that explains why John Fowler became so active on the Trust's behalf in the late 1960s and early 1970s, as is explained in a later chapter. And it is probable that what the Trust did in its houses not only had an influence on private owners, but influenced visitors in their expectations. We are still so close to those years, and the whole subject of restoration and decoration is so fraught, that it is difficult to be sure. Many private owners are critical of the Trust's handling of its houses, saying that they are dead because they are not lived in and that the Trust is extravagant; but there is also an element of envy and frustration over what the Trust has been able to achieve that springs from their uncertainty as to their own future.

The expectations of visitors to country houses has been fanned by photography, particularly colour photography, and, while even now the latter is seldom accurate, it not only gives people an impression of a house and sometimes catches its mood, but influences the way many people look at things. What has been

115 (left). THE CENTRAL HALL AT
MILLICHOPE PARK, SHROPSHIRE.
The walls were painted by David
Mlinaric in a warm biscuit-honey
colour and the architectural detail in two
shades of light-grey stone, with the
columns in the darker shade and the
frieze and capitals in the lighter.

116 (right). MILLICHOPE PARK.
In 1968-70 the neo-classical house was
reduced by suppressing the basement
entrance beneath the portico and
separating the house from the end
bays of the later service wing.

117 (below). HEYDON HALL,
NORFOLK. THE DRAWING ROOM
IN 1982. A house partly redecorated
with the advice of David Mlinaric. The
walls are painted yellow and
the seat furniture is upholstered
in blue and white striped ticking.

done and the way it has been illustrated have fused together to establish a view of the past that has become the basis of an influential style of decoration.

As it happened this growth of restoration and decoration in country houses open to the public coincided with the decline of purely private country house decoration. By the time John Fowler retired from full-time involvement with his firm in 1969, the particular kind of practice that he had built up in the 1950s and that had flourished during the 1960s was about to go into a marked decline, as he was aware. Most of his clients belonged to the generation who had grown up before the war, and there were fewer people in the younger generation with the houses, the means and the desire for that degree of detail. The mood had changed.

Of course some country house decoration continues, but costs, particularly for special materials and trimmings, are infinitely greater, and so the best decoration is much simpler. Here one of the most interesting houses that I have seen is Heydon Hall in Norfolk, because its recent history illustrates so clearly the links between agriculture and the landed estate and approaches to houses and taste. Captain Bulwer-Long came into Heydon in 1964, but the Hall, which had been let since 1932, became free only in 1970, and it was then that he and his wife had to decide what to

do with it. Clearly it was an impractical proposition to attempt to repair and modernize and live in the whole house, with all its additions, and so they opted for a scheme of reduction that kept the original Elizabethan core and gave them sufficient space to take the unusually large collection of family portraits; at the same time it would be of a size that could be furnished – much had been sold in 1949 when it seemed impossible that any member of the family would ever live there again – and it could be run easily. In 1974 David Mlinaric helped them with the decoration of the Red Drawing Room, the staircase hall and subsequently the drawing room [117]; and later at a sale in Ireland he found them the seat furniture for the last, and he had it upholstered in a simple blue and white striped ticking that works well with the pale yellow walls and also makes historic sense because it suggests the look of case covers. The whole effect is timeless and yet of today, and I sense that lying behind it is an understanding of the work of both John Fowler and David Hicks, the former in the overall synthesis and the latter in the directness and the clear, strong colours. Heydon is much the most encouraging country house I have seen in England in the past few years, not only for itself but for the way it shows how styles develop and move forward.

CHAPTER FIVE

FOUR DIFFERENT APPROACHES

In writing about attitudes to the past, to country houses, interiors and decoration in the twentieth century, there is a natural tendency to devote too much attention to the contributions of architects and decorators, and not give enough consideration to patrons and clients. Yet it is they who set the mood of the time, even if it is the professionals who give it form and style; and certainly that is important after the Second World War, even if many of their ideas had developed before it. It makes the Georgian enthusiasm of the twentieth century not only more drawn out but more fragmented and complicated. So it seemed helpful to write of four owners who have a complete understanding of houses and gardens and the Georgian tradition. They stand out because they have expressed themselves in their houses in a highly articulate way, but they do not belong to the same circle and they have different approaches, quite apart from the fact that their houses present different challenges.

The first of these is Mrs C.G. Lancaster, a Virginian whom I see as the last representative of the Henry James tradition in England, but with a completely un-Jamesian lightness and sparkle: as John Fowler's partner after the war she played a crucial role in his success and so in his influence, but even if she had never met him, she would still have had a significant influence on English and American taste. The second is Anne, Countess of Rosse, brought up with her brother, Oliver Messel, to look at every aspect of houses and gardens so that she became interpreter and

preserver of her family's houses, and with her husband, the late Lord Rosse, closely involved with the preservation movement. Colonel Roger Hesketh represents the tradition of the amateur classical architect so strong in the eighteenth century, but virtually extinct today. He rebuilt his family house in Lancashire around his family pictures and furniture, creating a visual unity that has also a historical reality. The fourth is Colonel Rupert Alec-Smith, who combined an appreciation of Georgian architecture with a feeling for local history that he expressed in his own house and pursued in his work for the preservation of historic buildings in East Yorkshire.

Obviously there are others I could have chosen, but I think that the enthusiasm of these four people throws light on the relationship between decoration and taste and attitudes to the past and to preservation that are shared by many more people.

MRS C. G. LANCASTER (MRS RONALD TREE)

As long ago as 1954 Cecil Beaton wrote in *The Glass of Fashion*:

Among those who energetically flout all contemporary obstacles or disparagements, Mrs Nancy Tree has a talent for sprucing up a stately but shabby house and making a grand house less grand. She has an adequate reverence for tradition, observes the rules of style and proportion, and manifests a healthy disregard for the sanctity of 'important' furniture

... Her love of colour, her flower sense, and her feeling for comfort have brought a welcome touch to many an English house sorely in need of such ministrations.

At that point she had been John Fowler's partner for about eight years, and, although she never worked with him on a regular basis, she made a contribution to his success and influence that is as important as it was involved and subtle, as will be explained. However, she had started to have an influence on English and American attitudes to houses and taste more than twenty-five years before that; and, what is so rare, she has continued to inspire not only her own contemporaries, but her sons' generation and the generation after that.

Her houses and gardens have been such complete expressions of the essence of England that it is all too easy to forget that she is in fact an American, or rather a Virginian – she always used to fly the Confederate flag over her house, not the stars and stripes – and that it is her early years in Virginia that provide the key to her approach. In particular she has what strikes me as a non-American appreciation of the romantic quality of old buildings that certainly existed in Henry James's day; and it has been inspired by her memories of un-selfconscious Virginian houses in mellow decline after the Civil War. It was in them that she grew to love faded colours and materials softened by time and to understand the mood of a house.

She first came to England in 1910, while at school in France, and then again in 1915, when she stayed with her father's sister and her namesake, Nancy, wife of Waldorf, later 2nd Viscount Astor. It was on that second visit that she became aware of the houses of Edwardian ladies of taste, among them Lady Essex, a great friend of her aunt and also an American (born Adele Grant, she was the second wife of the 7th Earl of Essex), Lady Florence Willoughby, the wife of Lieutenant-Colonel the Hon. Claud Willoughby and sister-in-law of the 2nd Earl of Ancaster, and Lady Islington, who lived at Dyrham and Rushbrooke. Philip Tilden, who worked for Lady Islington at 20 Portman Square, wrote of her: 'She adored all beautiful things, and never did I meet with more ecstatic enthusiasm for houses, furniture or works of art than hers.'

In 1917 Nancy Langhorne married Henry Field, a grandson of Marshall Field, but tragically he died within the year through medical incompetence. It was to encourage her that her aunt invited her to spend Christmas of 1919 at Cliveden, and on the ship coming over she met Ronald Tree, an American first cousin of her late husband but brought up and educated in England. They were married here in May 1920.

However, since Nancy Tree wanted to live in America, her husband, who regarded himself as an Anglo-American, decided that he should make his life there. So they rented a house in New York from Ogden Codman, which, looking back, must have been a good omen for their future involvement with houses; also he bought Mirador, the house in Virginia that had belonged to his wife's grandfather. This they restored with the aid of William Delano, one of the most sensitive classical architects of his day in America, and, what must have been unusual, for some of the curtains Nancy Tree used old, or at least second-hand, chintz. Even then she preferred materials that were not new. Compared with the two English country houses that the Trees lived in later, Mirador is a simple classical villa of the kind that Americans built with success in the South in the Jefferson period; but to her it has always meant more than any other house she has lived in, and it was a very sad day for her when finally she had to sell it in 1955. Indeed she has always had an eye for English houses that remind her of Virginia, and it was typical of her that when she was out hunting in Northamptonshire one day in 1927 and saw Eydon for the first time, she immediately told her aunt, Lady Brand, to buy it, recommending it because it was reminiscent of Bremo, a house by Jefferson not far from Mirador.

Ronald Tree had hoped to make a career in American politics, but realizing that his English voice and upbringing made that impossible, he decided in 1926 to return to England and stand for Parliament. It was with the idea of finding a seat that he took on the mastership of the Pytchley when it was offered to him, and that was the reason for renting first Cottesbrooke for a year and then Kelmarsh, a house by James Gibbs. Appropriately the best photograph of Ronald and Nancy Tree shows them on the steps there, Nancy dressed for hunting [118]; and this relates to the slightly later description of her by George Washington, who started as first footman at Ditchley in 1935 (see his contribution 'The Hall Boy's Son' in *Gentleman's Gentlemen* by Rosina Harrison, 1976): 'The picture of her sitting side-saddle on her horse before a hunt, immaculate in her top hat and veil and wearing a blue coat and long skirt, is one I shall take to the grave with me, and if afterwards I see her looking the same I shall know I'm in heaven. Her beauty though wasn't just skin deep, she was wonderful to be with ...'

Although Kelmarsh was only rented, her uncle, Paul Phipps, who had been a pupil of Lutyens, restored and modernized the whole of it, and they began to buy suitable furniture and pictures for it. Also they went to look at other eighteenth-century houses, among them Houghton and, a little later, Uppark. Visits such as those confirmed Nancy Tree's love of old colour, and so it was singularly fortunate that among the men working for one of the subcontractors was a painter called Kick, who had the best feeling for tone she has ever met. By using seven coats of distemper he was able to reproduce in the hall at Kelmarsh the pink in the hall at Rushbrooke, a colour that Nancy Tree remembers looking marvellous with the two hunting pinks that were so often to be seen there on winter days. Kick also painted the drawing room in what she describes as an atmospheric blue-grey [119]. Later Kick worked at Ditchley, and after the war Nancy Tree introduced him to John Fowler.

Several decorators helped the Trees at Kelmarsh, among them Mrs Mann, who had been a friend of Edward Knoblock, Margot Brigden, who had started with Mrs Guy Bethell, and Mrs Bethell herself, whom John Fowler regarded as the best English decorator of her generation in England. As well as making Nancy Tree's bed out of old silver brocade and damask [121], she made the curtains in the saloon, and it is clear from photographs of them how much John Fowler must have learned from her about drapery. Later

Nancy Tree took to Colefax & Fowler the valance that Mrs Bethell had made for the Exhibition Room [122] and so it became part of the Colefax language. For the garden Nancy Tree sought the advice of Norah Lindsay.

Not only was Kelmarsh unusually well decorated, but it was immensely comfortable, with a bathroom for every bedroom, a novelty in English country houses at that time; and the bathrooms were treated as rooms. Care was also taken with the servants' rooms, as George Washington wrote of Ditchley:

I remember when I first arrived at Ditchley and was shown my bedroom, I thought I had been put temporarily into one of the guest rooms. It had a fitted Wilton carpet, a comfortable bed with a matching chintz valance, bedspread and curtains, an antique chest, fitted wardrobe and washbasin, and of course central heating, an untold luxury for any servant's room at that time.

Altogether Kelmarsh seems to have set a new standard for country house life on both sides of the Atlantic, and Nancy Tree remembers the late Duke of Buccleuch telling her that she had cost his generation a great deal of money.

Since the Trees realized that they would never be able to buy Kelmarsh, they began after a time to look round at other houses, particularly those with Virginian connections. Knowing that, Colonel Cooper, who shared their enthusiasm for houses, sent them a

118. MR AND MRS RONALD TREE ON THE STEPS AT KELMARSH HALL, NORTHAMPTONSHIRE, IN ABOUT 1930.

119 (above). KELMARSH HALL. THE
SALOON IN 1933. The walls were painted
'an atmospheric blue-grey' and the room was
entirely lit by candlelight; the Bessarabian
carpet was flanked by two early Aubussons;
the carved and cane-backed chairs were bought
in Italy.

120 (left). THE CURTAINS IN THE SALOON
AT KELMARSH. These were made by Mrs
Bethell, a decorator who was much admired
by John Fowler and from whom he evidently
learned a great deal about drapery.

121 (top right). MRS TREE'S BEDROOM
AT KELMARSH. The walls were hung with
silk, and Mrs Bethell made the bed out of old
damask and old brocade.

122 (below right). THE EXHIBITION ROOM
AT KELMARSH. The bed was made of old
rose apricot brocade and the valance to the
window curtains was of ivory silk painted with
flowers trimmed in old rose. Both were done
for an exhibition by Mrs Bethell and bought
for Kelmarsh by Mrs Tree.

123. DITCHLEY PARK, OXFORDSHIRE. THE PARTERRE. Designed by Geoffrey Jellicoe, the parterre is shown here in a photograph taken by *Country Life* in 1941.

124 (right). THE DRAWING ROOM AT DITCHLEY. A comparison of this photograph with those published by *Country Life* shortly before the Trees bought it reveals how through Ronald Tree's taste for fine furniture and objects and through Nancy Tree's gift for decoration and arrangement they brought the great house to life.

postcard suggesting that they should go to see Ditchley in Oxfordshire. For a year they did not follow up the suggestion, but when eventually they did, they fell for the house, and within two weeks Ronald Tree bought it, with its estate of 3,000 acres, as it stood, still almost completely furnished and only lacking some of the most important historical portraits, which Lord Dillon had left to the nation.

Even in 1933 the task of refurnishing, re-arranging and modernizing such a large house was a considerable one, and it is only right to emphasize that it was an act of collaboration between two people with complementary gifts. Indeed it was Nancy Tree who said to me that it was her husband who had a much greater feeling for architecture and works of art. So it is fortunate that he wrote of Ditchley in his memoir *When the Moon is High*, which gives a sense of his deep love for the whole place, his appreciation of its design, the pleasure of his quest for fine furniture, both Kentian

and continental, and his desire to create an architectural garden worthy of the building. As confirmation, there is Heron Bay, the beautiful house in the West Indies inspired by Villa Maser that Geoffrey Jellicoe designed for him in 1948-9.

If Ronald Tree was a Palladian and a purist, it was his wife who had the feeling for the synthesis of centuries in a house. Her memories of Mirador led her to keep as much of the old paint and reveal more that lay beneath later coats, then probably a novel idea in England but already accepted in certain circles in America, and to introduce as few new materials and textures as possible; and it was she who had the gift of bringing the great rooms to life and work as a background to entertaining on a considerable scale.

Paul Phipps advised them once more, but they made only one major internal alteration on the ground floor, the formation of one large library out of two smaller ones, an alteration that in retrospect she regards as a

125 (left). A BEDROOM AT DITCHLEY. The late-eighteenth-century bed, with its early-nineteenth-century hangings and matching window curtains, was in the house when the Trees bought it, and the old chintz was carefully retained. Later the pattern was copied by John Fowler [LXVI].

126 (right). A BATHROOM AT DITCHLEY. At Kelmarsh in the late 1920s, and subsequently at Ditchley, Mrs Tree not only installed many bathrooms but treated them as furnished rooms, then a novel idea.

mistake because it upset the balance of the rooms. Several people were involved with the decoration, among them Stéphane Boudin of the Paris firm of Jansen, whom Mrs Tree had met in Paris with an American friend, Mrs Havemayr. Boudin made curtains of old material for her sitting room, which she had hung with nineteenth-century damask that she had bought and then bleached. From him also came Mauny wallpapers and light fittings that are still in use and have been subsequently copied by Colefax & Fowler. Boudin's involvement at Ditchley is a reminder that the Trees' approach was not just Anglo-American but was tempered by European experience, including familiarity with the enthusiasms of people like Charles de Bestigui, whom she had first met in China in 1919.

When the Trees went to Ditchley, there was no garden, and Ronald Tree asked his neighbour in Queen Anne's Gate, Edward Hudson, whether he could recommend a designer who could devise a suitable architectural layout [123]. That was how Geoffrey Jellicoe got his first big commission. Also working with him was Russell Page, who met Boudin for the first time and so embarked on what amounted almost to an unofficial partnership which lasted for the rest of Boudin's life and led to many commissions.

Photographs of Ditchley at that time were not published (Kelmarsh was illustrated in *Country Life* in 1933), but because hunting played such a big part in fashionable life and the Trees had so many people, both English and American, to stay for it, their houses became well known and influential.

By 1936 Ditchley was more or less finished. It had become a perfect expression of two people's enthusiasm for an eighteenth-century house and park, but it left Nancy Tree needing other outlets for her energies and talents. As George Washington wrote of her: 'We used to say that she was blessed with two brains not one, and that you needed roller skates to keep up with her.' She began to help others with their houses, including her aunts, Lady Astor and Lady Brand, and she bought for Marian Tiffany's shop in New York and for Sybil Colefax, who was a friend of her husband. (At the same time Sybil Colefax had worked for them, providing among other things a glazed chintz painted with morning glories for one of the Ditchley beds [90].) Indeed both Sybil Colefax and Syrie Maugham tried to persuade her to join them.

Of the Ditchley years, particularly during the war when Winston Churchill used to stay there for weekends 'when the moon was high' and he could not go

127. Haseley Court, Oxfordshire. The saloon in the 1960s. Traces of blue on the table, always in the room, suggested the colour of the silk for the walls, and the ceiling was picked out in two colours of gold. The room contained one of the finest English chandeliers, originally acquired in the 1920s for the saloon at Kelmarsh.

to Chequers, there is an excellent account in Ronald Tree's memoir. By that time Nancy Tree had become fully committed to England, and, because she thought America was being slow over entering the war, she decided to become a British citizen. The end of the war saw the end of their marriage, and the post-war situation made life at Ditchley impossible for Ronald Tree.

It was in the uncertain situation after the war that Ronald Tree persuaded his wife to buy Sybil Colefax Ltd from Lady Colefax; and in that he had the enthusiastic support of John Fowler, who had met her for the first time when he had been taken to Ditchley soon after it was finished. Nancy Tree never worked with John Fowler on a 9 to 5 basis, but in the late 1940s and early 1950s, while she was living in London after her short-lived marriage to Colonel Lancaster in 1948, she used to make appearances as dramatic as they were unexpected in the shop, always superbly dressed and bringing with her an air of a wider, international world. She and John Fowler often went on expeditions together either in search of stock for the shop or to see clients who were her friends or acquaintances. However, the business was always for her essentially a private activity rather than a commercial concern, its point being the convenience of being able to get the best of what was available at cost price. On the other hand a great many of the best jobs came through her, particularly through her Astor cousins and her Anglo-American friends. Thus it was that John Fowler worked at Mereworth for Peter Beatty, who was the son of Ronald Tree's mother by her second marriage, and at Grimsthorpe for Lord and Lady Ancaster; and it was she who took him first to Boughton and Wilton, to the Duke and Duchess of Windsor in France and who introduced him to Mr and Mrs Paul Mellon and Mr and Mrs David Bruce. But it was never a conventional partnership, and the late Duke of Norfolk, who summoned them to Arundel Park, said that he had never heard two partners argue so much.

Nancy Lancaster's influence on John Fowler, however, is something I find extraordinarily difficult to pin down, particularly her influence on his style. Often it was subtle and indirect, such as introducing him to Kick, producing things that she had had made in the 1920s and 1930s for him to copy, and persuading him to travel abroad. For instance, it seems likely that it was she who persuaded him to go to see the villas of the Veneto, because they had made such an impression on her when she saw them for the first time in the early 1950s. She also probably gave him greater confidence when it came to handling large and richly decorated rooms and may well have encouraged the development of his sense of comfort.

After Ditchley it took a long time for Nancy Lancaster to find another house in the country, but in 1954, after looking at 125, she discovered Haseley, which was then derelict; and she became absorbed in its restoration and decoration and the creation of its garden. It was the ideal house for her to work on with John Fowler, providing scope both for restoration and decoration, and it was perhaps the high point of their partnership. Its entrance front is deceptive, for within it is not a straightforward Georgian house, and therein lies its appeal: it has all the advantages of Georgian proportion and detail in its main rooms, but, since the core is much earlier, there are surprises and rooms of unusually varied character. The small early Georgian rooms in the centre are flanked on one side by a bigger library with an eighteenth-century gothick bow window and on the other by a neo-classical saloon rising through two storeys. So it is architectural enough to appeal to someone used to more important houses and with pictures and furniture brought from them, yet it is human in scale. Alas, I never saw it while she was living there, but it was photographed on several occasions, and so it is possible to imagine it as it was from the late 1950s to the late 1960s.

The saloon [127] must have been particularly successful, with its walls hung with blue silk that related to the colour discovered on the George II table always in the room, and its ceiling painted Ditchley white picked out in two colours of gold. The gilding answered the Ditchley trophies and the frames of the pictures and looking-glasses.

The contrast between the elegant formality of that room, the masculine comfort of the dining room and the library, and the rustic fantasy of the Palladian Room [XIII, 130] admirably demonstrate John Fowler's range as an architectural decorator and restorer, his sensitivity of conception and his attention to detail in execution, but there was evidently no striving after effect or of decoration dominating life there.

Of John Fowler's decoration there are two survivors, the painted paper in the Palladian Room and the *trompe l'œil* decoration of the Gothick Room, both in collaboration with George Oakes [XIV, XV, 128]. The King of Sweden had given Mrs Lancaster a small piece of painted paper from Drottningholm and John Fowler and George Oakes developed it into a complete design for the Palladian Room. The intention was that the

128. THE GOTHICK ROOM AT HASELEY. Mrs
Lancaster originally decorated it as a bedroom for her aunt
Lady Astor.

129. THE GOTHICK ROOM AT HASELEY AS IT
WAS IN 1954.

paper should be like an eighteenth-century European
imitation of a Chinese paper rather than a copy of a
Chinese paper as suiting the provincial character of the
room; and to that end they painted it on small sheets
of paper with the joins showing.

The key to the Gothick Bedroom [128] in the chapel
wing was set by its 'east window' and the plaster ornament in its reveals: that suggested the stone-coloured
cornice, which is inspired by the one in the drawing
room at St Michael's Mount; the ochre colour of the
walls is based on that in the saloon at Ditchley. All the
rest of the decoration, except for the central roses for
chandeliers, was painted in *trompe l'œil* by John Fowler and George Oakes. So convincing is it that when
Mrs Lancaster saw it for the first time, she said, 'Damn
John, he has plastered the room, not painted it as I
asked.' Over the chimneypiece is a *trompe l'œil* grisaille relief of Diana with branches of oak leaves that
recall the plasterwork of the Bristol stuccoist, Thomas

130. THE PALLADIAN ROOM AT HASELEY AS IT WAS IN 1957. In 1954 Mrs Lancaster had found the house lying derelict and immediately began work on its restoration.

Stocking; and there are more sprays of oak in the spandrels, with a hound's head reminiscent of plaster-work on the staircase at Russborough in Ireland.

In 1958, about the time that Haseley was finished and the shop was doing badly, it was decided that Nancy Lancaster should have as her London *pied-à-terre* the back of the building in Avery Row that overlooks a garden court. On the first floor is a long room with a shallow barrel vault [XVI] that Wyatville had added as a reception room and that the shop had used as its main showroom for antique furniture. Characteristically Nancy Lancaster referred to it as her bed-sit, but to many people it was the most glamorous room in London, being both visually stimulating and immensely comfortable. The decoration, needless to say, was done by John Fowler, but how much of the thinking behind it was his and how much was Nancy Lancaster's I find impossible to say, although all the detail bears his stamp. The strong yellow walls with their high-gloss finish were intended by him to be slightly shocking at a time when gloss paint was not only regarded as being out of fashion but was looked down on; but the idea of the colour went back to a suggestion of a butter-yellow library made to Nancy Lancaster by Paul Phipps years before. To add to the sense of surprise there were the full-length Elizabethan portraits of the Fitton sisters from Ditchley, which were not yet fashionable in the late 1950s. The room, in fact, was immensely full, of pictures, furniture, chairs, sofas and banquettes beneath the three large Venetian chandeliers; and there were lots of books, all wrapped in red paper, to give it the calm of a library. Yet it never seemed crowded, and, although it was very complicated in its planning, because it was both an eating and a sitting room, it never seemed over-elaborate, even when just two people were in it.

It was a sad day when Avery Row came to an end, and it is even sadder that of the many houses that

133. THE TOBACCO BEDROOM AT HASELEY IN 1957. A French sepia wallpaper with an early-nineteenth-century bed and Brussels carpet, both of which were bought at the Ashburnham Place sale. The carpet was subsequently copied by John Fowler as 'Rose and Ribbon'.

131 (top left). THE LIBRARY AT HASELEY. The draw curtains had false valances attached to them, an idea Mrs Lancaster learned from Edward Knoblock.

132 (below left). MRS LANCASTER'S BEDROOM AT HASELEY.

Nancy Lancaster has lived in almost all that survives are drawings, watercolours and photographs. And posterity is bound to wonder about their secret and why, ever since Kelmarsh, her houses have been so much admired in England and also America. In part the answer lies in their respect for scale, their boldness and their mellowness, their unaffected elegance and their avoidance of pretension. They do have an American desire for perfection, but the result never becomes leaden, as it so often does, and Virginian confidence and naturalness is combined with wit. Indeed she has always tried to bring out the personality of a house and give it what it needs rather than stamp her own personality on it. She breathes her spirit into a house, as George Washington wrote at Ditchley, and that gives them their tantalizing mystery, which many seek to capture and none succeed in imitating.

ANNE, COUNTESS OF ROSSE

If Mrs Lancaster is always associated with eighteenth-century houses, Lady Rosse is most often thought of in connection with 18 Stafford Terrace, Kensington [1], the house that her maternal grandfather, Linley Sambourne, took when he married in 1874 and her mother, Mrs Leonard Messel, lovingly preserved until her death in 1960. Lord and Lady Rosse then lived in it for almost twenty years while they worked out how it should be preserved in perpetuity. The house is a unique survival of Victorian middle-class artistic eclectic taste, with immense human appeal; and while it is also vivid evidence of Lady Rosse's approach to houses, it is not truly representative of her own taste.

If given a completely free hand, her sympathies would be with the eighteenth century, but it has so happened that only with her first house in London did she start from scratch: the other houses in which she has lived have been family houses and of an unusual, even bewildering range of character, partly seventeenth-century and Georgian gothick at Birr Castle in Ireland, mainly Georgian classic at Womersley Park near Pontefract, 1920s romantic Tudor Revival in what survives of her parents' house at Nymans in Sussex, and 1870s artistic in Stafford Terrace. She has not needed to buy much furniture, so her experience has been very different from that of Mrs Lancaster, but they both have an innate sympathy for the same kind of rooms, enjoying the romantic and the mellow. While Mrs Lancaster talks of the deadness of perfection and liking 'music, houses, gardens with a

minor note', Lady Rosse talks of the need to muck up good taste; and she always urges the wives of those who inherit houses to let them speak for themselves and not to make them a reflection of their own personalities.

Lady Rosse's own reaction to styles is a fascinating microcosm of the past sixty years. One key is that she is the sister of Oliver Messel, and the talent that with him emerged in theatrical design, in her has been expressed in the houses that she has lived in. The sense of tone and texture, the feeling for scale and the understanding of theatre are gifts that came to them from their parents and developed through their upbringing.

Their great-grandfather was a banker in Darmstadt and he sent two of his three sons to England – the third remained in Germany, practising as an architect. Their grandfather, Ludwig, who founded L. Messel and Co., lived at 3 Hyde Park Gardens and started the gardens at Nymans; he also bought a number of pictures. Their father, Colonel Messel, was a much more passionate collector, with several specialist interests, such as fans and botanical books; and their mother, the daughter of Linley Sambourne, was an artist by temperament. They lived in two houses of contrasting characters (and differing kinds of discomfort): 104 Lancaster Gate, decorated in the handsome classical style developed by Lenygons and furnished with pictures and objects bought with advice from Sir Hugh Lane and with a special museum room where Colonel Messel kept his early glass, oriental ivories and classical antiquities; and Nymans, which Mrs Messel transformed into an evocation of a West Country manor house [36–38].

The Messels did not believe in schools for a daughter, and so Lady Rosse had no formal education, but her father and his friends in the London museums introduced her to the collections in their charge. At houses where she stayed, such as Stoke Edith, Chillington and Sherborne Castle, her mother also taught her to notice everything, from the whole building down to the details of the design of a damask table cloth. That was not a conventional English approach, and many people would have thought it rather bad form, but the result is a remarkably sure eye and a clear visual memory. Mrs Messel was also a skilled needlewoman, and so when her daughter grew up it was natural for her to help her brother Oliver with his productions and make clothes for them; for a time she worked at Victoire in Sloane Street, cutting and sewing.

However, much as their daughter admired their

houses and what they contained, they were not a natural taste for someone emerging in the 1920s. So not surprisingly when her father gave her the lease of 25 Eaton Terrace in 1925, at the time of her marriage to Ronald Armstrong-Jones, she gradually decorated it and furnished it in a late-eighteenth-century and Regency style. By the early 1930s the drawing room was pale grey and white, with a little gilding; the curtains were Regency satin and the furniture was white and gold. Such schemes were soon to become generally fashionable, but at the time the enthusiasm of her circle for English classical architecture was still novel, expeditions to look at City churches with Nancy Mitford and Robert Byron were not obvious pursuits, and the fun of architecture was recognized by few people. Robert Byron also liked Victorian things, but it was Mark Ogilvie-Grant who introduced her to the designs of William Morris.

Robert Byron had been at Eton both with her brother Oliver and Lord Rosse; then Robert Byron, Harold Acton and Lord Rosse were at Oxford together; and fairly soon after Lord and Lady Rosse were married in 1935 he, Robert Byron, Lord Derwent and others were involved in the formation of the Georgian Group, which took place in 1937 to save what little remained of Georgian architecture in London. Prevention of destruction and the preservation of the past thus became a thread in their lives parallel to what they were doing at Birr. Lord Rosse's father had been killed in the First World War when he himself was only twelve, and Birr had received no sympathetic attention after its occupation during the Civil War and its damage by fire: 'Not one room was agreeable, everything was cheap and out of proportion.' However, since they both loved the place and saw the potential of the garden, they decided to make it their home.

The saloon [XVIII] was a particular challenge, for although it is one of the most beautiful rooms in Ireland it lacked any suitable furniture. So Lady Rosse used the money her father had given her for her trousseau to buy one of the sets of furniture made by Chippendale for Sir Lawrence Dundas. It was the most significant purchase the Rosses made, but they also bought a Kent table for the same room, *garnitures* for chimneypieces and mirrors for the Yellow Drawing Room. Appropriate door furniture was ordered and Coles brought out old blocks to make wallpapers. Lady Rosse repaired old curtains and bought new braids and fringes to trim them. Years later she was able to add to the house more pictures and furniture

which she inherited from her parents' house in Lancaster Gate (it was at that time that the house was photographed for *Country Life*). The synthesis was quite remarkable, because the Parsons inheritance was topped up with objects chosen by the Messels, who had more adventurous eyes, and the two elements were fused together and arranged with imagination and a sense of theatre; and also set off with spectacular flowers done by Lady Rosse. Harold Acton, an old friend, described in *More Memoirs of an Aesthete* how 'On Friday morning the whole floor of the entrance hall was carpeted with flowers which Anne arranged for the vases all over the house, opulent harmonies of colour and form ... She had a way with flowers and they had a way with her. This was extended to her decoration of the rooms, of the dinner-table. Her personal touch with *objets d'art* never allowed them to congeal as in a museum.'

When Lady Rosse started on Birr, she bought excellent chintz at 1s. 6d. a yard from the shop of Miss Frith, the daughter of the painter, and with the aid of a resting actress friend and two women living in the town at Birr, she made all the curtains. Her natural inclination is to hunt for an old piece of material, whether velvet, damask or chintz, and work out how to use it in such a way that it looks as if it had always been there; and many hours were spent at Stafford Terrace darning and patching the old upholstery so that there was as little new material as possible to disturb the effect. It is an approach that is pictorial and practical, but also takes pleasure in the crafts of housekeeping. However, that spirit was combined with a willingness to go all out after the Dundas furniture and get Victorian wallpapers copied; and probably the first time Lady Rosse had professional advice was in 1958, when she asked John Fowler, whom she had first met in his Peter Jones days, to paint the drawing room at Womersley [XIX] at the time Lord Rosse's mother, the Dowager Lady de Vesci, went to live there.

Womersley is a rambling, understated friendly manor house of many dates but with the principal Jacobean front Georgianized and one of its wings devoted to a great room almost certainly designed by John Carr. The place went through a hard time in the 1920s, when sales of contents were held and the property failed to find a buyer; and in the 1930s it was let. It was only when war became imminent that the Rosses decided that the house was the place for Lady Rosse to take the children, but there was virtually no furniture and not even a floor in the drawing room – it had been sold – and much of the house was requisitioned. However, friendly relations were soon established with the troops quartered there, and they helped Lady Rosse make a knot garden with M A R in box as the principal motif and a frame for old-fashioned roses. Gradually the house was pieced together and made the charming place it remains. John Fowler's treatment of the drawing room is an excellent illustration of his understanding of the feeling of rooms and houses as well as Georgian architecture and colour. It would have been all too easy to make the room jump against the rest of the house, but so subtle are the shades that they do not cause that to happen; instead they bring out the balance of the design and the quality of the detail while never looking contrived. And after twenty-five years the room is still completely harmonious.

Nymans as it exists today is a substantial fragment of the manor house burned in 1947. Lord and Lady Rosse kept it because of the garden, which Colonel Messel had left to the National Trust and which they wanted to continue to direct so that it kept the flavour of a private garden. Thus the house was more in the nature of a perch than a permanent home – Lady Rosse describes it as her potting shed – and little was spent on it. However, a certain amount of the contents of the complete house had survived the fire, and there was one long room, a garden hall, and that became the main sitting room. John Fowler's advice was: 'Don't try to make it look like a drawing room but keep it looking as if it was a passage leading to big rooms beyond' – another excellent illustration of his sympathy for the individuality of houses. The leaded lights make it rather dark and mysterious and the white walls are mostly hung with tapestry in green tones, picked up in the old greens of the sofa at the far end. There is nothing about the room that is decoration in the normal sense, but the way an atmosphere is created is remarkable.

Seeing these houses it becomes easier to understand why the National Trust's Country Houses Scheme got going and took the form it did. James Lees-Milne, who was the first Secretary of the Historic Buildings Committee from 1936, became a close friend of the Rosses in the late 1930s, and during the war, when Lord Rosse was serving with the Irish Guards, he was invited to join that Committee; from 1945 until shortly before his death the care of the Trust's historic buildings and gardens was one of his main fields of activity. The Trust's Scheme was thus an extension of a private world, which was one of the main reasons why it won the confidence of benefactors.

And the same was true of the Georgian Group and of the Victorian Society, which was formed at Stafford Terrace in 1958. From 1948 Mrs Messel had allowed the Rosses to stay in the house from time to time, when their house in Eaton Terrace was let, and to invite people who might appreciate it; and it was through that gradual process of getting to know what had become a Sleeping Beauty kind of house – Mrs Messel had never allowed her brother any freedom there and continued to keep all the keys until her death in 1960 – that a circle came together who formed the Victorian Society there under Lady Rosse's presidency. The whole story is not only a remarkable illustration of the vitality of romantic taste but shows how we move forwards by looking backwards.

COLONEL ROGER HESKETH

The country house in the eighteenth and nineteenth centuries owed a great deal to the amateur tradition, and a surprising number of owners were competent architects, but the twentieth century has become increasingly inimical to that tradition and there have been few owners who have aspired to be their own architects, let alone exponents of the classical style. So Colonel Roger Hesketh, who designed the remodelling of Meols Hall in 1960–64, would be unusual even if he was not in addition a highly original, rounded figure in the Renaissance tradition: a composer as well as an architect, he was called to the Bar before studying architecture and becoming an architectural journalist; later he became a landowner, farmer and forester; he has also served as Mayor of Southport and as its Member of Parliament. He was elected as a Conservative, but he is really a Whig, a progressive traditionalist.

But seeing Meols for the first time none of that could be guessed, and, as I wrote in *Country Life* in 1973, the first impression is of a spreading North Country manor house with an involved building history but evidently untouched for some 150 years [134]. The core dates back to the seventeenth century, but the gabled section is all that is visible of the old house on the east front. The Gibbsian centre block, the Regency wing at the south end and the battlemented gazebos are all designed by Colonel Hesketh and were executed under his supervision, without the aid of a clerk of works and by direct labour. And the interior was arranged round the hanging plan that he made for the family portraits, which were left back to him by a cousin, Thomas Parr. The result is what I believe to be the most successful substantial country house

134. MEOLS HALL, LANCASHIRE. THE EAST FRONT. In 1960–64 Colonel Hesketh remodelled
the old house to his own designs, creating an impression of a seventeenth-century house altered about
1740 in a Gibbsian style and extended at the end of the eighteenth century.

created in England since the war. Its balance of architecture, pictures and furniture and of decoration is one
scarcely ever achieved; and, it has a sense of life,
because it embodies so many threads of history that
have reality for Colonel Hesketh but can never exist
with a made-up collection. What he has created for
himself and his family is a lasting statement representing the country house in our time.

Indeed history and architecture have been potent
forces in his life, but what makes them particularly
interesting is his unexpected involvement in the 1930s
with the publishing of modern architecture in the *Master Builder*, which he owned from 1930 to 1934. Even
as a boy Roger Hesketh was aware of his family's deep
roots in north-west Lancashire, and he was particularly fascinated by Uncle Peter, Sir Peter Hesketh
Fleetwood, who nearly brought about the family's
complete ruin through his scheme to build the town of
Fleetwood in the late 1830s; and as boys he and his

younger brother, Peter, created an architectural dream
world. At Eton he developed his talent as a watercol-
ourist, and sketchbooks from Eton and Oxford days
show his understanding of classical architecture. At
Oxford he read law and then was called to the Bar,
but he was advised that he was much more suited to
architecture and so, after a short spell at Chatham
House, he decided to go to the Architectural Association. Not that he envisaged practising: his decision was
based on the hope that he would eventually inherit
what remained of the family property round Southport
and then would be able to act as his own estate architect. However, before he reached the AA, his father
suddenly sold the estate and dashed that hope, at least
for a few years.

While he was at the AA, he heard that the *Master
Builder* was for sale and he decided to buy it so as to
present a much broader picture of current architecture
than existed at that time, with an emphasis on what

was being done abroad. In 1927 he, his brother Peter and John Summerson had done a tour of Northern Europe in which they looked closely at the work of Schinkel and his school and had their first contacts with the Modern Movement; and the following year he went to Germany and laid the foundation for his enthusiasm for Central European Baroque and Rococo architecture, about which little was known in England. He was essentially catholic in his tastes, and saw no reason why classicism and Modernism should not exist side by side, both being based on rules of good proportion; and in this he had much in common with Christopher Hussey, whom he had got to know in the late 1920s. The *Master Builder* was an excellent vehicle in which to proclaim that view, and he was able to persuade friends such as John Summerson and Christopher Hussey to contribute. To him architecture was both deeply important and a source of pleasure and fun. Sometimes commercial pressures conflicted with aesthetic standards, but he managed to build up a good coverage of new buildings; he also wrote about regional planning and urban design, ways of grouping buildings that show his appreciation of vernacular architecture, and even about tax exemption for historic parks; and he included designs for houses by his brother, including some slightly improbable ones such as a three-bedroom villa in the style of Nash with an upstairs library. There were also lighter pieces in which he and Peter collaborated over the illustrations that look forward to Osbert Lancaster's books of the later 1930s. Indeed 'Pillar to Post' was originally Roger Hesketh's phrase. The *Master Builder*, however, could not be made financially successful, and so late in 1934 he gave it to his somewhat surprised, and reluctant, staff, and he turned his attention to re-establishing an estate round Meols, buying back what he could of what his father had sold and augmenting it with more land at Hale.

The change of direction distracted his attention from disagreements, doubts and disenchantments with Modern architecture that developed in the mid-1930s and, although he made some small alterations at Meols in 1938, it was clear the war was coming and it was not the time for ambitious schemes. Afterwards most new architecture seemed so anti-social and destructive to him that he had little interest in it, and his rejection of it for aesthetic reasons was combined with frustration at not being allowed to carry out his own plans for a model town at Hale. At the same time restrictions made building at Meols virtually impossible. Then from 1952, the year that he married Lady Mary Lum-

ley, until 1959 he served as MP for Southport. His years at Westminster gave him the time to finalize his plans for Meols, and in 1960 he was able to acquire materials from Tulketh and Lathom, two houses with family connections, so uniting practicality and sentiment.

The result is a house of strongly individual character, because it manages to combine comfort, informality and intimacy with a sense of parade; and it works equally well with and without staff. The entrance hall, being low and quite narrow, gives no sense of what lies ahead. To its left lies the Yellow Room, also in the old part of the house and with the same low ceiling, and beyond it is the library [135] that he added on, the largest room in the house and really a library-sitting room in the Reptonian sense. The library leads into a small drawing room [136] in the new east front, really an ante-room, and beyond it into the Garden Hall [137], both rooms intended for the display of portraits. To the south of the latter is the dining room, and separating it from the kitchen in the new wing, is a pantry in the old part of the house lined with old library bookcases painted black for the display of china and glass. Thus, using the house one way the hall, Yellow Room, dining room and kitchen link up well; or, after sitting in the library, there is the pleasure of walking through two formal rooms before reaching the dining room; or as a third alternative the Yellow Room, Garden Hall and dining room link together.

The planning of the house, the design of the rooms, and the hanging of the pictures were worked out together, as can be seen from Colonel Hesketh's sketch for one wall of the dining room [138], and although naturally some rehanging has been done in the course of the past twenty years, partly to accommodate more inherited portraits, the basic scheme has changed very little. The pattern remains essentially Georgian and architectural, with walls considered as a whole. It is often thought that good pictures get lost in an overall pattern, but, as can be seen at Meols, the reverse happens, because the lesser pictures throw up the better ones while at the same time receiving support from them; and the hanging of portraits over doors balances pictures over chimneypieces and the rooms are strengthened in consequence.

Colonel Hesketh's approach, with his sense of architecture and feeling for family history, needs restraint in decoration. On the other hand changes in colour and texture are significant, and historical knowledge and architectural sense led him to have water-gilt fillets made for the rooms that are hung (they were

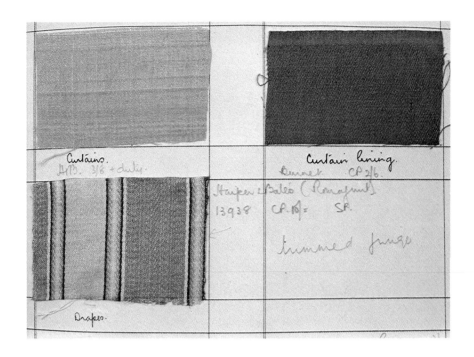

XXII. SAMPLES OF MATERIALS USED IN THE
DRAWING ROOM AT 15 KENSINGTON PALACE
GARDENS, LONDON, IN ABOUT 1938. According
to the order book, the walls were painted in two
shades of grey; the striped satin (cost price 10s. a
yard) trimmed with blue and brown bullion fringe
was used for the continued drapery, with curtains of
gold shantung (cost 3s. 8d. plus duty) lined with
purple and tie-backs of blue and white silk cord,
with heavy tassels and rosettes. The curtains are
shown in illustration 153.

XXIII. SAMPLES OF BLOCK FRINGE AND
WALLPAPER USED AT 15 KENSINGTON
PALACE GARDENS. The Mauny *coquille* pattern
in flock was a favourite one with John Fowler, and
he continued to use it after the war, as at
Lennoxlove and Holyrood [XXXVII and XXXVIII].

XXIV. 'VOGUE' REGENCY TREATMENT OF THE STAIRCASE WINDOW OF A WEST COUNTRY FARMHOUSE DECORATED BY JOHN FOWLER IN ABOUT 1939/40, AS IT WAS IN 1984. The drapery is in a white weave overprinted with a small rosette pattern and trimmed with a pink and scalloped green ruffle; it is held by rosettes and tasselled cords. The fixing of the blind is masked by a wooden valance painted in with the walls, and the blind is of a painted material that he frequently used from the mid-1930s and later had printed.

XXV. SAMPLES OF MATERIALS AND PAPER USED IN THE PRINCIPAL BEDROOM AT THE FARMHOUSE.

XXVI. THE CURTAINS IN THE PRINCIPAL GUEST ROOM AT THE FARMHOUSE IN 1984. The material is a copy of an old dot-and-cross lining chintz printed for John Fowler, which cost 1s. 6d. a yard [see also LXIII], lined with dark blue and trimmed with flounces of the same blue, scalloped and pinked, and with yellow and blue cords and rosettes.

XXVII. THE PRINCIPAL BEDROOM AT THE FARMHOUSE AS IT WAS IN 1984. The feeling is Anglo-French, with a Mauny wallpaper of grey and white drapery and columns of foliage, finished by hand at the top with cut-out rosettes and a painted braid and at the bottom with a painted knotted fringe. The carpet is an early version of the revived 'Moss' pattern. The orange-pink curtains are trimmed with a block bullion fringe relating to the carpet. The muslin is embroidered with a design of lilies of the valley.

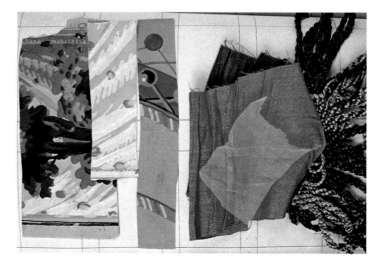

XXVIII. RADBURNE HALL, DERBYSHIRE. THE
HALL. The architectural decoration of the room is
painted in three tones of white. The darkest echoes the
stone chimneypiece, which had been painted over, and
the walls are a pale duck egg colour which moves
between blue and green in the changing light and which
is continued in two tones on the bed of the ceiling.

XXIX. UPHOLSTERY IN THE HALL AT
RADBURNE. Two of the chairs were already
upholstered in old green stamped wool velvet and the
rest of the set has been covered in a bold red mohair
velvet stamped with an eighteenth-century pattern; the
curtains are of the same material but unstamped.

XXX. THE SALOON AT RADBURNE. Here the walls
were painted a pale pink, to go with the white and old
gilding of the architectural decoration. John Fowler only
added a little extra gilding to some of the mouldings.

XXXI. A DETAIL OF THE SALOON CEILING AT
RADBURNE. Gilding had stopped at the cornice and so
John Fowler repeated the style of the gilding of the
walls, using two colours of gold for the reliefs in the
corners of the ceiling.

XXXII. THE CURTAINS AND
VALANCES IN THE DRAWING
ROOM AT RADBURNE.

XXXIII. THE LIBRARY AT
RADBURNE. The walls are hung
with a striped paper in single and
double flock that gives the effect of
two tones of green. The green is
picked up in the lining-out of the
skirting, dado rail and cornice, while
the colour of the marble
chimneypiece is answered in the
slightly later frieze. The curtains are
of green wool rep with borders of
old gold velvet that appears to match
one of the stripes of the flock.

XXXIV. LENNOXLOVE,
LOTHIAN. THE ENTRANCE
HALL.

XXXV. THE YELLOW DRAWING ROOM
AT LENNOXLOVE. Here the decoration
started with the hanging of the decorative
seventeenth-century portrait of Lord Bellasis
over the chimneypiece. The yellow tops of his
boots provided the key to the painting of the
panelling in three tones of yellow with white.

XXXVI. DETAIL OF THE PAINTING IN
THE ENTRANCE HALL AT LENNOXLOVE.
This shows the relationship of the apricot,
yellow and white to the marble in the
chimneypiece.

135. THE LIBRARY AT MEOLS.
Colonel Hesketh revived the early-
nineteenth-century idea of the library-
drawing room, making it the largest
room in the house. A clue to its design
lies in James Ward's picture of an Arab
stallion, which had belonged to Sir Peter
Hesketh and was recovered by Colonel
Hesketh in 1936. It dictated the height
of the wall between the dado and
the cornice.

136. THE DRAWING ROOM AT
MEOLS. A small room of parade built
in 1960–64, hung with a pale-grey
watered material and finished with a gilt
fillet made in the house.

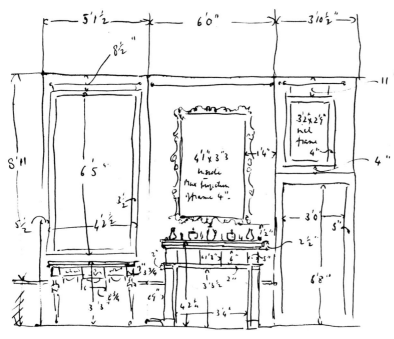

137 (above). THE GARDEN HALL AT MEOLS.
The walls are hung with a plain forest-green flock
paper and the woodwork is clear white. The white
and gold furniture was copied in 1934 from furniture
in a *schloss* near Vienna.

138 (left). COLONEL HESKETH'S SKETCH FOR
THE DINING ROOM AT MEOLS. This shows the
close attention to scale everywhere in the room,
down to the placing of the china on the
chimneypiece. The arrival of more portraits since the
design was made has led to the revision of the
scheme but not its principles.

139 (right). WINESTEAD, EAST YORKSHIRE.
THE HALL. After Colonel Rupert Alec-Smith
acquired the house in 1947, he incorporated into it
many fittings saved from demolished and bombed
houses in and around Hull. He introduced the black
and grey stone floor and the simple cornice in 1955,
and a chimneypiece from Etherington Buildings in
Hull. He also made the recesses to take the small
busts of George III and Queen Charlotte.

made on the spot). Thus the flash of gilding is important in the library, which is essentially low in tone with its *café au lait* coloured walls, dark upholstery and dark picture frames. From *café au lait* one moves to pale blue watered material in the drawing room and then to plain green flock in the Garden Hall, a marvellous background that I have never seen elsewhere, and after that to plain red paper in the dining room. All the curtains are simply designed, and so is the upholstery.

COLONEL RUPERT ALEC-SMITH

To all four of the people described in this chapter, the eighteenth century has spoken very strongly, but naturally in rather different ways. To Colonel Alec-Smith it spoke very early. He remembers being taken at the age of ten in 1924 by his parents to see the Red Hall at Winestead, a sober mid-Georgian brick house near Hull, and thinking not only that it was the most beautiful building he had ever seen but that Georgian build-

ings meant more to him than anything else. That discovery was one that he made entirely for himself, for his parents did not encourage him to use his eyes, and the simple masculine house was not to his mother's taste. However, his parents tolerated his enthusiasm and in the following years for his birthday and at Christmas gave him pieces of antique furniture that he still has. The fascination for houses, and for the Red Hall in particular, grew during his teens into a life-long interest in local history, fostered first through books and then by pictures, and that developed into a deep affection for the City of Kingston-upon-Hull and the East Riding of Yorkshire and Holderness in particular.

When he left school he went into the family business in Hull, Horsley Smith and Co., and from 1933 to 1936 worked in its London office, but he did not enjoy life in London and met few people who shared his architectural interests, never encountering the circle who were about to form the Georgian Group. By the time its formation was announced, he was back in

140. THE LIBRARY AT WINESTEAD. The cornice and chimneypiece came from Etherington Buildings in Hull and the doors from the Red Hall at Winestead. Francis Johnson designed the north wall.

141. THE DRAWING ROOM AT WINESTEAD. Added on to the back of the house in 1775, the room has a chimneypiece and overmantel from 37 High Street, Hull. The curtains and the painted chairs came from Grimston Garth in East Yorkshire. Most of the portraits are of members of the Maister family, Hull merchants who owned part of Winestead in the eighteenth century.

142. THE DINING ROOM AT WINESTEAD. The double doors link the dining room to the room behind, so forming one larger room, with the inner part, which gets the morning sun, also serving as a breakfast room.

143. THE WEST BEDROOM AT WINESTEAD. The woodwork came from 20 High Sreet, Hull, but the shell drops on the chimneypiece are new carving.

Hull, and being discouraged by the destruction of Carr's Assembly Rooms in Beverley, the growing dereliction in the High Street of Hull, and the demolition of the Red Hall in 1936, he decided to form the Georgian Society for East Yorkshire. Just as the Georgian Group was the offspring of the SPAB, his Society was founded early in 1937 under the wing of the East Riding Antiquarian Society. Through it he met Lord Derwent, the first chairman of the Georgian Group, who lived at Hackness Hall near Scarborough, and the following year he got to know two people who shared so many of his interests, Holman Sutcliffe, a member of the Georgian Group Committee who lived in Boston, and Francis Johnson, who had just set up in independent practice as an architect in Bridlington. After the war a triangular friendship blossomed that proved to be mutually encouraging in their work for historic buildings in the East Riding and Lincolnshire.

During the war Colonel Alec-Smith served in the Green Howards, and it was then that he met Sir Richard Sykes. Brought up at Sledmere, Sir Richard naturally preferred the second to the first half of the eighteenth century in terms of architecture and decoration, and after the war both he and Sledmere came to mean a great deal to Colonel Alec-Smith, confirming his feelings for the past and in particular the fusion of mercantile and landed threads in the East Riding (which he believed in very strongly as a Hull man and Sir Richard was inclined to forget). When peace came, Colonel Alec-Smith went back into the family business and in 1947 he bought the Old Rectory at Winestead [139-143]. Naturally he turned to Francis Johnson for advice on its repair and improvement, and together they battled through the intricacies of licensing, incorporating in the house many fragments salvaged from bombed houses in Hull and from the Red Hall. It is rare to find a patron and an architect so completely in accord with one another in terms of taste and historical feeling; and for me Winestead has always had the quality of a complete work of art. It is unusual for imported features not to look like new arrivals, but Francis Johnson's re-use of old work is so skilful that the whole house is completely convincing, and the sense of visual balance of pictures and furniture is reinforced by a rare historical feeling. Perhaps it is also that, while great care was taken with the colours in the house and some of the curtains were ingeniously designed by Francis Johnson, Colonel Alec-Smith has always been basically anti-decoration. When young he was deeply suspicious of London decorators. He may have softened a little through working on Winestead, but there is no striving after effect and no dressing-up of rooms. Instead the harmony comes from a study of Georgian architecture, with its strong sense of order and balance.

Winestead is a smiling house, but there is a strong streak of melancholy in Holderness, just as there is sadness in the raped City of Hull; and this feeling for melancholy, unloved places has been an integral part of Colonel Alec-Smith's pleasure in Georgian architecture and local history. It has been an inspiration to him in his civic work in Hull – he was a City Councillor for many years and Lord Mayor – and in his work for the Georgian Society for East Yorkshire, which culminated in the Society saving, largely through his initiative, two houses in the High Street of Hull, which it subsequently gave to the National Trust, and Blaydes House.

Before the war Colonel Alec-Smith was very much a lone voice, and only after it did he get to know people outside the East Riding who were actively involved in preservation. It was through local Conservative work, for instance, that he first met Lord and Lady Rosse. Others he got to know when he became a member of the Georgian Group Committee about 1953. His contribution to Hull and the East Riding was recognized when he was appointed Lord Lieutenant of Humberside.

*

Rupert Alec-Smith died on 24 December 1983, but I decided to keep the account as it stood because it was written after what proved to be my last visit to him, in March 1983, when, despite ill health, he was still planning improvements at Winestead, and it was not intended to be in memory of him.

CHAPTER SIX

JOHN FOWLER AND THE BIRTH OF HUMBLE ELEGANCE

The rise of decoration, the enthusiasm for country houses, the rediscovery of the eighteenth century and the revival of the country house after the Second World War all have a meeting point in the figure of John Fowler, who in the English tradition drew inspiration from the past and created a new style out of it. He is a figure who not only has a place in the history of the country house in the twentieth century but has made a contribution to decoration that is far more widespread than is knowledge of his work or even of his name. However, in order to understand his unique practice after the war, it is necessary to trace his development before it and see how his approach grew out of his early struggle and the post-Slump mood.

In later life he seldom talked about his family background or his upbringing; he had been devoted to his mother, but seldom if ever mentioned his father and never his elder brother. As far as most of his friends were concerned, his life before he got his first job in decoration in 1926 or 1927 was a virtual blank except for his admiration for Thaxted church and what the Reverend Conrad Noel had done there. His Fowler forbears were Hampshire and Buckinghamshire yeomen who prospered for much of the nineteenth century but then went under during the agricultural depression; and his father, Robert Richard Fowler, who was Clerk of Lingfield Racecourse, did not make a great success of his life. He died in 1915, when John was nine. He left his widow very badly off, and,

although John went to Tormore, a preparatory school near Deal, and then in January 1921 to Felsted, where his father had been before him, he had to leave in April 1923. There was no money for him to have any kind of professional training, but he was found a job in an estate agent in St James's which he hated. As a result he had some kind of breakdown and spent a year with a cousin, who had a small farm in Kent.

How he got his first job in decoration, with Thornton Smiths, who were a big commercial firm in Soho Square, is not recorded, but during his year there he learned a good deal about painting, particularly wallpaper, and he used to describe how he was taught to do chinoiserie designs, first the leaves, then the flowers and finally the birds. After that he worked on his own for a short time, but it was an impossible struggle, and in 1930 he would have joined Mrs Guy Bethell, the decorator whom he most admired, had she not died. The following year he was asked to run the studio attached to the new department of decorative furniture at Peter Jones, where he stayed until the autumn of 1934. Then he and his most talented colleagues in the studio left in order to set up his own business called John Beresford Fowler, operating from the house where he was already living at 292 King's Road, not far from Lady Colefax at Argyll House, and Syrie Maugham who had moved to 213 King's Road in 1927. The firm of John Beresford Fowler lasted until 1938, when Lady Colefax asked him to join her in Bruton Street.

The outline of the story is simple enough, but what is remarkable is how he developed his individual style, combining artistry with scholarship and simplicity with sophistication to produce a fresh, country style in London in the wake of the Slump. He had a natural flair for painting which he had put to good use at Thornton Smiths, so that when he began to paint furniture for Margaret Kunzer before she took him to Peter Jones she recognized that he had a special talent. He also had a searching eye, an accurate historical sense with a particular feeling for dates, and a photographic memory, and, although he had no opportunity to travel abroad, he spent a great deal of time in museums, particularly the Victoria and Albert Museum, which he used as Sir Henry Cole intended as his university. As well as being marvellous company and the warmest of friends, he possessed a remarkable ability to inspire devotion and command unquestioning loyalty; he was good at spotting and releasing talent; and he had a special knack of creating a mood of happiness and laughter. Those gifts masked his fundamental insecurity, which emerged in the less happy side of his nature, his need to dominate, in his intolerance and his tendency to bully. However, what is more significant is that his Peter Jones colleagues who went with him to 292 King's Road still look back with such warmth to the happiness of those hand-to-mouth days; and several of them worked for him on and off for many years to come. They started the business as a near co-operative, with virtually no capital other than what was provided by the fathers of two of the girls, and there was no shop window, only a glazed box in the garden that had to be dressed every day; but such was the freshness of his eye, their skill at painting and the originality of the detail of their upholstery that they soon attracted the attention of clients, mostly Chelsea people, and the press.

The first account of their work appeared in *Harpers Bazaar* in February 1935, written by a friend of Gwen Jervis, who ran the studio attached to 292:

A band of enterprising young people have opened a studio in King's Road, Chelsea, under the name of John Beresford Fowler. They will decorate your home from top to bottom (they are all practical craftsmen as well as artists); they will change your present scheme in the twinkling of an eye into something fresh, gay and charming; they will paint, lacquer, pickle and embellish shabby old furniture until it looks completely rejuvenated ...

These youngsters are adept at copying old designs and transforming dreary old chairs and cabinets and what nots with delicate seventeenth and eighteenth century scrolls and flourishes, till you don't recognize your old things. Besides that they have a flair for picking up old furniture, china, pictures, chintz and things like that - you know - they are the sort of people who can go to the Caledonian Market and come back with a treasure instead of a moth-eaten waste paper basket. Anyway, they will look out for just the things you have wanted for years - and find them. And they can combine periods and create flattering backgrounds and generally make themselves useful.

They have a charming showroom as well as a studio in the King's Road house so you can see what they can do.

From a commercial point of view it was a haphazard enterprise, but in several respects it was a good moment for talented people to start out in a new direction. The Slump in 1929 had forced people to think more modestly, but it had not quenched the growing desire for more attractively decorated houses, and by 1934 a swing against the starkness of Syrie Maugham's first white manner was under way with a return to colour and pattern; and people were discovering the Victorian period. That is apparent in an article in *Harpers Bazaar* for November 1934 by Rosamund Harcourt-Smith under the title of 'Victoriana':

During the past year we have grown tired of decorating as chastely white as a christening robe, of furniture stripped bare to the grain or composed of steel tubes and the skins of wild animals, and have cast about for something a trifle more lively. We have ransacked the ages, and oddly enough in the dark green swamps of the Victorian era our search has ended.

In 1936 *Vogue* revived *House and Garden*, publishing it as a double number of *Vogue* twice a year, and it was an immediate success. The first room decorated by John Fowler and illustrated under his name in *Vogue* was in the issue of 13 April 1938: it was in Mr Ayscough's house, 14 Gayfere Street, Westminster. The caption starts: 'Elaborately early Victorian is the drawing room ...', and the text describes how 'the natural result of the return to humanity in decoration after the years in the wilderness of straight lines and neutral colours, has been an outburst of extreme decorativeness'. Thus one senses that his talents were absolutely right for the moment.

A few weeks earlier, on 24 March, the flat in Sussex Gardens [145], which John Fowler had decorated for Lady Patricia Ward, the sister of Lord Dudley and a contributor to *Vogue* and *House and Garden*, was illustrated in the *Evening Standard*, but without any mention of his name. 'The whole thing is early Victorian. Even the radiogram in the hall has a case of

144. JOHN FOWLER IN 1971. A photograph by Paul Tanqueray, a friend from school days.

145. LADY PATRICIA WARD'S FLAT IN SUSSEX GARDENS IN 1938. Anne Scott-James remembers vividly the impression it made on her, the fresh country look, the light bright colours, the simple materials, the lamps.

artificial flowers on it,' wrote the Home Page editor. If the rooms do not look early Victorian to us, the colours and materials were typical of John, curtains of percale striped in white and pink, the carpet moss green, the cushions piped in mauve, and the sofa cover white with grey stripes. The lamps beside the bed were Victorian vases: 'Victorian vases may be a joke to some people, but they are coming back to fashion all the same – converted to useful purposes.' The photographs do not make the flat look very special to us, but Anne Scott-James, who was working on *Vogue* and knew Lady Patricia, remembers vividly the impression it made on her, the fresh country look, the light bright colours, the simple materials, the lamps. It struck her as being both different and eminently desirable. And Lady Patricia's sister, Lady Morvyth Benson, must have thought so too, because she asked him to decorate her house in Cowley Street.

By then John had begun to develop his particular feeling for upholstery and curtains and for the details of their finishing. Some of that came from studying eighteenth-century costume at the Victoria and Albert Museum, while the sense of colour owed a good deal to the ballet and the theatre, but the ideas were translated into simple materials. One scrap of material gives an excellent idea of that. It is a trimming made of theatrical slipper satin combined with a simple chintz; the edges of both layers are pinked [LXIII]. He used that kind of trimming throughout his career, as on curtains he made for Lady Gunston in 1969. Another survivor from that time and related to some he made for Send Grove is a cushion cover made of three colours of slipper satin, once crisp and now limp, the main cover in no colour and then edged with a double band of points, one in yellow and one in purple, the cushion being corded in purple, the yellow points edged in no colour, and the purple points edged in yellow. Even in its battered state it suggests that he had looked at ballet costume and devised something fresh and simple-looking which must have taken the nanny of one of the girls, who did much of the sewing at 292, a remarkably long time to make. John Fowler was already interested not only in how things looked in the past, but how they were made, and he and Joyce Shears would unpick what came their way in order to study its construction. 'Shearo' would work out how to adapt ideas for drapery and cut out the curtains as well as make such special details as the rosettes.

Very little of the work carried out at 292 can survive now, but it was essentially simple and romantic and it brought a country look into London. All three aspects were responses to the mood of the time and were not in themselves original, but what was new and fresh was his own synthesis, born out of his own circumstances: that was what he called 'humble elegance'.

However, fortunately there is one virtually complete house in Chelsea that John Fowler did in about 1935/6 for a client who had discovered him through the show case at the front of 292; and that has been maintained just as it was ever since, with only minor replacements when necessary. The dining room on the ground floor is painted a dark green dragged over a white ground, and the cornice mouldings are wiped off rather than picked out; the doors are painted in with the walls, and the skirting is a darker green. The colour is darker than he would have used later, but already there is the light ground, the broken colour, and the darker skirting. On the other hand later on he would have turned against the wiping-off just as he would have made features of the doors. His approach is already painterly but less architectural than his mature work. The curtains are of green silk reversing to pink; the chairs are black japanned Regency parlour chairs.

At first-floor level, outside the drawing room door and facing the stairs, is a niche, which is lined with a Regency-inspired wallpaper of sprigs of ivy set within garlands of cords and tassels, and it is framed with draped curtains made of plain wine-coloured glazed chintz trimmed with fringe. The walls of the double drawing room [XXI] are painted a gloss pale lilac, lilacs and mauves always being among his favourite colours, with the pilasters and cornice marbled to relate to the grey marble chimneypiece. The treatment of the curtains is reminiscent of dressmaking, exploiting not only the contrasts of colour but the variation in the sheen of the materials as well.

In the principal bedroom the walls are pale blue and the curtains and the draped canopy over the bed are in striped and plain copper-coloured taffeta, again with dark red fringe. The breaking of the colours and the elaborate working of the upholstery, with close attention to the details of trimming and sewing, look forward to John's mature work, and even now the rooms give a sense of unusual personalities lying behind them; but of course, instead of seeming up to the minute, they have become a remarkable relic of a period of decoration that has all but vanished.

Much of the inspiration for what John Fowler did in that house and for other clients lay in the simpler aspects of the Regency style, which as we have seen had been discovered some years before but only became widely fashionable in the early 1930s, when it seemed to offer a parallel to the Modern Movement. Indeed Peter Jones had its first Regency exhibition in 1935.

What John's attitude to the Modern Movement in architecture or design was at that time, I do not know, but the natural presumption that he turned his back on it is unlikely to be correct; it is more likely that he followed the new developments, while recognizing that they were not for him. Certainly rather later, in the years when Ian McCallum was working for the *Architectural Review*, from 1943, John subscribed to it. Indeed one of his favourite phrases, 'pleasing decay', came from the title of an article by John Piper in the *Review* in 1947.

It was not just the look of Regency things that appealed but also its raffish romantic character as expressed in Regency Brighton. John and Hardy Amies, whom he met in 1934, the year that the latter went to Lachasse, often went on expeditions there together in pursuit of the Regency, which struck them as new and undiscovered. Indeed Hardy Amies still speaks of their excitement, and in *Just So Far* he wrote: 'I would be amazed to notice with what assured eye John would choose his colours for a decoration scheme'; and of their visits to the Pavilion at Brighton: 'I would listen to long arguments and explanations of English furniture and taste.'

Fortunately the most revealing photographs of early Fowler rooms are of his own at 292 King's Road, the first set being taken in December 1934 and the second in June 1939 [146-150]. The first one of the L-shaped drawing room on the first floor shows it when it was a shop in 1936.

In the next photograph, which shows the room in 1939, when it was his sitting room, it is noticeable that the Victorian elements have disappeared and its own restrained Regency character comes through more strongly, not only in the choice of Regency and Empire furniture and ornaments and the ivy-leaf chintz, possibly one produced for Lady Colefax before he joined her, but in the greater sparseness of the treatment.

The development is interesting because by 1940/41 those who knew his work associated him completely with the eighteenth century. When Lady d'Avigdor Goldsmid's husband inherited Somerhill in Kent soon after their marriage in 1940, a friend actually put her off going to John Fowler, saying that it was a pity it was a Jacobean house because he only liked the eighteenth century.

There was also a garden room at 292 King's Road [149], where later visitors to the Hunting Lodge will recognize many old friends among the simple furniture and objects, and such characteristic touches as the carefully float-tufted pad on the chair on the left. The photographs show his growing mastery of the simple style that enabled him to cope with grand rooms later and make them human. It is possible to see why the romantic atmosphere he created made such an impression on those who went to see him, among them Jean Hornak, who worked with him at Peter Jones and saw 292 for the first time about 1933. 'The room was lit by candles and a blazing fire and was scented by a huge vase of lilies. There was a beautiful orange vermilion chair of Spanish make and dated about 1690. There was a spinet which John played and there were Spanish torchères, "Charlie" chairs, a beautiful rose cope, rush matting, and grey and white ticking on an old seat.' That was the essence of 'humble elegance'. John loved early music and played not only on that instrument but on those collected by Benton Fletcher and then housed at Old Devonshire House, Bloomsbury. Friends also remember that he was an excellent cook, and more than one says that he not only opened their eyes to decoration but taught them about food as well.

John greatly missed a garden, which is partly why he took a primitive clapboard cottage at Rolvenden in Kent, which he rented for 5s. a week. Jean Hornak remembers bundling off there by train at the weekend with John clutching the *New Statesman*; and very happy times when they got there, with too much local cider and John doing cartwheels in the nude. The snapshots of the cottage are, sadly, too poor for reproduction, but Joyce Shears still remembers a bed hung with old mauve toile-de-jouy bound with cerise pink. Life, however, was not all fun. In London he used to take part in anti-fascist marches, carrying banners and wearing sandals. And Anne Talbot, one of the girls at 292, used to sell the *Daily Worker* outside South Kensington station.

Foreign influence, particularly that of France and Italy, was obviously intriguing. When John was in his twenties he had no chance to travel, but he had an extraordinary ability to absorb essential information from illustrations in books, and he built up an amazing knowledge about the look of places that he had never visited. But photographs are no substitute for reality, and the influence on him of France, and to a lesser extent and later of Italy, was direct as well as indirect. Mrs Hourigan remembers him going to Paris for the first time in 1936 (and the occasion is etched in her memory for the absurd reason that he split his only

146. 292 KING'S ROAD, LONDON. THE TOP ROOM IN 1934. The presumably French screen and the English printed pottery and creamware are two aspects of John Fowler's personal tastes.

147 and 148. THE DRAWING ROOM AT 292 KING'S ROAD IN 1934. The formal arrangement of the room, the balance of small pictures to the plain wall and the choice of objects all suggest the Regency Revival, but the valances of presumably old *toile de jouy* with striped cotton curtains, the emphasis on painted furniture and the matting on the floor all suggest the way John Fowler's own individual style was developing.

149. THE TOP ROOM AT 292 KING'S ROAD IN 1939. The simple chair, the three-legged table and the long stand for plants, the rush matting on the floor, the English creamware on the shelves, and the tin flower stand painted in stripes are of the essence of John Fowler's personal tastes throughout his life. Many of the objects would be familiar to visitors to the Hunting Lodge thirty-five years later.

150. THE DRAWING ROOM AT 292 KING'S ROAD IN 1939. Regency and Empire furniture. Over the table, 'hanging' from a coloured cord with a bow and tassels, is a portrait of John Fowler's Irish forbear, whom he believed was an illegitimate daughter of Archbishop Beresford and after whom he was named. Over the chimneypiece is a marble relief that was later given a marbled frame.

151. A DISPLAY AT 24 BRUTON STREET IN ABOUT 1938. A photograph taken shortly after John Fowler joined Lady Colefax, showing characteristic materials used at that time.

152. LADY COLEFAX'S HOUSE IN LORD NORTH STREET IN 1940.

pair of trousers the day before he was to set out). What he saw in Paris must have been a revelation to him in many ways but particularly in terms of finish and detail and in the handling of colour in paint and materials; and it was after that visit that he began to make use of Mauny wallpapers, which have a special life of their own. Mauny was a firm started in 1933 that produced, and still produces, wallpapers made in the traditional way as *papiers peints*, with paint colours mixed by hand, painted grounds, and block printing by hand.

Perhaps it was at that time he developed his romantic passion for Marie Antoinette, who also became a kind of patron saint of all that he admired most in light, elegant and highly sophisticated decoration. Every book on her that appeared he bought, and scarcely a weekend at the cottage went by without reference to her. Indeed, one of his most treasured possessions was a pair of her gloves, which with characteristic generosity he gave to Versailles, making a special pilgrimage to present them.

To what extent he fully absorbed the French sense of scale and feeling for formality I am less certain – perhaps it did not occur until his immediate post-war visits. Certainly there is a French quality about the layout of his garden at the Hunting Lodge [169] that has a freshness about it suggesting an immediacy of response to an experience. In the late 1940s and early 1950s he paid fairly frequent short visits to Paris, staying at the Hôtel de Beaujolais in the Palais Royal, particularly when he was painting a room for the Duke and Duchess of Windsor at their mill house in the country, and it was then that he bought some fine pieces of old toile-de-jouy which he later gave to the Victoria and Albert Museum. Also he picked up a smattering of French phrases that so amused the late Lord Pembroke that he used to call him 'Quand-même'. However he travelled less extensively than might be presumed.

Accounts vary of how John joined Lady Colefax, but the year was 1937 or 1938. According to Richard Fisher in his book on Syrie Maugham, it was she who first suggested to John Fowler that he should join up

with her, but he refused. However, her daughter, Lady Glendevon, who became a friend of John after the war, says that he used to tell her that he had asked her mother for a job and she would not give him one.

It must have been about the same time that Peggy Ward, later Countess Paul Munster, suggested to Lady Colefax that John Fowler should join them. Lady Colefax, who had naturally good taste that had been admired by her friends for many years, started to decorate on a professional basis in 1933 when she joined up with Stair & Andrew, who were antique dealers in Bruton Street. The following year she bought the lease of their premises from them and started Sybil Colefax Ltd, and Peggy Ward became her partner. Immediately it was considered smart: Sir Henry Channon, for instance, in his diary entry for 19 December 1934 records going Christmas shopping with Lady Diana Cooper and buying 'dozens of presents; most from Lady Colefax's chic shop'.

Peggy Ward might have come across John Fowler through Peter Jones, but it is more likely that she met

him after he set up on his own at 292 King's Road. So he went to Bruton Street, and was paid about £8 a week. Lady Colefax did not want his studio, and the only people to go with him were Joyce Shears as cutter and Mrs Hourigan, who looked after the accounts.

It is not clear how distinctive Sybil Colefax's work was at the time John Fowler joined her, but photographs of Old Buckhurst, her house in Sussex, published by *Country Life* as long before as 1919, suggest that while she did not have as romantic or imaginative an eye as Sir Louis Mallet, E.G. Lister or Colonel Cooper, who was a close friend, she would have felt a certain affinity with the simplicity of John Fowler's taste. It is a surprise, for instance, to find her using Hardwick matting at Old Buckhurst. However, there seems to have been a divide between her own rooms at Argyll House and later at 19 Lord North Street, which look unselfconscious and undecorated, and what she did for other people. That is brought out in *The Glass of Fashion* by Cecil Beaton (1954): the delightful rooms in her own house:

153. 15 KENSINGTON PALACE GARDENS, LONDON. THE DRAWING ROOM CURTAINS. The
striped material and the block fringe used on the continued drapery were also used on the sofas. The
deep bullion fringe in blue and white hid the radiators. The festoon blinds were purple or mauve.
Samples of some of the materials used can be seen in illustration XXII.

154. THE REGENCY BEDROOM AT 15 KENSINGTON PALACE GARDENS. Lady Colefax was
commissioned to do the decoration and soon after John Fowler joined her. The wallpaper was coral
sprigged with white, the curtains were grey and blue, and the paintwork sage-grey lined with mauve;
the hangings of the bed were of striped mulberry lined with blue and trimmed with a block fringe.

XXXVII. THE BLUE DRAWING ROOM AT LENNOXLOVE. The decoration of the room
started out from the nineteenth-century greeny-blue damask curtains woven with the Hamilton
emblem of the oak leaf and the nineteenth-century Savonnerie carpet, also from Hamilton Palace;
and their colours meet in the floral chintz. The curtains are too fragile to draw and so the
windows have festoon blinds. Some of the gilt chairs are upholstered in the floral chintz and
some in silk; the big sofa and armchair are upholstered in the trellis chintz found at Ramsbury.
The Mauny *coquille* wallpaper is used in other colours both at Lennoxlove and Holyrood and is
shown in illustration XXIII.

XXXVIII. THE DUKE OF
HAMILTON'S APARTMENTS AT
THE PALACE OF
HOLYROODHOUSE, EDINBURGH.
The drawing room. The main feature
of the apartment is the run of three
big rooms, the drawing room, hall
and dining room. For practical as
well as visual reasons John Fowler
moved their main doors from beside
the windows to the middle of the
wall, remaking them as double doors
with architraves. The drawing room
is hung with the Mauny shell
wallpaper in pale lilac-mauve and the
curtains are of matching taffeta
trimmed with a gimp specially woven
to match the old one re-used in the
hall; the ground of the frieze is tinted
in a tone related to the lilac-mauve
and the picking-out in gold was done
at the same time.

XXXIX. THE HALL OF THE DUKE
OF HAMILTON'S APARTMENTS,
WITH THE VIEW THROUGH TO
THE DINING ROOM. The walls are
hung with a blue-grey broad-striped
wallpaper that John Fowler first
devised as a replacement for damask
(it is also seen at Shugborough in
illustration 188). There is no picking-
out or gilding.

XL. THE DINING ROOM OF THE
DUKE OF HAMILTON'S
APARTMENTS. The Charles II
ceiling is complemented by the
wallpaper copied by John Fowler
from an early-eighteenth-century
damask and printed from four blocks
on small sheets of paper. The reds in
the room were suggested by the
nineteenth-century stamped wool
velvet on the chairs. The late Duke
of Hamilton bought the Panini of
The Coronation of the Pope for
historical reasons, but it provides a
focus when all the doors are open;
and John Fowler found the Italian
table to go beneath it.

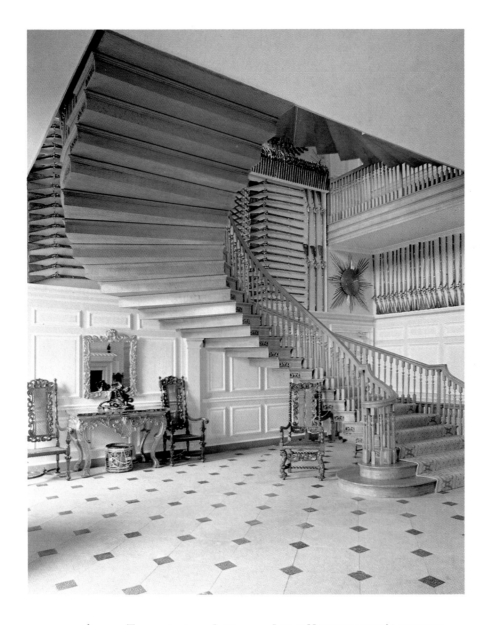

XLI and XLII. TYNINGHAME, LOTHIAN. LADY HADDINGTON'S SITTING
ROOM. The idea was to give the room a Georgian character but not to create a
complete eighteenth-century room. The eighteenth-century marble chimneypiece is an
introduction, as is the pedimented doorcase; and John Fowler designed the flanking
bookcases, which, like the rest of the woodwork in the room, is painted in stone white
and picked out in gold. The key to the colouring came from a stock of Victorian braid,
which was almost enough for two sets of curtains, and the walls are hung with a
golden yellow corduroy.

XLIII. CHEVENING, KENT. THE STAIRCASE. John Fowler cleaned the woodwork;
he also painted the panelling in off-whites and the upper walls a broken yellow to
provide a warm background for the display of arms apparently first arranged here in
the 1720s.

XLIV. CHEQUERS, BUCKINGHAMSHIRE. THE GALLERY. John Fowler arranged this room for the use of the Prime Minister and guests. To relate the bookcases to the Elizabethan style of the windows, he used his 'Berkeley Sprig' wallpaper [LXVII and LXVIII]. Compare this room with the gallery at Sudbury [50 and LXXVI].

XLV. Ivy Lodge, Radway,
Warwickshire. The hall. John
Fowler recommended using only patterned
wallpapers in the hall and passages. The
lilac spray pattern provides the key to the
house.

XLVI. The drawing room at Ivy Lodge. The many now faded colours in the decoration of the room echo the
colours in the bold, still strong colours in the nineteenth-century carpet and complement the changing arrangement of
pictures.

XLVII. THE SITTING ROOM AT THE HUNTING LODGE, ODIHAM, HAMPSHIRE, BY SERABRIAKOFF. John Fowler's sitting room changed little over the years. On the right wall stood his best piece of furniture, an eighteenth-century commode, probably Swedish, and it was flanked by a pair of bell pulls, a favourite device of his to frame an object as well as to pace out and give height to a room. The pair of flower stands flanking the open window came from the Blithfield sale. Characteristically he left them to Lady Bagot for Blithfield and on them stood a pair of painted tin flowerpots. The black dog, a present from Nancy Lancaster, was not real.

were decorated with all the restraint of an eighteenth-century intellectual ... Influenced in her taste by The Souls Lady Colefax created an atmosphere that was without any quality of pretentiousness, regardless of where she lived ... She purposely avoided the inclusion of any grand pieces of furniture in her rooms, obtaining her effects through the use of off colours - pale almond green, greys and opaque yellows - and an overall discretion ... When in later years Lady Colefax took to decorating professionally, her individual flair was missing, and she assembled rooms that were singularly unlike her own.

Among her great friends was Lady Anglesey, and Sybil Colefax's name appears in the Plas Newydd visitors' book, but how much she helped Lady Anglesey with the house does not seem to be known. However, it suggests the kind of rooms that she liked.

Among the first big commissions that the firm did after John Fowler joined it was Sir Alfred Beit's house in Kensington Palace Gardens [XXII, XXIII, 153, 154]. The ornate architectural work was done by Trenwith Wills and Lord Gerald Wellesley as a background for Sir Alfred's pictures, and Lady Colefax, an old friend of Sir Alfred's mother - she had been one of her bridesmaids in 1897 - was asked to do the colours and upholstery. It was probably the first grand house that John ever worked in, and, seeing photographs of it forty-five years later, one might not immediately guess that he had a hand in it, because the combination of the splendid objects and the formal atmosphere is not one associated with him; but once told of Sybil Colefax's involvement certain John Fowler hallmarks are identifiable. Fortunately it is possible to follow them through in the samples pasted into the order book, which Mrs Hourigan kept, and they confirm that many elements of John's style were already present then.

It is interesting to compare that house with Send Grove in Surrey, which he decorated for Countess Paul Munster about 1937/8. When it was illustrated in *House and Garden* on 11 May 1938, the author of the article wrote: 'In England, decorative spirits run equally high. In a sitting room in her country house, Countess Paul Munster hangs vivid yellow face-cloth curtains against pearl-grey walls, puts a bright crimson stair carpet in a hallway papered in blue and white stripes.'

By 1938 John Fowler was recognized in his own right in the field of decoration, as can be seen in an article in *House and Garden*, which consists of interviews with eight leading decorators, and, since it is apparently his first interview, it is worth quoting John Fowler's answers in full.

Such a welter of news in decor. Such a flood of ideas, colours, styles. Such a ticklish job to sort out the wheat from the chaff, that we decided to consult the oracle in the shape of eight of the foremost decorators of today. We asked them these seven questions.

1. What do you consider the most important feature of decoration today?
2. Do you consider that taste and feeling have changed very much in the last six months?
3. Towards which period and style do you think there is the greatest trend today?
4. What do you think about colour? Is the new feeling for bright colours, or pastels?
5. What new fabrics do you consider important? What textures and what designs?
6. What do you consider the greatest lack or fault in decoration in England at the present time?
7. What is your own personal enthusiasm in decoration at the present time?

John Fowler's answers were:

1. That decoration is a logical compromise between comfort and appearance. A room must be essentially comfortable not only to the body but to the eye.
2. No, I do not. Fashions in decoration evolve more slowly than fashions in clothes. They usually change for some political, social or economic reason to satisfy an emotional need.
3. I do not think we can say there is any definite trend towards one particular period. The styles of the Regency and Empire have not lost their popularity and Victoriana has by no means had its day. Thus the last five years have shown evidence of a romantic revival using rich colours and furniture of a sophisticated type. Again there is a greater appreciation of French furniture, particularly of the Régence period, and Austrian furniture in the Biedermeyer style.
4. I think there is a very healthy tendency to use bright colour. Pastel colours can be beautiful, but in England most of us have come to limit the use of that term to 'pinky-beige', peach and pale blue. There is a feeling for richer colours and a greater daring and understanding in mixing them.
5. Most fabrics can be given significance if used in the right way. I am frankly bored by the endless variety of oatmeal cloths and nigger tweeds and the usual galaxy of insipid artificial satins. Cotton has been largely ignored in serious decoration but many of the English striped cottons and the Provençal flowered ones are delightful. These by no means look 'cottagey'. Used with a sophisticated background they possess a chic of their own.
6. The limitation of colour and the lack of originality in design of furnishing materials.
7. I like the decoration of a room to be well behaved but

free from too many rules; to have a sense of graciousness; to be mannered, yet casual and unselfconscious; to be comfortable, stimulating, even provocative, and finally to be nameless of period – a 'fantaisie' expressing the personality of its owner.

Send has changed hands on more than two occasions since then, but one house which John Fowler began to decorate in 1939 and completed after the outbreak of war still survives more or less intact; and it was done for the same client as the Chelsea house. It is a West Country farmhouse skilfully remodelled to suggest somewhere in France, with stone walls, a pantiled roof and big white painted cornices; and within he continued that idea, making it Anglo-French, Empire and Regency, not at all a simple English country house. The front door is in one corner of the big forecourt, and the first surprise is to find a stone staircase climbing round a solid pier to the principal floor. At its head, glazed double doors lead into a cross-corridor painted a bluish pink, a favourite colour of the client and providing the colour key to the house. One end of the corridor opens out enough for 'a room' to be made out of it by papering it with a small Empire rosette pattern in gold on blue-grey, with a ceiling of paler pink. (The same pattern is used against a different ground colour in the dining room.) Off it opens the drawing room, where the pattern of the paper is enlarged in scale and simplified, being printed in gold on lilac-mauve. It is an excellent French background for more Empire than Regency furniture and for an Aubusson carpet, carved trophies, Empire porcelain lamps and a French marble chimneypiece. The French headed curtains are of yellow ottoman lined with mauve and are trimmed with yellow and mauve bullion fringe; behind them are festoon blinds trimmed with fringe; and the yellow is picked up in the green of the felt planned to the floor with a grey border. And even the view out on to the lower garden is more French in feeling than English. The dining room furniture is more Regency than Empire, and the now worn stone floor is uncovered. Again the chimneypiece is French, and the violet in the marble relates to the purplish cast to the brown ground of the wallpaper.

The principal bedroom is again Anglo-French [xxv, xxvii]. The bed head is of the same orange pink as the curtains and has a drapery of white muslin and a bedspread of muslin embroidered with lilies of the valley and mounted on pink. With the continental commode and painted chairs are *arte-povere* bedside tables made to John Fowler's design. Here and in several rooms there are painted slatted blinds as at 292.

Some of the curtains were repeated by Colefax & Fowler later, but even so it is interesting to see John Fowler's decoration evidently becoming crisper under French influence, which had become direct after his first visit to France in 1936; and also to see how he ran themes of colour and pattern through a house, so creating a sense of unity. Much of the detail and many of the ideas were to recur in his post-war work, but the overall feeling of the house is not really what I associate with his approach. But then perhaps we expect a simpler, more relaxed, style in what is still basically a farmhouse; and the French Empire and Regency styles are at present out of fashion in England.

With the outbreak of war, decorating came almost to a halt. The staff, except for Lady Colefax's secretary and Mrs Hourigan, were paid off; the younger craftsmen were called up; and good materials vanished. However, John Fowler and Mrs Hourigan kept the business ticking over, moving from Bruton Street to 66 Grosvenor Street and then in 1943 to 39 Brook Street.

Most of John Fowler's time was devoted to the ambulance section of the A R P, but he had one day off a week, and that he devoted to the shop, where he worked out pretty schemes with unlikely materials, dying sheets and damask table cloths and making cushions out of old dresses bought in Brighton.

How he made ends meet is unclear, and the rent from the two let rooms at the top of 292 was probably a significant part of his income throughout the war, and afterwards. Friends remember the warmth of the welcome there, the cosiness of the house, jolly parties beneath his prized Venetian chandelier, and the retreats to his Anderson shelter in the garden. James Lees-Milne was one friend who used to take refuge there towards the end of the war, and part of his entry in his diary for 1 July 1944, runs: 'Slept in John Fowler's Anderson shelter on the top bunk, which was very luxurious, although there were as many as five of us in the shelter. A noisy night, but quieter at dawn. Incessant jokes and hoots of laughter non-stop. In fact we laughed ourselves to sleep.'

It was during the war that John ventured into the theatre. He designed the sets for two H. M. Tennant productions [155, 156]. One was *The Circle* by Somerset Maugham, which was part of a John Gielgud season at the Theatre Royal, Haymarket, and opened on 11 October 1944; the other was *Another Love Story* by Frederick Lonsdale, which opened at the Phoenix Theatre on 13 December 1944. He also designed and he and Mrs Hourigan painted the sets for *La Parisienne*, which Michael Redgrave, who was a friend of

155. A SET FOR 'THE CIRCLE' DESIGNED BY JOHN FOWLER IN 1944. A Fowler country
house drawing room as it might have been, but adapted for the stage. The attention to the treatment of
the architectural decoration, the line of the upholstery, the formal disposition of the pictures, and the
use of flowers anticipate rooms decorated by him in the 1950s and 1960s.

156. A SET FOR 'ANOTHER LOVE STORY', 1944. The bedroom is papered with a painted
enlargement of a Mauny design that John Fowler had used before the war. The treatment of the
drapery on the bed and dressing table recalls a bedroom like that in illustration XXVII.

157. JOHN FOWLER PHOTOGRAPHED AT 39 BROOK STREET IN 1946. In later years his own
room in the shop was an Aladdin's cave of old fragments of wallpapers, carving, trimmings and so on,
as well as trials of designs he was working on and a bank of materials as colour samples.

John, put on at the St James's Theatre. John loved
that kind of work, and it was a great disappointment
that more of it did not come to him after the war; but
apparently he fell foul of Binky Beaumont, who con-
trolled H. M. Tennant, over a matter that was nothing
to do with his work, and as a result he was prevented
from getting any more commissions. So, if that was a
dead end, the photographs of the sets are interesting
because they show what were really Fowler rooms set
up on the stage and so show how his style in decoration was developing.

John had met James Lees-Milne for the first time in
1944. They shared a passion for buildings and a hatred
of destruction, and contact with someone of James
Lees-Milne's romantic and historical cast of mind must
have been important to him. It was James Lees-Milne
who introduced John to Margaret Jourdain, by then
the high priestess of historic decoration and furniture,
whom he had long wanted to meet; but he was amazed
at the bareness and austerity of the flat which she
shared with Ivy Compton-Burnett, and the starkness
of its decoration and the lack of relationship between

their few pieces of good Georgian furniture and their setting. His reaction, which James Lees-Milne describes in his diary, is an interesting comment on two very different approaches to the past.

The ending of the war did not mean the end of restrictions, particularly in luxury trades like decorating, and for several years it was a case of make-do. But John Fowler, with his background of practical skill, was not daunted. The kind of thing that he was asked to do was well illustrated at the Brighton Pavilion, then being restored by Clifford Musgrave. Some samples of painted linen in pale grey with a chinese trellis in gold had been found in store, but, since in 1948 it was impossible to get enough gold leaf, Lady Birley suggested that John should be asked to restore it; and he did, in yellow paint, working with three assistants through the whole night in order to get it finished.

It was at about this time that two events occurred which were of vital importance in John's life. First, as was explained in the last chapter, at the very end of 1946 or beginning of 1947 Ronald Tree persuaded his wife Nancy to buy the business of Sybil Colefax Ltd from Lady Colefax. Nancy Tree, or Lancaster, as she was soon to become, contributed much more than capital to the business: she and John sparked each other off in a remarkable way, but it is only right to say that it was not a case of peaceful collaboration, because both were strong characters used to having their own way. There were marvellous expeditions in search of stock for jobs, which often meant Nancy's houses, and a great deal of laughter; but also blistering rows that did not always evaporate overnight. Quite what they learned from each other in visual terms is hard to pin down: it seems to have been a case of two people being very much in accord over what they admired. However, probably Mrs Lancaster did teach John a great deal about comfort and the comforts that rich people expect and encouraged him to develop a bolder sense of scale that was to be essential in his success as an architectural decorator in the 1950s. Also, of course, many of the clients came through her and her houses, and that dictated the character of the business, as will be explained later.

The second key event was John's discovery of the Hunting Lodge near Odiham [XLVII, 167–171], which he saw advertised in *Country Life*, and bought in 1947. He immediately set to work on it, and by 1949 *Harpers Bazaar* thought it so special that they devoted to it four pages of rationed photogravure. Over the years John enlarged the cottage a good deal, but in essence it did not change and the old familiar much-loved possessions continued to be found there.

Thereafter the shop in Brook Street and the Hunting Lodge provided the framework for his life, but since an alternation of hard work during the week and precious weekends in the country is not the stuff of biography, it seems more satisfactory to consider his work by subject than by date.

However, there are aspects of John's life that cannot be dealt with that way, one of which is his battle against ill health throughout the last twenty years of his life. He always had bad eyesight and was not fit enough to serve in the war; but from the middle to late 1950s there were much more serious problems. In 1963 cancer of the throat was finally diagnosed and he had his first operation for it, but, according to those who had worked with him before, the trouble may have started several years earlier. After the operation he was told that if he was clear for five years, he would probably be completely free of cancer. But, alas, just at the end of that period it was discovered that he had Hodgkin's disease and he had another operation. From then on he lived with the disease, having to pay regular visits to the Marsden Hospital, for which he always had the highest praise, and living on cortisone for the last six years of his life. In addition he had a bad heart and also suffered from Ménière's disease. John always talked about his cancer in a very matter-of-fact way, because he believed that helped other people; and so his friends and colleagues grew to accept it too, with the result that the physical and mental struggle necessary for him to continue with his work was all too easily forgotten. He had immense inner strength and spirit, but inevitably after 1973 the drugs seemed to affect his concentration. Also the burning of the garden room that he had built was a blow from which he never really recovered. Characteristically, however, he rebuilt it, making it as much like the old one as possible.

Somehow he managed to continue to cope with a gruelling schedule, and it was only during the summer of 1977 that it finally became clear that the challenge of yet another great house was more than he could take. That July he felt himself start to falter, but even then he would not give in and he continued to try to concentrate on his Trust work. The end was coming, but what his friends dreaded was a long-drawn-out final illness during which it might not be possible to look after him at the cottage. Mercifully, after all the years of anxiety, John died at home on 17 October 1977.

CHAPTER SEVEN

JOHN FOWLER
AND THE
ENGLISH INTERIOR

John Fowler's great contribution was to the English country house, to its decoration, preservation and understanding. He was essentially an architectural decorator – he always used to say, 'Don't call me a designer, I'm a decorator' – who was a master of unity and balance, of texture, colour and pattern; and he possessed a remarkable historical sense as well as a rare gift for bringing life to rooms and houses. At the beginning of his career he brought a country style to London, and in maturity he was able to take back to country houses all that he had learned.

The sheer quantity of his work is amazing, and it is extraordinary that he should have built up such a practice in the difficult years after the Second World War and continued it despite years of ill health; but, of course, it included a great deal of bread-and-butter decorating, particularly in London flats, that did not stimulate him, and in the end he came to dread telephone calls from exigent ladies in Eaton Square. 'I'd pay not to do it,' he used to say in a pained voice. That aspect of his work can be passed over, but just as his practice was considerably broader than country houses, so was his influence. Indeed he made a major contribution to English taste and preservation, and the traditional style of decoration as it is understood today both here and in America is really based on what he did.

When working on a worthwhile building, he always tried to put its character before that of the client, but the personality of the client was of enormous impor-

tance to him, and it is impossible to understand his approach to houses without understanding his relations with his clients, collectively and individually. They explain why he was essentially a decorator of private houses and why the challenge of commercial work was not for him. Some important public commissions came his way, as will be seen, but in every case he needed a figure who was able to take on the role of client and act as touchstone and sounding board.

In this respect 44 Berkeley Square in London [158] was particularly interesting. At first sight it might seem odd to have asked John Fowler to decorate a gambling club, and equally surprising that he should have accepted the commission and enjoyed it. Characteristically he took the opposite view: after all it was one of the few fine houses left in London, with noble, dramatic interiors by William Kent and elegant ones by Henry Holland; it was built by Lady Isabella Finch, who always intrigued him, because he could never understand why a prim lady-in-waiting to George II's unmarried daughters and supposedly of modest means could have built such a sparkling house; also a later owner (after whom it was called the Clermont Club) held extravagant gambling parties there, and the raffish aspects of the eighteenth century always had a special appeal for him. His client, John Aspinall, was someone for whom he had worked before and whose boundless enthusiasm and spirit of adventure were qualities that he appreciated. The architect was Philip

158. 44 BERKELEY SQUARE, LONDON. KENT'S GREAT ROOM. This was carefully restored by
John Fowler for use by the Clermont Club. The rooms without historic character were decorated so as
to suit its use as a gambling club.

Jebb, for whom he had great respect as well as affection and with whom he worked in satisfying harmony (in fact they had first met through Mr Aspinall).

John Aspinall, who had bought the house after the passing of the Gaming Act of 1960, gave them more or less *carte blanche* in terms of expenditure. John Fowler in his turn restored the historic interiors with immense care and at the same time decorated up with equal attention other parts of the house so that they just stopped short of outrageous vulgarity. The relationship between client and decorator was obviously mutually stimulating, and there was room for teasing and laughter as well.

It is revealing to compare 44 Berkeley Square with the Turf Club in Carlton House Terrace, which John Fowler also decorated. That too is a fine house, but of a type with little appeal to him and done for members for whom he had neither understanding nor sympathy; and what he did there has no conviction.

He liked to work for men with a streak of the adventurer in them and whom he could not fathom completely, and for that reason he got on well with such different characters as Mr Aspinall and Mr Harry Hyams, whom he helped at Ramsbury. But rich people *per se* did not interest him; nor was he impressed by money. Naturally, however, most of his clients were well-to-do, and women; and most of his best work was done for glamorous, spirited and often gifted, highly intelligent people, who stimulated him; and the combination of a striking, sympathetic personality and a worthwhile house usually meant the development of a lasting and affectionate relationship.

It would be invidious to give a list of those clients with whom he got on particularly well, but there were certain of them whom his close friends realized had a special place in his affections. Apart from Nancy Lancaster, there was her cousin, Lady Ancaster, who always called him 'Folly'; she was immensely generous to him and took a great deal of the worry out of his life when he became ill. Another was Mrs Jack Dennis, who always seemed to get the best out of John, because, although she did not know much about pictures or furniture, she had a natural eye for enchanting things; and she was pretty, elegant and fun. She adored John: indeed she appeared to move house in order to be in constant touch with him. He, for his part, had a special affection for her, and it always appealed to him that she had been in C. B. Cochran's chorus and ended up in Grosvenor Square. (On the other hand there was the occasional client who encouraged him to go over the top with disastrous results.)

If the spark between John Fowler and his client was vital for success, his upbringing left him insecure, and he always was nervous when a client came to see him for the first time. If telephoned for an appointment by someone whom he did not know, he would seldom grant one under six weeks away; and when the dreaded first meeting took place in his room in Brook Street, he would often keep the client waiting for ages; he was even known to slip away in the middle of a meeting for no other reason than to unnerve the client and so establish the upper hand that he felt was essential for any job. (When Mrs J. F. Kennedy came to see him, she had to wait while he finished watching an episode of *Coronation Street* on the television.) His domination was such that even someone whom I would take to be confident in most situations remembers the courage it took when eventually she had to disagree with him over something that he was doing for her.

He had a reputation for being expensive, and no doubt that discouraged a number of people who really needed his advice and were able to afford it from going to him; and there are a considerable number of houses where it is a great pity that he did not pay even one visit. He was never extravagant with the thought of his own profit, but a good deal of money was spent, because he took little account of it when ordering work to be done again. As an old friend and client said, it was not that he was extravagant, but that he introduced people to expensive things.

There were quite a number of people whom he refused to take on as clients, even though they had houses that would have interested him; and a few he would not even see. Others who proved to bore him were disposed of; and he was quite prepared to reprove a client in a sharp, schoolmasterly way: 'Do pay attention. Do you know what a cornice really is?' He particularly disliked clients whom he thought pretentious and patronizing: they would be dismissed as 'people playing at ladies and gentlemen'.

On the other hand he was always sympathetic to those whose lot he felt was hard, and there would be one or two surprises among a complete list of clients, including an unknown lady who lived in Half Moon Street in London. When she telephoned the shop and asked to speak to Mr Fowler she would not take no for an answer, and on a second attempt she was put through to him; she explained that she was not his usual type of client and she did not want to embarrass him by coming to the shop, but would he, please, come round and advise her about her flat? He did, but history does not, alas, relate what he devised for her.

If relations with clients limited the range of his work, he was able to vary the balance of house and client. On the one hand he loved to pull out all the stops if a building called out for it and the client had the means, the personality and the will; but equally his appreciation of buildings and his sympathy for people was such that he would take enormous trouble to stop clients doing what would have been damaging or unnecessary, even if it would have been profitable for his firm, suggesting how a house could be transformed as simply as possible or how to get the right results without spending a lot of money in his shop. For instance, when Mr and Mrs Christopher Hussey moved into Scotney Castle, he suggested that they bought the material for the upholstery in the library from him, but that they should get the covers made locally because his people would make them too well to suit the character of the house. He had, as Philip Jebb said to me, the ability to make a rich man enjoy spending a great deal of money, even more than he had ever intended, but he was just as happy to save other people as much as he could. Both threads run through his post-war work.

His approach was always that of an artist with a romantic eye, the nose of a detective and a strong historical sense, never that of a man of business. No one had less feeling for money. What made his unique practice possible was his partnership with Nancy Lancaster, and, later, although he would never admit it, the way in which the firm was re-organized by her elder son, Michael Tree, and run by Tom Parr. He had found 39 Brook Street in 1943, when property was very cheap; and Mrs Lancaster, then still Mrs Tree, did not pay much for the business in 1946/7. So throughout the late 1940s and most of the 1950s the shop ticked over. It was the equivalent of an industrialist's hobby farm, with John getting a very modest salary and Nancy Lancaster seeing very little profit on her investment, and even losses, which she says she met by writing a cheque at the end of the year. It was a marvellous way for her and her friends to get their work done, but it was a hopeless way to run a business and particularly one doing that quality and quantity of work.

By the late 1950s it was obvious that the business would have to be re-organized if it was to continue, because even the ground floor of 39 Brook Street had been let off to a bank and with it the shop window. So Michael Tree asked Tom Parr, at that time in partnership with David Hicks, whether he would like to join Colefax & Fowler. A little later, in 1960, that idea was revived, and Tom Parr bought half the business (John Fowler had no shares in it). Immediately John Fowler was given a share of the profits, which soon became a reality, and within five years the profits were equal to the total turnover of the business in 1960. Thus he had the financial benefit while not having to alter his way of working.

In the last eighteen years of his life John Fowler was well paid, but he always chose to misunderstand the arrangements and constantly tried to win sympathy from his friends for his hard lot. The details are not significant now, but his attitude was characteristic, and it disguised the fact that, unlike anyone else involved in the world of *haute couture*, whether in decoration or fashion, he was able to go on in his own way.

Here parallels with fashion in dress come to mind, and in particular the experience of his old friend, Hardy Amies. The *haute couture* side of the latter's business is still the mainspring of design, but commercial success depends on the good boutique clothes and on licensing, with, on the one hand, the mood of the boutique clothes influencing the style of the house, and, on the other, the *haute couture* and boutique clothes providing the authority for the licensing business. That kind of equation had no appeal to John,

and he did not look beyond *haute couture*. The elaboration of his work continued when the equivalent was disappearing from the clothes of most of his clients; and perhaps unconsciously he gave them the kind of finish and fantasy that some of them missed both in their clothes and in their lives. His decoration became increasingly out of step with fashion in dress, and the only bond lay in the parallel between the essentially country style of his decoration and the athletic and sporting emphasis in clothes.

On a practical level too he never really adjusted to change. Even his simple decoration was based on the presumption that there would be well-trained staff, even if reduced in numbers, to look after it. I remember him saying to a client for whom he was doing a bed: 'There will, of course, be always two people to make it, won't there?' Although his rooms look beautiful when mellow and even when shabby, considerable attention to detail has to go into keeping them going, and, however natural and effortless they look, the naturalness does not really come all that naturally.

During the war he had done his best to provide clients with touches of fantasy, and after it his understanding of humble elegance was of crucial importance in the straitened circumstances of rationing and licences. His ingenuity continued to be important, but, since his wartime work has been in almost every case redone, it is now forgotten. It is equally difficult to judge what effect his colour sense and his revival of pretty designs had on English manufacturers: that will only become apparent when the whole period is surveyed. Just occasionally, however, something comes to light, such as the curtains in the drawing room at Little Durnford in Wiltshire, illustrated in *Interiors* for December 1981, which it described as having been inherited from a previous owner of the house, though without explaining that John Fowler made them for Lady Gunston in 1951 out of Moygashel dress material.

In spite of rationing, there were marvellous country house sales to go to, when there was sufficient black market petrol to get to them, and he and Mrs Lancaster had many hilarious and rewarding sorties to find stock for the shop, with the prettiest things invariably ending up in her houses.

With the easing of restrictions and the possibility of getting wallpapers and materials specially made once more in this country or imported from France, John Fowler got into his stride and he gave his clients the equivalent in decoration of the romantic, nostalgic New Look in dress; but whereas the New Look was quickly over, his has continued to appeal. There were not all that many jobs, but most of the good clients were connections or friends of Mrs Lancaster, with American money behind them and with that distinctly American appreciation of the purpose of decoration. They see it as creating a total look that will last for a period of years and then be redone, whereas English people tend to see decoration rather reluctantly as a necessity intended to last a lifetime. John Fowler worked not only for Mrs Lancaster's aunt, Lady Astor, but for two of her sons, William and Michael Astor, and for her daughter, Lady Ancaster; and he worked at Mereworth for Peter Beatty, who was the second son of Ronald Tree's mother by her second husband. And among Mrs Lancaster's old American friends he worked for Mr and Mrs David Bruce.

It was that circle that really gave him his chance to develop as an architectural decorator. 'Architectural decoration,' as he said to Philip Jebb, 'was not a matter of scattering paterae about the place,' but was to do with bringing out the essential quality and strength of rooms as they were expressed in their proportions and with understanding balance not only in one room but in a whole house and in the relationship of a house to its setting. He was very good at creating a sense of progression in a house and a sense of flow between rooms, and then underlining that flow by using patterns and colours that echoed each other. However, while it is the range and strength of John Fowler's colours that remain most vivid in one's memory, Christopher Wall, who worked with him on many occasions in National Trust houses, noticed that he invariably chose patterns before colour, establishing in his mind the needs of progression first, then those of scale and only afterwards the medium and the colour.

Within a room unity and balance meant establishing a proper relationship between the different classical members, the entablature, or at least the cornice, the dado rail, and the skirting, and their relationship to chimneypiece, doorcases and window architraves. He developed an extraordinarily fine eye for proportion, knowing when to increase the weight of a cornice, when to raise or lower or add a dado rail, when to add an overdoor to a doorcase. Even chimneypieces spoke their own language to him: of a chimneypiece that Philip Jebb had installed in a client's dining room John Fowler observed: 'Nice chimneypiece, but what a pity it was intended for a library.'

His understanding of classical proportion was all the more remarkable because he had never studied architectural drawing and probably he never actually drew the complete classical orders. However, he took immense care with drawings of mouldings and other architectural details, even if his sketches were often very free, quickly done in 3B pencil on any scrap of paper that came to hand or straight on the wall, even on new paintwork, or in charcoal. Plasterers, joiners and upholsterers were expected to be able to interpret his ideas. However, his sketches were expressive: as Peter Atkins, who did upholstery for him, pointed out to me, they had what he called 'movement'. That is particularly interesting, because it underlines his understanding of the nature of architectural decoration: almost certainly he encountered the word and the concept reading about the architecture of Robert Adam, and the idea of applying an eighteenth-century concept in his own work would have appealed to him.

His knowledge came from looking at details and painting them, and no one had a better understanding of painting architecture or how to convey the language of classicism through varying tones, how to balance in paint the different elements of an entablature, order, wall, dado and skirting, when to bring out the flutes of a column and when to dull the detail down. If one thinks of classical architecture as music, he was a conductor interpreting a score; but perhaps partly because he had no professional training in design, he had to feel his way through a scheme: he seldom if ever designed the decoration of a room in a formal sense. He did not produce perspectives or elevations of a room with the furniture all drawn in, nor did he make models. Indeed, he did not believe that it was possible to decide everything in advance. Instead he used to build up the decoration of a room gradually, working on it as a painter develops a picture. Hours would be spent on site making up his mind and assuring himself that all the details were correct, and if, for instance, at the end of the day a scheme for painting did not completely satisfy him, the painters would have to wait until it did. This element of growth was significant in the success of his decoration, because it allowed for that sense of life which is much more difficult to achieve in a scheme completely designed on a drawing board.

In setting out to achieve unity and balance he was fully aware of the flatness of perfection and also the stiffness and deadness that arises from having too many grand things in a room. He knew how to avoid the obvious and exploit a discord to give a sense of life and wit, particularly by creating slight clashes of colour and using unexpected contrasts of texture. His best rooms are sparkling and comfortable at the same time, apparently simple but actually very elaborate, saying a great deal but never confused, appealing to the eye and, although one does not realize it, to the mind as well. The elaboration was partly a matter of the number of paint colours and how the colour was applied, and the number of materials used for the upholstery; and it was also the way colours and materials related to each other and to furniture, pictures or objects in a room. It is well known that he liked pairs of objects: Mark Birley counted forty-eight pairs in one room at 44 Berkeley Square, and I have counted sixteen pairs in a medium-sized London drawing room. But somehow they never became insistent. Indeed, one is never really aware of how the unity is achieved.

He often liked to have what he called a 'dash of French' in a room. French architecture and decoration, which he greatly admired, had a profound influence on him, the influence coming through photographs as well as what he saw on visits. He found that one piece of French furniture made a valuable contribution to an English room, perhaps because of its greater discipline of line, its different sense of scale and its obvious foreignness: it was not only a visual matter but an associational one as well. However, the stiffness of French rooms had no appeal to him.

In his early days John Fowler evidently had little interest in providing comfort, but it became an essential ingredient of his mature work. His generous chairs and sofas of unfussy shape, basically Edwardian and looking as if they hailed from a smoking room or a library, not only look but are comfortable, and even luxurious, with their down-filled cushions. Chairs are invariably in the right positions to promote conversation – he used to speak of chairs talking to each other – and a light of the right brightness at the right height on a table big enough to hold a book and a drink made it always possible to read; and switches had to be at the right height. 'Why have you put the switches at council house height?' he asked Philip Jebb the first time he met him. Perhaps such points sound obvious, but in fact how rare it is to find a room that works in all the basic ways.

Yet another element, and one that closely related to his feeling for colour, was his feeling for light, for the play of sunlight and shadow on architecture and materials. Many of his drawing rooms seem to be infused with the spirit of a sunny June afternoon in the country; even in London he seems able to suggest bees buzzing among roses. It was probably his feeling for the play of light that made him dislike dark shiny floors and dark patterned oriental carpets, because they absorbed too much of the light. Whenever an owner would consent to it, he would have a floor stripped to give the effect of dry scrubbing, a traditional practice in eighteenth-century English houses like Uppark. And from his earliest days he used rush matting for the same reason, or, if he wanted to cover a floor completely, he would use a plain wool carpet in a shade of grey-fawn he called 'mouse's back' that would not be noticed. Thus he used historical arguments for dry scrubbing to justify visual decisions; and then, when the balance between decoration and restoration was tipped in favour of restoration, he would lay more emphasis on the historical arguments.

As far as artificial light was concerned, he liked to create atmosphere in a room by breaking up the space with pools of light. Even in the mid-1930s he had used what were then unusual bases for lamps, but he also liked simple wooden columns painted in different tones which appear in photographs of his work in 1946; and he always chose shades of simple shape with a steep slope. Waisted shades and coolie hats were never admitted; nor were rich materials, elaborate braids and bobble fringes. The sole trimming, and that only occasionally, was a plain deep silk fringe on a plain silk shade. Apart from card and plain silk shades, he liked pleated and gathered silk shades that were the grandchildren of the type used above billiards tables, and also shades covered in chintz, all of which break the light in different ways.

Colour and light lead on to two other aspects of his approach to interiors, his use of flowers and plants within a house and the way he liked to link an interior to its garden. As far as flowers are concerned, it is no accident that he started work at the same time as Constance Spry was making her name. Born twenty years earlier, she opened her first shop, Flower Decoration, in Belgrave Road in 1928 and by the mid-1930s she had achieved fashionable recognition. Rather surprisingly Gertrude Jekyll had written a book *Flower Decoration in the House* as early as 1907, and John Fowler's concern to link interiors and gardens grows, albeit unconsciously, out of her association with Lutyens. Perhaps the outstanding example of how this worked in his case was his own garden at the Hunting Lodge [169], which is described on pages 180-81, but it is also apparent in the simpler garden that he helped Miss Elizabeth Hanley lay out at the Ring at Audley End. The main feature of this is an avenue of apple trees lining the slight slope down from the gothick loggia of the cottage to a gazebo that reflects it and that he told her to copy from one in his own garden.

His influence as a gardener is difficult to pin down, because, although it is clear that he helped many of his friends and clients with their gardens and taught many of them about plants and about scale, it is hard to point to Fowler gardens as one can to Fowler rooms. The Duchess of Devonshire in her book about Chatsworth, *The House*, has put it very well when she described how he became 'as interested in gardens as he was in curtains: he used to leave the client in the drawing room and go into the garden, stop and raise his arms above his head shouting, "I'm a lime." The client was supposed to know if he was in the right place and had the rare chance to assert his authority by moving him a foot or two to right or left. Then John would throw himself on the ground in an attitude of prayer murmuring, "I'm prostrate rosemary." '

However, as well as the physical and visual aspects of his decoration there was also something more fundamental, what I can only call a feeling for mental comfort, of creating a settled timeless look in unsettled times and of building a bridge between the past and the present, of leading the present backwards in time and of bringing the past forwards. Not only did he help open his clients' eyes to the past, he also helped them to come to terms with the weight and challenge of family tradition and of social change. He was able to do that, I suggest, because the basis of his approach was 'humble elegance', with its understatement and its element of de-granding. Indeed he disliked rich objects in simple settings and anything that smacked of Chatsworth in a cottage. As two different people said to me, his decoration was never snobbish: what he loathed was genteel taste. He learned how to combine informality and grandeur and make formality acceptable. In this there are parallels to dress: as Hardy Amies said of Digby Morton, he transformed the suit into an 'intricately cut and carefully designed garment that was so fashionable that it could be worn with confidence at the Ritz'.

John Fowler's ability to do all these things came out of his early struggle and the sense he always retained of being at one remove from his clients who owned notable houses, however well he knew them and however affectionate was their relationship; and ultimately out of his historical sense, his unceasing curiosity and his inquiring mind.

He might be asked to advise on a drawing room or a hall, but he was almost certain to escape to attics, basements and store rooms and hunt for old wallpapers, chintzes and scraps of carpet and for all manner of obscure things that had been cast out and forgotten or overlooked. Lady Bagot has written a vivid account of his first and only visit to Blithfield in Staffordshire in 1953:

It didn't take long to decide just what had to be done [in the Great Hall] and we spent the rest of the day exploring the old house from cellar to attic, rushing about opening cupboards, looking into chests, like two excited children.

There was a cupboard full of oil lamps and lamp glasses, and John showed me how some of the glasses were meant to fit on the colza oil hanging light fittings in the Library. He discovered some Bitter Apple in an oak chest and told me it was to deter moth from devouring the woollen materials. We found an oak box in an attic room, which proved to be a neat portable 'loo' with a pretty blue patterned bowl, ivory handle and painted tin bucket. There were masses of old chintz and holland covers stored in the attics, curtains, and hand-made braids which seemed all the more mouth-watering after the war years.

In the large Walnut chest we found some beautiful men's suits, the earliest must have belonged to Sir Walter Wagstaffe Bagot, a mulberry coloured coat and canary yellow waistcoat heavy with silver embroidery. Three or four of the suits of a later date had been worn by the 1st Lord Bagot. John went into ecstasies over one in particular; the breeches and coat are made of corded silk consisting of very fine stripes in bronze, pale blue and olive green, the general effect being bronze, very elegant and understated. I'm sure John would have loved to have worn it . . .

That was the kind of experience that stimulated his imagination and gave him ideas and solutions to problems.

Part of the appeal of attics and store rooms for him lay in the evidence they produced about daily life in the past, for that interested him as much as the history of style and fashion. Indeed in some ways his approach anticipates that of Mark Girouard in his *Life in the English Country House* by more than one generation. Thus it is not surprising that David Hicks, right at the beginning of his career, saw the connection between the windows of Colefax & Fowler and Georgian conversation pictures. At weekends John would talk for hours about how houses used to be organized and the ceremonies that took place in them, from those relating to births and christenings to funerals, which had a special fascination for him. It made his day if he found traces of black in a house and soon he visualized whole schemes of mourning decoration.

Over the years he developed the knowledge to deal confidently with decoration of any decade from about 1700 to 1820, although his feeling for pattern went on a little longer, to about 1850. However, it was the third quarter of the eighteenth century that appealed most to him – the pretty patterns, the painted furniture and the simple fashions that came into prominence then, and the way life was conducted at that time. Not only was he enamoured of Marie Antoinette, but he loved her English contemporaries who came alive in the pages of Mrs Delany, Mrs Lybbe Powys and in the letters of the Lennox sisters; and he had a way of identifying himself with the characters involved in the history of a house he was working in, particularly humble ones like the dairy-maid at Uppark and Betty Radcliffe, 'the best maid in England', at Erdigg.

The dairy-maid at Uppark had a special place in his affections, but then of all English houses it was Uppark that meant most to him. Indeed it may well have been the first country house he ever saw. In a letter to Lord Roscoe in 1970 he said that he went there in 1930, which, if he is right about the date, would mean that he saw it before the Meade-Fetherstonhaughs inherited it.

Today Uppark [LXXIII, 183–185] is no longer able to cast the strong spell that it did in that generation, but the magic it had can be sensed in Christopher Hussey's articles in *Country Life* in 1941.

There is an enchanted air about this lovely beloved house, perched on the crest of the downs with all West Sussex at its feet ... It is the kind of house where you feel you might look through the window into the life of another age. If you could, it would be a fine, full, civilized, at times surprising life ...

In the second article he wrote:

The atmosphere of Uppark is as delicate and fragrant as the bloom on a grape. For nearly 200 years this untouched perfection might have lain under a spell, so little has been changed since Sir Matthew Fetherstonhaugh and Sarah Lethieullier finished unpacking all the treasures they had bought for Uppark in Paris, Naples, Venice and Rome.

And at the end he wrote of recent times:

After 190 years of day-long sunshine through the tall seaward windows the silk curtains were hanging in threads; the big pictures were black; the old wallpapers, tapestries, and chair-covers, well saved yet falling apart. Admiral and Lady Meade-Fetherstonhaugh have devoted the past decade to preserving with the most tender care all that was entrusted to them: the roof and cornice have been taken down and replaced bit by bit: the tattered, sun-rotted curtains have been darned from head to foot by the ladies of the house almost where they hung; their faded crimson or ivory brought to life again by lotions of saponaria; the colours of the carpets and petit point nursed back to life. This ten years' labour of love is the latest chapter, and not the least wonderful, in the fairy tale.

All that had an immense appeal to John Fowler, and the influence of 'pleasing decay' at Uppark was of crucial importance in his approach to old houses, as was the sense of its revival in the 1930s. Indeed his whole approach was based on a combination of survival and revival, and that was the kind of effect that he sought to create through his decoration.

I am not sure when John Fowler first did any work at Uppark, or rather discouraged it from being done, but another house that has a comparable magic and made a great impression on him is Boughton in Northamptonshire [105–110]. There, after the war, he helped the Duchess of Buccleuch, doing little decoration: he helped her arrange the house, he taught the painter how to clean and retouch old paint and he taught the carpenter how to upholster chairs in the French way; but it is perhaps only in the way the library was arranged, with the soft tones of the materials and the underplayed furniture [110], that someone who knew his work well might detect his hand. It was help and advice that he was giving and the business of helping houses was always an important part of his work. But at the same time he learned a great deal there, not only about decoration but also about traditional ways of housekeeping.

What he did at Blithfield is an admirable illustration of that process of helping. He went to look at the gothick Great Hall [159], because the room was to be used for a luncheon given for Queen Elizabeth at the opening of the Blithfield reservoir, and the Water Board were paying for the work. Lord and Lady Bagot had been warned that John Fowler was expensive, but when 'John arrived and looked at it, all he asked for was whether he could have a bucket of water and a scrubbing brush; and then he proceeded gently to scrub a small patch of the wall, removing the grey distemper that gave the room a flat depressing look, and revealing the original painted blocking-out of the stucco so that it looked like stone. After a few minutes he straightened up, put his glasses back on his nose and smiling said "You know, all this wants is a really good wash."' Years later, when he was consulted about the decoration of Wilkins's Hall at King's College, Cambridge, he suggested that it should be painted in the same way as Blithfield.

The combination of his knowledge about and his feeling for the past and his awareness of the present heightened his romanticism, and he responded to places redolent of the past, so that he valued very highly his marvellous opportunities to get to know such places so well. But his approach was inevitably

159. BLITHFIELD HALL, STAFFORDSHIRE. THE GREAT HALL. John Fowler washed off the
later flat distemper to reveal the original blocking-out of the stucco so that it looked like stone, an idea
he later copied in the hall at King's College, Cambridge.

different from that of people like Sir Osbert Sitwell, Vita Sackville-West or Christopher Hussey, whose inheritance was that past. In that respect, John Fowler bore more resemblance to H. G. Wells, and the latter's descriptions of life at Bladesover in *Tono-Bungay* (which is based on Uppark) brings John Fowler's approach vividly to mind.

In considering John Fowler's work I have written generally about his approach to interiors and their decoration before considering him as a restorer of historic decoration for two reasons. The first is that his work as a restorer grew out of his practice as a decorator, and his whole approach to restoration was conditioned by what he had seen while working as a decorator and looking as a student. Second, the concept of restoration of interiors started to change both radically and rapidly in the last decade of his life as a result of a combination of new academic attitudes and knowledge and the development of new technical skills. (More will be said about that in the chapter on his contribution to the National Trust.)

Before the war I doubt whether there was any significant degree of restoration in John Fowler's work as a decorator, because the opportunities did not come his way. It developed after the war, when, largely through Nancy Lancaster's introductions, he started to help owners of notable country houses. Also his approach to restoration developed gradually, starting by advising people not to do things, and by seeing whether what he had read and observed could be applied in his clients' houses.

As with all his work, the process was an empirical one, and his approach developed in the late 1940s and the 1950s as he saw more and more and hunted out for what was hidden from view by later decoration. Thus, as his memory became more richly stored with detail, his work became more serious and historical.

In all his country house work he struck a balance between restoration and decoration. At the end of our book *English Decoration in the Eighteenth Century* is a chapter called 'A Matter of Balance', which we included largely to explain how John's approach worked in practice and to show how he applied his knowledge of historic decoration. Of Mrs Lancaster's Yellow Room in Avery Row [XVI] and the saloon at Haseley [127] he said and I wrote:

What is significant about those rooms is not what was done but what was not done. Chintzes and silk were freely mixed; and there was an avoidance of materials and colours matching and of sets of furniture that would give a static character, or indeed of a 'period' feeling in the usual meaning of the term. And yet none of the original decoration of either room was disturbed. Indeed at Haseley the plaster work was most carefully restored. Thus history was respected but re-interpreted to meet the needs and tastes of a particular person.

A younger generation which does not know that world finds the element of interpretation in his schemes of restoration hard to accept, not recognizing his eye for detail, or his interest in how things were done, or his ability to get the best work out of other people, all elements that came together when he dealt with complicated problems such as the restoration of eighteenth-century wallpaper and painted furniture. He, of course, never had the back-up of an equipped conservation section as now exists at the Victoria and Albert Museum: instead he relied on the artist–craftsman tradition. However, his skill and sensitivity in that direction is apparent in the wallpapers he restored at Clandon and Erdigg [LXXVII, 193, 194], in a painted bed now at Syon (of which Plate XL of *English Decoration* is a detail) and in his careful replacement of the curtains in the saloon at Sezincote [176].

John Fowler's approach to interiors, however, cannot be considered just in generalities, as has been done so far in this chapter, and it is necessary to examine how it worked out in practice in a variety of commissions. Some of those that I have seen or been able to discuss with the help of good photographs are described here and others are treated from different points of view in the succeeding chapters on colour and pattern and upholstery. (However, sadly, some of the commissions by which he set particular store and which his admirers might expect to find here, like Daylesford, have disappeared without a proper record having been made, and since I never saw them, I feel I cannot write about them convincingly.)

One of John Fowler's first big country house jobs outside Nancy Lancaster's immediate circle was the Earl of Wilton's Ramsbury Manor [160–166], which he had bought in 1954; and even that came about partly through her. Lord Wilton had been a friend of Michael Tree at school and so in the late 1930s he had stayed at Ditchley, which made a deep impression on him. Although at the time not especially interested in houses, he realized that it was quite different from any other country house in its grand elegance, its comfort and the perfection of all the details of life in it. His grandfather having sold Heaton Park, Manchester, and all its contents, he had no family house, and so, when Ronald Tree left England in 1949, he decided to buy Ditchley. The house was far from being complete, and therefore about a year later he turned to John Fowler, whom he had already met with Nancy Lancaster. Fairly soon he found that what had been possible in a country house in the late 1930s was impossible in the early 1950s, and the house did not readily lend itself to compromises. So when Ramsbury, which he had always wanted, came on the market in 1954, he bought it; and again he turned to John for help. The latter, for his part, had appreciated the difference in approach and eye between a male client – Lord Wilton was not yet married – and a female client; also he accepted that Lord Wilton did not like some of his own favourite greens, lilacs and mauves, and yellows. On the other hand he was keen to buy fine furniture and carpets and spend money on materials of the right quality. In the end Lord Wilton lived in the house only for four years, but shortly before he sold it to Lord Rootes, he allowed *Country Life* to photograph it (although the articles are illustrated with some photographs showing changes made by Lord and Lady Rootes). Naturally the articles do not concentrate on what Lord Wilton and John Fowler did together, but their approach is worth recording now, because it is indicative of the opportunities to buy and John's position at that time.

In the hall and saloon [160-162] they combined things bought with or for Ditchley and new purchases. As to the arrangement of the hall, Lord Wilton liked to use it as a sitting hall: John would have preferred it to be a bare architectural space.

For the curtains in the saloon [161] he made festoons, because Lord Wilton had liked the uncluttered windows during his first summer there and would not have drawn curtains with draped valances. Lord Wilton says that it was the first time that John had ever made them and that initially they gave a good deal of trouble. He had made festoon blinds before, but not curtains of heavy material and with deep fringes. However, he knew that they were an appropriate eighteenth-century idea for such a room and complemented the pier glasses and console tables, and he had seen eighteenth-century ones at Uppark and in other undisturbed houses.

In the Burdetts' time the dining room [164, 165] had been hung with portraits, and although Lord Wilton bought them so that they should stay in the house where they belonged, he preferred to put other people's ancestors on the staircase. That left the badly stained panelling unacceptable, and so it was painted in tones of white with the intention of finding pictures for it.

Going through the photographs with Lord Wilton

twenty-five years after he left the house, what is striking is the restraint of the decoration and the marvellous opportunities that there were if one was tackling a largish house. Today not only would it be infinitely more difficult to find suitable fine things, but it would be unbelievably, and unenjoyably, expensive; and anyway most of the old gilding would have been redone in the interval and the old Kimbolton velvet would have gone (in fact Lady Rootes removed it). But above all what Lord Wilton did naturally might now seem rather forced.

John Fowler subsequently did a little work at Ramsbury for Lord Rootes and later more for Mr Harry Hyams, with whom he had a great *rapport*. With Lord Wilton too the friendly association continued, and over the years he helped him with two other houses in the country, with London flats, and finally, just before he died, with a dining room in London.

The late 1950s and early 1960s were probably John Fowler's most successful years, and one of the most complete and best preserved jobs of that time is Radburne Hall near Derby [XXVIII-XXXIII]. It is a handsome, masculine house built for Major Chandos-Pole's ancestor, German Pole, by Smith of Warwick, probably in the 1740s, with enrichments carried out for his nephew, Colonel Edward Sacheverell Pole, who inherited in 1765; virtually unaltered after that, it still retains furniture listed in the 1765 inventory. It is the kind of house that brought out the best in John Fowler, because it demanded that overall understatement and restraint in which he excelled, and yet its principal rooms are sufficiently varied in character to provide scope for variations in the mood of his decoration.

He first went to see the house in November 1957, after Lady Bagot, a friend and neighbour of the Chandos-Poles, had suggested that they should consult him. The bulk of the work – he decorated the whole house – was carried out as part of a thorough restoration and modernization of the house in 1958-60.

The centre of the main front is devoted to a large hall [XXVIII, XXIX] with a screen of Ionic columns across its inner end, and since the balancing saloon behind is arranged as a room of parade rather than as a drawing room, it is the hall that is used for sitting in when there are more than six or eight people in the house. The drawing room, the present dining room and the library are all smaller, two-bay rooms.

There are two keys to John Fowler's decoration of the hall, the carved stone chimneypiece, which had been painted over and was successfully cleaned, and a pair of handsome mid-eighteenth-century armchairs

XLVIII and XLIX. COLOUR SAMPLES. In 1947 John Fowler produced a set of colour samples for Christopher Hussey for use by the Georgian Group. Although apparently intended for external use, they relate very closely to the colours he liked to use in decoration and they show how his palette had matured by then. On the back of each sample he wrote how he made it. Thus there is a pale green consisting of white, emerald, cobalt blue, chrome and burnt siena; a second of yellow ochre, cobalt blue, chrome yellow, black and white; the grey-white is made of white, black, cobalt blue and Venetian red; and the yellow has white in it, emerald green, cobalt blue, chrome and burnt siena.

The second group consists of crimson lake with cobalt blue, black Venetian red and a little white; the pink is white, crimson lake, vermilion, black and cobalt blue; the green has emerald, black, burnt siena, ochre, chrome and white; the white has black, burnt siena and raw umber; the top has no pink.

L. SYON HOUSE, MIDDLESEX. THE
HALL. Instead of painting the room a
single white or off-white, John Fowler
apparently used four basic tones, a light
grey, a stronger blue grey, a warm white
and a soft white, painting up the
architecture to emphasize the elaboration
of the concept and tie in the marble
statues and the grisaille roundels. But
there is a sense of mystery, because the
play of light leaves one uncertain about
the variation in the tones.

LI. A SECTION OF THE UPPER WALL AND
THE CEILING OF THE HALL AT SYON.

LII. THE PEDESTAL TO THE STATUE
OF APOLLO AT THE NORTH END OF
THE HALL AT SYON. This shows the
variation in tones.

LIII. THE CIRCULAR CLOSET AT SYON. In one of the turrets off the Long Gallery is this closet, which
was repainted by John Fowler.

LIV. A DETAIL OF THE FRIEZE IN THE CIRCULAR CLOSET AT SYON, SHOWING THE
PICKING-OUT AND THE GILDING.

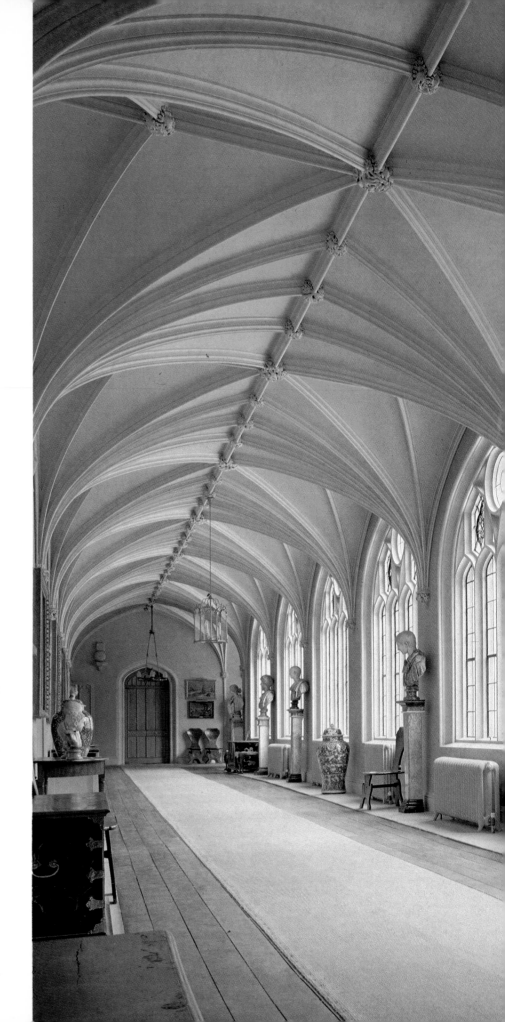

LV. WILTON HOUSE,
WILTSHIRE. JAMES WYATT'S
CLOISTERS. The main colour is
an apricot terracotta, stippled over
a yellow ground. The four ranges,
including the eight narrow arches
between the thin shafts at the
intersection of the four ranges and
the vault, are painted in three
related tones; the skirting, the
shafts, the capitals and the ribs
are in stone white. The plaster of
the walls is scored to represent
blocks, and although the blocks
are not painted individually,
which they might have been
originally, as at Blithfield [159],
the stippling prevents the colour
going solid.

LVI. A DOORCASE IN THE LIBRARY AT WILTON. This is made up of mainly seventeenth-century woodwork, with painting, gilding and marbling suggested by John Fowler. He liked the effect of two colours of gold and here the treatment of the terms and the carving in the pediment is inspired by the treatment of the standing figures in the overmantel of the Double Cube Room.

that were covered in mid-nineteenth-century green stamped wool velvet. Together they suggested the colours and textures of the room. Apparently John said that the colours would improve within two or three years, and in that he was right, for they have fused together so that it is now quite hard to tell what is variation in tone and what is the effect of light and shade.

The architecture of the hall is strong, as is the furniture – a set of six chairs and two settees and very handsome mahogany side tables – and John Fowler emphasized that strength by retaining the old green velvet while restoring the proper line of the chairs and covering the rest of the set in a brilliant singing red mohair velvet stamped with a bold eighteenth-century pattern.

The saloon is rather different in character: all the architectural decoration including the picture frames is original, but the gilding was presumably introduced when the cycle of pictures by Wright of Derby and J. H. Mortimer were installed in the 1770s by Colonel Pole. Here John Fowler's main contribution was to paint the walls a pale pink as if it was contemporary with the white and gold scheme, choosing a warm tone, because it is a north-facing room without a carpet or a set of seat furniture.

The woodwork was all carefully repainted in three tones of white so as not to disturb the old gilding, and he added only a little more gilding to improve the balance. The original gilding had stopped at the cornice, and he not only carried colour into the bed of the ceiling but repeated the style of the gilding of the doorcases and overmantel in the ceiling, using two colours of gold, lemon for the grounds of the medallions and yellow for picking out the ornament, as can be seen in illustration [XXXI].

If the saloon is a statement of neo-classical connoisseurship – and formal – the drawing room has the character of a boudoir. The Chandos-Poles bought for it an Aubusson carpet and that provided the key to its colour scheme, but what makes the room are the curtains with their elaborate valances, tails, scarves, choux and bows [XXXII].

The library [XXXIII] presumably acquired its present cornice about the time the pictures were installed in the saloon, but the chimneypiece of purple and white marble is original. Through colour John tied the two together and through textures he linked the room to the hall. The bookcases he painted white, like the dado and the architraves to the doors, and the natural wood of the doors goes well with the old leather bindings. And there are *coups de rouge* in the

hunting pictures. This room seems to me to be the essence of John Fowler's country house decoration, well mannered and comfortable, strong and sure, subtle and sophisticated; but unselfconscious and completely relaxed.

At Ramsbury, John Fowler was involved in the refurnishing as well as the redecoration of a fine house. At Radburne he was dealing with a historical unity. At Lennoxlove in Scotland [XXXIV–XXXVII] he had to create a sense of unity between an ancient house and one of the most important historical collections in Scotland. It had come there only in 1948, when the Duke of Hamilton bought the house. John already knew the Duke and Duchess, having decorated their London flat in about 1964/5 and having also worked with Philip Jebb on a mews house for them. The Duchess, who had been recommended to go to him by Lady Kennedy, a friend of the Astors, knew that she had to make definite suggestions, even if they would change – she wanted apricot in the hall and she liked using blue as a decorating colour – and she understood the point of a running debate with him and how 'to argue him off the extra bow'. The last point was important at Lennoxlove, where the collection of mainly seventeenth- and eighteenth-century portraits representing one of the great families of Scotland is much stronger than the architectural decoration of what is essentially a large laird's house and where colour is needed as a background for the portraits as well as to stand up to them. Colour was also needed to bring warmth and life to rooms in a land where there is a great deal of grey light. Elaborate decoration, however, was out of place, not only because of the character of Lennoxlove, but because of the tastes of the Duke and Duchess. On the other hand what would have appealed to John was the way the pageant of Scottish history expressed through portraits also created a formal rhythm thanks to their hanging by the Duke and Duchess.

The two drawing rooms are on the first floor, the principal one having a mid-eighteenth-century plaster ceiling and the second being panelled in the late seventeenth century. In the principal room, which became the Blue Drawing Room [XXXVII], the starting-off points were the nineteenth-century curtains of greeny-blue damask and a nineteenth-century Savonnerie carpet which, to most people, would have been irreconcilable. John Fowler, however, produced a meeting point in a bold floral chintz that ties everything together.

The idea of the Yellow Drawing Room [XXXV] arose because the white panelling did nothing for the

160 (above). RAMSBURY MANOR, WILTSHIRE.
THE HALL AS IT WAS ARRANGED BY LORD
WILTON IN 1957. The pair of portraits flanking
the saloon door, on the right, were bought at the
Ashburnham Place sale; the tables below came from
the Duke of Kent's collection; the high-backed chairs
with their original upholstery were bought at the
Kimbolton Castle sale; the big lantern was copied for
Ditchley; the curtains were ordered by the Trees
from Boudin for the saloon at Ditchley.

161 (left). A PIER GLASS, CONSOLE TABLE AND
FESTOON CURTAIN IN THE SALOON AT
RAMSBURY. This was the first time that John
Fowler revived the eighteenth-century idea of festoon
curtains of heavy material, as opposed to blinds.

162 (top right). THE SALOON AT RAMSBURY IN
1957. Lord Wilton bought at Christies the pier
glasses and console tables shown in illustration 161,
as well as the carpet, all of which belonged to the
room; the gesso tables and torchères were bought for
Ditchley; the chandelier came from Wentworth
Woodhouse; and the two French chairs were pattern
chairs used by Boudin and sold to Sir Philip Sassoon.

163 (below right). THE LIBRARY AT RAMSBURY.
Here John Fowler used the Owen Jones wallpaper
which he encouraged Coles to revive. The globes on
the bookcase are copied from a print by Marot,
possibly by way of Boudin.

164 (above) and 165 (left). THE
DINING ROOM AT RAMSBURY AS
IT WAS IN 1954 AND IN 1920. It
was decided to repaint the room after
Lord Wilton had taken down the
Burdett portraits that he kept in the
house, but the intention of finding
suitable pictures was not realized.
The carpet was brought from
Ditchley and the Rococo glass came
from Bramshill.

166 (right). THE SMALL
DRAWING ROOM AT
RAMSBURY. John Fowler found the
damask pattern at Warners, had it
specially woven in silk for use here
and subsequently used it on other
occasions in
different mixtures.

seventeenth-century portraits. Choosing for the over-mantel a full-length portrait of Lord Bellasis in a red suit, which was brightest in colour, John Fowler took the yellow tops of his boots as the key to the room.

Later the Duke and Duchess of Hamilton asked him to help them with their apartment in the Palace of Holyroodhouse [XXXVIII–XL], the Duke's perquisite as Hereditary Keeper of the Palace. Although the rooms are arranged so that the Duke and Duchess can stay there, they are mainly used for official entertaining, particularly when the Court is in residence, and the object of their re-decoration was to create a suitable background for such occasions and to house pictures and furniture formerly at Hamilton Palace that could not be accommodated at Lennoxlove. John Fowler suggested that their basic problem lay in their narrow doors adjoining the windows, and, although there are historical arguments against his solution – indeed probably it would not be permitted today – his arrangement of double doors with bold architraves between the three main rooms transformed them both from a practical and a visual point of view; and a sense of unity was achieved by the hanging of the pictures, originally the work of the Duke and Duchess and John Fowler together.

It was his idea that the drawing room [XXXVIII] should be mauve, but so subtle are the colours that at first sight the wallpaper might be read as being in warm greys, and it is only gradually that the pale lilac cast to it becomes apparent. In the middle room, which is the hall of the apartment, there is no gilding in the architecture and no colour in the frieze, just the different whites of the woodwork and the blue-greys of the broad-striped wallpaper [XXXIX]. Both rooms are underplayed, but in the dining room [XL] there is one of the fine Charles II plaster ceilings in which the palace is so rich, and here John Fowler used the wallpaper that he derived from a piece of early-eighteenth-century damask. He found the Italian table to go beneath the Panini *Coronation of the Pope*, which the Duke bought because he felt that it should be in Scotland since it includes portraits of the Pretenders. The picture is splendidly placed, and it is a memorable experience to turn round to see it balanced by the huge view of Venice that hangs at the far end of the drawing room.

It was not often that John Fowler was given the opportunity to decorate up in an established country house and to produce an elaborate scheme that was not bound by existing elements. That makes the sitting

room done for the Countess of Haddington at Tyninghame in Lothian all the more interesting [XLI, XLII]. It was the only one of the principal rooms that he decorated completely, but there is evidence both of his hand and his influence in other rooms, and certain ideas sprang from his visits. As the house exists today the layout and most of the architectural detail is due to William Burn, and fortunately the gallery, the ante-room and the drawing room retain their original early Victorian flock wallpapers – a most sympathetic background for an unusually varied old family collection. Thus there is a rich mellowness of texture and colour in the house without any feeling of precise date, and what drew Lady Haddington to the house – and the garden – also made her sympathetic to John Fowler's approach. Like many of his clients she says that she learned a great deal from someone she regarded as a friend, and he in his turn regarded her as one of his best clients because it is abundantly apparent that she was one of the few who had a natural feeling and flair of her own.

Such an introduction is important, because, when illustrated on its own, the sitting room might appear so dramatically decorated as to be difficult to imagine as part of a sequence of rooms. It has both a sense of sparkle and an air of comfort about it that makes it a delight for visitors as well as a warm refuge for Lady Haddington, with its beautiful view over the park and the river down to the sea. Her idea was to have a warm, sunny room, but the scheme of decoration actually started out from a good stock of Victorian gimp in yellow and gold. Thus it is a room in yellows, whites and gold, with an imported fine white marble Rococo chimneypiece from the House of Elie and above it an overmantel glass in white and gold whose central portion suggests the name of Booker of Dublin. At the same time John Fowler introduced the eighteenth-century doorcase with its carved frieze and pediment and the flanking pyramidal bookcases. The total effect is rich, warm and full, but also easy, because of the use of simple materials, in particular the Brompton stock chintz for the upholstery and even the lampshades. There is no sense of John Fowler setting out to create an authentic eighteenth-century room: rather does he borrow from the eighteenth century – the period is Lady Haddington's and his own.

As with any designer, ideas recur in John Fowler's work: materials, colours and textures which he liked continually suggested themselves to him, as can be seen in the rooms described already; and naturally solutions worked out in one place came to mind when he was faced with slightly different problems in another. But it is both fairer and more relevant to consider the development rather than the repetition of ideas. A particularly interesting comparison can be made between his treatment of the Long Gallery at Sudbury [LXXVI, 50] for the National Trust and the Gallery at Chequers [XLIV], because, while his solutions are quite different, he must have had Sudbury in mind when he considered Chequers.

His involvement at Chequers in 1970–72 came about through Earl Jellicoe, who as Lord Privy Seal was Chairman of the Chequers Trustees. Lord Jellicoe had first consulted John Fowler about his own house ten or eleven years earlier at the suggestion of his mother-in-law, Mrs Peggy Willis, an old friend and client of John, whose own house is illustrated [XLV, XLVI]. Although John Fowler himself had not done that job, he seemed to Lord Jellicoe the obvious person to turn to for Chequers when it became possible, thanks to a benefactor, to produce a plan that would make the interior into a country house worthy of a British Prime Minister.

It was the kind of house that had appealed to and challenged rich people in the opening years of the century, an Elizabethan house that had been unfortunately Victorianized and was ripe for restoration. That was what Lord and Lady Lee did after they leased it in 1909 (Lady Lee was the daughter of a New York banker). Avray Tipping apparently gave advice over the South Garden, and Sir Reginald Blomfield took charge of the house. The work was skilfully done by the standards of the time, but by the 1960s it appeared 'boiled' (Christopher Hussey's vivid word for a special type of over-restoration), as well as suffering from the impersonality and visual dullness of an official residence.

Lord Jellicoe wanted it to look like a credible country house, traditional and yet of the present day, comfortable and relaxed while suitable for official entertaining and meetings, and a welcoming retreat for a Prime Minister, human without being too personal. That is a surprisingly difficult combination of requirements, and Chequers was all the more difficult for John Fowler in that he actively disliked its particular kind of bogus pretension. That made Lord Jellicoe's personality crucial: in John Fowler's mind he became the client, as later did Mr Heath.

At Sudbury the seventeenth-century wainscot of the Gallery had been lined with nineteenth-century bookshelves with portraits over them and the room was partly furnished. What he did is explained on pages 212–13. At Chequers not only was the architectural treatment much simpler but it was the stained glass and the eighteenth-century bookcases that gave it its character. So instead of making it into a gallery for parade, he made it into a long sitting room, which was how such galleries were often used in the late eighteenth and nineteenth centuries, where groups of people could talk or someone could happily read or write on their own.

Looking at a photograph of the room, what is striking is the simplicity of the treatment, the deliberate playing-down of a space that almost everyone else would have played up, given the use of the house, and his way of giving a sense of ease to the occupant through presuming that the ease can be taken for granted. Thus it is a matter not only of simple decoration but also of subtlety of mind.

Chequers led on to some work at Chevening, because Lord Jellicoe as Lord Privy Seal was Chairman of the Chevening Trustees. Donald Insall had already restored the fabric of the house, removing the top storey and later refacing, so returning it to its early-seventeenth-century form and making it once more into a brick house. However, nothing had been done to the decoration of the interior, which the Trustees wished to tackle so that the house could be occupied by one of the figures nominated in the late Earl Stanhope's will, with the Prince of Wales as first choice. It was the kind of unclear situation, with conflicting interests, in which John was not likely to be able to achieve his best results, but he was flattered by the commission and he began work with enthusiasm, perhaps closing his mind to the likely difficulties. In the end his contribution was mainly restricted to the Tapestry Room, which he saw as a room of parade and painted to relate to the set of the tapestries, and to the hall and staircase [XLIII], which is the most remarkable feature of the interior. The hanging staircase was apparently constructed about 1720 by Nicholas Dubois for General James Stanhope, later 1st Earl Stanhope; and it is from his time that the display of arms also dates. As on other occasions, notably in the saloon at Lyme, John Fowler found that the effect of the much darkened woodwork was dead and oppressive rather than showing the true patina of age, and so he cleaned the staircase; the panelling he painted in stone whites and the walls he coloured to throw up the pattern of the arms, which he was at great pains to retain.

The houses and rooms so far considered are all of architectural and historical importance, but they represent only half of John Fowler's work. What are equally significant are his simple rooms in modest houses, not only because his treatment of them is the basis of his style, but because they influenced his approach to grand rooms; also they explain why his work continues to have such a broad influence on traditional decoration. Obviously his own house, the Hunting Lodge, is one that needs to be considered, but another, which gave him particular satisfaction, stands out: Ivy Lodge at Radway in Warwickshire, which he did for Mrs Peggy Willis in 1958. Mrs Willis had first met him in the war when he decorated a flat in London for her; after Ivy Lodge he worked for her on two occasions. Work led to great mutual regard – Mrs Willis says that he was one of the only two geniuses she has ever known – and to a firm friendship; and although they did not see a great deal of each other, the affection is apparent in the little velvet cushion that he had painted years before and left to her.

Like other clients of his, Mrs Willis had been enormously impressed by Kelmarsh and then Ditchley before the war. Also she had bought from Kathleen Mann pretty japanned furniture of the kind that he liked. Her own definite personal tastes, including a liking for lilacs and mauves, were thus to an unusual degree in accord with his; but, while she has always been interested in decoration, that has been secondary to her pleasure in pictures, which is expressed in a wide-ranging and entirely personal collection. The result is a house where decoration plays second fiddle to pictures, supporting them in a general way through textures and colours; on the other hand there is no sense of a contrived relationship, because over the years the arrangement of pictures has gone on changing. It is a very rare situation, but John would have been the first to appreciate the point of the challenge and the discipline in the decoration. Naturally, after twenty-five years his colours have faded a good deal, but it is remarkable demonstration of his feeling and skill that the house has developed a marvellously unaffected mellowness.

There is nothing grand or architectural about Ivy Lodge: basically it is a three-bay stone farmhouse doubled in size in the last century, so that it is quite deep; at the front there is a sitting room and a dining room flanking a stone-flagged staircase hall leading back to a larger drawing room formed out of two rooms by Mrs Willis. When she and John Fowler first discussed the house, he recommended using patterned wallpapers not in the rooms but in the passages; and it is the lilac spray wallpaper in the hall that provides the key to the house [XLV]. The stone-flagged floor

with its octagonal squares is in tone with the mouse's-back carpet up the stairs; and a note of formality is introduced by the facing pair of brass-nailed baize doors to the cloakroom and kitchen.

The sitting room is partly a picture room and partly a book room and he devised a layout of shelves to accommodate both, with one pair of narrow bookcases flanking the fireplace, a pair facing them and another pair flanking the bay window.

The green of that room is balanced by the red of the dining room, both stippled and stronger colours than he generally used in small rooms, but at the same time the balance is also reversed in that the green walls with red covers of the former reverses to red walls (the reds are not the same) with a lot of red and some green and white in the floral curtains and in the pads on the chairs in the latter.

The drawing room [XLVI] is cooler and paler, but there is great variety of colour. The decoration started out from the bold nineteenth-century carpet with a moss green ground and plenty of mauves, pinks, oranges, yellows and whites. That has kept its colour, but the modern dyed colours have faded.

The walls are dragged in a very pale mauve that might be taken for a warm grey, and, although one is not aware of it, it answers the lilac of the wallpaper in the hall. Mauves and lilacs with yellows was a favourite combination of his, and here the curtains are of a subtle yellow shantung, french headed and finished with a green gothick gimp that relates to the pattern of the glazing bars and answers a gilded glass over a japanned cabinet. Even when faded the many colours used for the upholstery echo the pictures and pick up notes in them. There is plenty of black and near black, in the furniture and in the French bronze and ormolu candlesticks on the chimneypiece, the only obviously 'grand' things in it and suggested by John. Here perhaps because of the pictures it becomes apparent that John's decoration was indeed a kind of painting.

Ivy Lodge gave John Fowler great satisfaction, but naturally his own house, the Hunting Lodge near Odiham in Hampshire [167-171], was the most fully developed expression of his approach, in particular in the balance between simplicity and sophistication. Like any designer's house it was the subject of constant thought and attention as well as a source of inspiration. When he discovered it through an advertisement, it was almost a rural slum, without services, but the appeal of its enchanting eighteenth-century gothick front and the possibility of a country garden with a view were overwhelming. Within two years and at a time of official restrictions and very limited resources on his part, he had made it into a show house and started to create a setting for it that made it seem not only grander than it was but also larger. In fact it was *au fond* a tiny and inconvenient cottage, and, although over the years he enlarged it, that was what it remained: he built on an entrance hall and a kitchen and then in the mid-1970s provided accommodation for a couple, who in fact never materialized; a little earlier in the garden he built a studio that immediately became a sitting room. It is only right to mention the drawbacks, because the contrast of discomfort and luxury was an integral part of staying there in his later years: it was a fantasy that John made real, an English Petit Trianon.

There was no gate on the road, just a turning on to what was for many years a track and never became a wholly successful drive. There was, however, a sense of mystery and secrecy as it wound through the dark wood; and then suddenly it came out into the light, and there was an unpainted wooden gate in a hedge and the brick house. One arrived at the back, where there was no hint of the gothick façade, and in summer the house was disguised by the spreading branches of an apple tree in the *rond point*. The first sign of architecture was a Georgian doorway flanked by lanterns set in a clapboard addition, standing out white against a warm stone colour. That led into a diminutive but classically treated hall with a simple cornice and chair rail, and two pairs of doors. It was painted in two tones of biscuit and off-white that toned with the dry scrubbed floor, on which there was a fragment of an eighteenth-century Aubusson floral carpet with a brown ground. Facing the front door was a Louis XVI table painted soft white with a marble top, and over it hung an old friend from King's Road days, a marble relief of a Caesar that had been given a marbled frame to match the table top. Over the window was an eighteenth-century bowed and fretted pelmet cornice that had its original painted decoration. In every way the room was a perfect introduction to John: it was a completely classical interior, yet scaled down to a cottage, cool and disciplined yet played up in the French table and marble relief, completely English yet given breaths of France and Italy.

The hall was an addition on to the original cottage and so the door into the first room was in one corner. That room ran the depth of the cottage, but it was very narrow, being originally lit by a single gothick light, and it had an uneven square tiled floor, a difficult shape for an eating room; and since John did not like the dead look of a dining room not in use he gave it the feeling of an ante-room, with a round brass-rimmed Regency table in one corner. The uneven plastered walls were lined out to suggest *trompe l'œil* panelling, and on them hung part of a group of early botanical prints in painted wood frames.

At the gothick window was a shaped valance and a pair of curtains in his strawberry-leaf pattern in brown and red, but the other windows were done in a different material with french headed curtains of yellow diamond cloth, and there were blinds of the printed version of the painted slat design that he had used frequently in the late 1930s.

Naturally great trouble was taken with the laying of the table, with charmingly arranged flowers, often in a painted tin basket sprouting painted tin tulips that held the candles; and he always avoided a formal set of china, preferring groups of old moulded and printed English plates and the simplest of glasses.

Until the first garden room was built there was a charming simply painted Italian commode to the right of the fireplace. It was replaced by a simple English walnut chest of drawers that he had inherited.

The sitting room in the centre of the gothick front was also very small, but the seat furniture seemed so generous and was so well planned that the room did not seem cramped and it was never apparent that there was only one way of using it. The focus of the room was a mid-Georgian carved-wood chimneypiece painted in several whites and over it a light and spirited seventeenth-century French drawing of a horse that fitted into a pyramidal composition with the five main objects on the chimneypiece. John always liked the idea of a five-piece garniture, but typically he achieved it through variety rather than uniformity. So here was an urn-shaped clock that could be filled with camellias or roses for a party, and it was flanked by candlesticks, eighteenth-century English enamel or light French ormolu; and at each end were pairs of plants, in basket holders or miniature Versailles tubs. On the wall to the right of the fireplace was a sofa, extra stuffed with feathers, and over it a fragment of the big Seymour painting of the St Johns of Dogmersfield Park, now in the Tate Gallery, that came to light in the early 1970s. John loved it because it suggested the character of the park in its heyday, and every guest was given the full story of how he acquired it and what the dabs and dashes depicted in the way of follies. But it was also an essentially undemanding picture. The rough walls were a soft pink, and the gothick shape of the windows was reflected in cotton curtains

167 (opposite top left). THE HUNTING
LODGE, ODIHAM, HAMPSHIRE. In 1947
John Fowler acquired this mid-eighteenth-
century gothick folly, originally one of the
ornaments in Dogmersfield Park, and planted
the formal layout of hedges that frame
the house.

168 (opposite top right). THE FAÇADE OF
THE HUNTING LODGE.

169 (opposite below). THE GARDEN
LAYOUT AT THE HUNTING LODGE FROM
THE AIR IN ABOUT 1970. John Fowler said:
'I wanted to create a sophisticated "room" in
which the dolls' house could sit. I wanted both
an air of grandeur and a cottager's garden.'

170 (above). THE DINING ROOM AT THE
HUNTING LODGE.

171 (right). THE BOOK ROOM AT THE
HUNTING LODGE. The wallpaper came
from Mauny.

made of a trellis design hand-printed by Nancy Nicholson and designed by John.

Beyond the sitting room was a tiny book room where John had his desk, an Empire secretaire, but there was nowhere else to sit, because the stairs, the walls of which were covered with a bold Mauny wallpaper, went up from one end.

Over the book room was John's tiny bedroom. There was a double bedroom over the sitting room, a tiny bedroom beyond it with a bathroom behind it, the two corresponding to the dining room, and at the back another tiny bedroom and John's bathroom. If all the rooms were occupied, there was a good deal of conspiracy to avoid being put between the front bedroom and the bathroom, but it was characteristic of John that he never wanted for himself more than a slip of a room and the simplest of furniture. But he did enjoy the luxury of his bathroom – though he even shared that.

In essence the cottage changed remarkably little over the years and that too was typical of John. By 1947 his style was mature, and he never felt the urge to change what he had done. But he loved building projects, and had a great affection for the craftsmen who worked for him, and so there was invariably some scheme in the pipeline, if only a shed for the logs and dustbins lovingly built out of clapboard and old tiles.

For John the garden [169] was as important as the house, and, since plants and flowers mattered so much to him, no description of the Hunting Lodge would be complete without an account of the garden written by a gardener. In the latter part of his life he grew to know well his cousin, Barbara Oakley, who now looks after the garden for the National Trust. She did not know it in the early years, but she has written a description of it that she has kindly allowed me to quote from here:

For John house and garden were indivisible and he designed his two enchanting summer houses to complement the unique façade of the folly. Within a strong framework of clipped hornbeams apparently incompatible plants rubbed shoulders with one another. Old-fashioned roses – the Gallicas, Bourbons, Albas, Moss roses and their relations were his predominant passion both in the garden and for the house but in later years he was heard to murmur 'they *are* dull in August' and added a few modern varieties such as Iceberg and Rosemary Rose. He always loved the highly scented hybrid musk roses. Felicia, Cornelia, Penelope and Prosperity were his favourites. But roses were never segregated and tumbled over clumps of campanulas, peonies, phloxes and daisies.

Suddenly plates of harsh yellow achillea contrasted with roses and soft blue campanulas. Hot-coloured *Euphorbia griffithii* jostled next to soft pink sidalcea. A great clump of shasta daisies fought for lebensraum with fine flowered hardy fuchsias and clouds of sprawling herbaceous clematis. Alpine strawberries, mint, thyme, marjoram all strayed through mixed planting, and everywhere *Helleborus orientalis* made glossy cushions of evergreen leaves, their smoky mauve and smudged white flowers discreetly adding texture and charm to narrow borders all the year round. The architecturally satisfying evergreen leaves of *Bergenia cordifolia* spilled on to paths made elegant with small patterns of cobbles and bricks; clumps of white anemone japonica sparkled, upright through slanting autumn shadows. Falling apple trees – that never fell – supported waterfalls of frothing rambler roses. Adelaide d'Orléans with strawberry buds and creamy clouds of scented flowers tumbled with misleading ease from lichen covered branches. About the house the blush white rose Mme Alfred Carrière, prolific in summer and tolerable in autumn, grew beside Paul's Lemon Pillar, sumptuous in June but sulky thereafter. The sunset copper flowers of Lady Hillingdon galloped to the eaves intertwined with honeysuckle – *Lonicera tragophylla* – but somehow room was made for vines weighed down with grapes in good summers. Most cherished of all, *Magnolia grandiflora*'s glossy green leaves, suede backed, and crowned after years of waiting by great goblets of velvet cream-coloured flowers, scented the night air shining under harvest moons.

Clipped box in painted tubs flanked the front door. Banks of glossy camellias, red twigs of cornus and the flat white flowers and dark green leaves of *Viburnum tinus* ensured a welcome all the year round.

Winter Sweet, so dull for most of the year, would be allowed to ramp so that bunches of inconspicuous waxy brown flowers could be brought into the house in the worst winter weather to fill a whole room with their delectable scent. In spring little clusters of flowers bespangled orchard grass. Wild daffodils, species narcissi, fritillaries, clumps of Crown Imperials, blue and white anemones and later marguerites and Pheasant's Eye narcissus filled the air with smells of spring and early summer. All round the garden self-seeded honesty, sweet-scented rocket, foxgloves, tansy and many others grew unexpectedly. On the woodland edges bluebells, primroses, wild violets, blue lungwort and hellebores thrived. The unexpected invader might be allowed to stay a year or so apparently misplaced but unwanted predators were firmly removed and weeds never allowed to take charge.

In spite of a passion for cottage flowers he loved to include elegant rarities. *Indigofera potaninii*, exotic tree peonies and rare species tulips were cherished and cared for. Within the garden boundary a pale lemon Ukon cherry joined old orchard trees. Wherever there was space his beloved amelanchier found a place – its frothy flowers in spring, its unassuming summer aspect and its flaming autumn colour endeared it to him beyond all other small trees. Hollies, oak, wild cherries, ash and willows were planted on the common land beyond the boundary and round the pond. Yet even here nature was tamed in the eighteenth-century tradition and a wide path cut through rough grass linked an elegant gateway to shining water with no rubbishy weeds allowed to clutter the romantic view of pond, farmhouse, woods and fields.

John's gardening was a metaphysical part of his whole personality. It exemplified his passionate belief in perfection without pedantry, romanticism without sloppiness and an unfailing instinct for quality whether perceived in the sparkle of a celandine or the elegance of a rose. A cluster of snowdrops showing through half-melted snow probably gave him as much pleasure as summer's pink geraniums spiked unexpectedly with scarlet tumbling from his elegant tubs on gothic stands placed symmetrically on the brick terrace by the house.

Who else could have used dashingly unexpected plantings, cottage charm and elegant formality on the grand scale as he did? His gardening was as subtle and surprising as his interior designing.

Stylistically John Fowler's work did not change very much in the 1950s and 1960s, but from the late 1960s, largely because of what he did for the National Trust and because so many of his old friends and clients ceased to need significant decoration, there was a change in the balance of his work, with less emphasis on decoration and more on restoration and historical suggestion. It was with some relief that he was able to give up bread and butter work in 1969, but naturally he continued to help some old friends and his neighbours at the Hunting Lodge. By then the list of places where he had worked was as impressive as that of anyone involved with English architecture during the past 300 years. I have not attempted to compile a complete catalogue, but at least the principal buildings must be named, if only to give an idea of the scale of his activity.

The country houses on which John Fowler worked (excluding his work for the National Trust, which is listed separately on page 200) include:

Alnwick Castle, Northumberland
Arundel Park, Sussex
Basildon Park, Berkshire
Bletchington Park, Oxfordshire
Blithfield Hall, Staffordshire
Boughton House, Northamptonshire
Bruern Abbey, Oxfordshire
Chequers, Buckinghamshire
Chevening, Kent
Cholmondeley Castle, Cheshire
Cornbury Park, Oxfordshire
Daylesford, Gloucestershire
Ditchley Park, Oxfordshire
Eythrope, Buckinghamshire
Grimsthorpe Castle, Lincolnshire
Hackwood Park, Hampshire
Haseley Court, Oxfordshire
Houghton Hall, Norfolk
Howletts, Kent
Kelmarsh Hall, Northamptonshire
Keir, Stirling
Lee Place, Oxfordshire
Lennoxlove, Lothian
Little Durnford, Wiltshire
Mereworth, Kent
Nant Clwdd, North Wales
Notley Abbey, Buckinghamshire
Oakly Park, Shropshire
Plas Maenan, North Wales
Radburne Hall, Derby
Ragley Hall, Warwickshire
Ramsbury Manor, Wiltshire
Sezincote, Gloucestershire
Syon House, Middlesex
Tyninghame, Lothian
Wilton House, Wiltshire
Womersley Park, Yorkshire

Other major buildings include:

Buckingham Palace
The Palace of Holyroodhouse
The Bank of England
44 Berkeley Square
Doncaster Mansion House
Brighton Pavilion
Winfield House, London

CHAPTER EIGHT

JOHN FOWLER'S USE OF COLOUR AND PAINTING IN ARCHITECTURE

Some people enter the profession of decorating through dealing in furniture and works of art; some through upholstery; others through a training in architecture and design; and others through painting. The differences in approach are naturally apparent in the results that they achieve. John Fowler came to decorating via training in Thornton Smith's studio as a painter of wallpaper, and that proved to be of fundamental importance to him in his feeling for the range, weight and texture of colour and possibly for close toning as well. Also he developed an eye that was highly sensitive to the language of classical architecture and the nuances of pattern and ornament; and, having looked a great deal at Impressionist pictures, he had a feeling for the play of light and for the effects of shade and fading. Thus it was a remarkable combination of responses that gave such individuality and distinction to his painting of rooms.

The effect could be light, pretty and feminine; it could be grand and formal, with lavish picking-out in gold ('pulling out the stops', he used to say); it could be intentionally slightly shocking and stimulating, with near clashes of colour and discords; or it could be calm and relaxed. And while invariably it looked simple, the one certainty is that it wasn't. That emerges when anyone else has to paint rooms alongside those done by him. The difficulties lie not just in the colours, but in the combinations, the methods, the build-up and the texture of the top coat.

The best introduction to the range of John Fowler's colours that I know is a set of samples that he sent Christopher Hussey in connection with a pamphlet that the latter was preparing for the Georgian Group in 1947 [XLVIII, XLIX]. The samples give a good idea of his range of delicate colours throughout his mature period, and each slip says on the back what went into the colour. Even now they strike one as remarkably fresh and lively; in 1947 they must have seemed a revelation to most people, who were much less used to colour in decoration than they are today and had had to exist on utility paint after the creams and beiges of the early thirties. Since then his colours have been widely imitated, but even so his own use of them was quite distinctive and personal. On the other hand it is relevant that there was a revival of colour in decoration and dress design in the years when he started to work on his own; and the palettes of contemporary painters and designers have to be borne in mind, in particular those of Rex Whistler and Oliver Messel. The introduction to the catalogue of the Oliver Messel exhibition at the Victoria and Albert Museum in 1983 said:

What are thought of now as colours typically Messelian – a claret-pink, sage-green, turquoise, ultramarine, a feverish yellow and pearly grey – can be found also, to a greater or lesser degree, in the work of his contemporaries such as Burra, Piper, Richards, Nash and Whistler. These tones were characteristic of that period. However it was in the very personal way Messel used them that in the end gave his work its painterly look, and a unity of mood on the stage which is more poetic, nostalgic, than that of his contemporaries.

As far as the influence of couturiers is concerned one writer on John Fowler said: 'It was fashion – namely Chanel and Schiaparelli – that encouraged [him] in the early thirties to be daring with colour.'

The colours he produced for Christopher Hussey were historical colours for external use, but it is striking how well they capture the spirit of decoration in the 1760s and 1770s, the kind of colours that Mrs Powys described at Fawley Court in 1771 with its hall in French grey, eating room in Quaker brown, breakfast parlour in pea green with a gold border and chairs in pink, green and grey, Mrs Freeman's dressing room in dove colour, and Indian papers with grounds in pink, green and buff. The pinks, the pale blues, light yellows, lilacs and greens had started to come into fashion in the late 1750s with James Stuart and remained in fashion until the palette became heavier again in the 1790s.

What are missing from the samples John Fowler produced for Christopher Hussey are the strong colours that he began to use in the 1950s, in particular the Italian pinks and orange-terracotta colours that he liked in halls and staircases [LV, LVII]. The pinks may have come partly from Nancy Lancaster, who had copied a pink from Rushbrooke at Kelmarsh in the late 1920s, just as the idea of the strong, glazed yellow of her room in Avery Row [XVI] was first suggested to her by her architect uncle, Paul Phipps. They may also have come from the chalky grounds of eighteenth- and nineteenth-century chinese wallpapers, which he used to look at a great deal in the late 1950s and 1960s, particularly when he and George Oakes were painting chinoiserie decorations for clients. But probably the most important influence of all was his sight of the villas of the Veneto during a Georgian Group tour in the mid-1950s, which encouraged him to use stronger and more freely applied pinks and terracottas.

If he particularly liked a client, he might tell them what he put into the colours he made for them. That happened with Lady Bagot at Blithfield, who has kept the notes he gave her. In the L-shaped Drawing Room yellow stainers were mixed into white Walpamur distemper – yellow-ochre, chrome yellow and also black. The lilac-mauve in the vestibule was made of permanent red, cobalt blue and black into white. In the New Drawing Room blue, cobalt blue, chrome, raw umber and black went into white.

What is so striking about these samples is what a good eye he had for close tones, which is not at all easy to convey through illustration in a book. But it is apparent from one of the few notes that he kept, a sheet of alternative materials which he suggested for the Queen's Audience Room at Buckingham Palace [178]: it gives an excellent idea of how he set about the process of selection and suggestion for an elaborate scheme.

Invariably he thought in terms of three colours or three tones of a colour, and Mattei Radev, who restored gilding on furniture and picture frames for him and therefore knew him well, suggested to me that it was probably partly derived from practices in wallpaper painting.

Small samples do not give any idea of how his colours build up in a big room. While he is particularly associated with the use of secondary colours and an infinite variety of whites and no-colours, it is important to remember that he could go from *pianissimo* to *fortissimo* in a quite remarkable way and use not only strong colours but a great many colours in a room. He used to say that young decorators never used enough colours, for he believed that the more there were the greater were the possibilities of mixing. What bored him was what he called 'Sloane Street good taste' with 'genteel colours'.

He liked giving colours names. There were colours named after houses, like Ditchley white and Rushbrooke pink; there was Blithfield red and Bowood pink. Then there were colours with basic names – sugar bag blue and cooking apple green – and ones with suggestive names such as shadow colour, elephant's breath, straw-left-out-in-the-rain and mouse's back; and also some Fowler-French ones such as *caca du dauphin* and *vomitesse de la reine*. And he could be scathing too: 'That is the sort of blue that an expectant mother would put in a nursery for her boy child.'

His painter's eye and his historical sense made him prefer water paint to modern emulsion paint, which he despised. It was the dry look of water paint that he liked, and he thought that more important than a perfect finish or long life: also it gave the worn effect of old colour if applied in thin glazes. John White has written: 'His insistence on translucent overpainting of white to give the effect of texture was masterly. Although not authentic, it did however reproduce, in modern materials, textured effects which, because of the poor grinding of pigment, in previous generations could not be avoided.' He is now often associated with dragged paint, and while he used it a great deal and to marvellous effect, it was not he who revived the fashion: it was going strong in the 1920s and 1930s. On the other hand it was he who established the post-war fashion for it.

It is striking that all his colours are light and clear, never muddy; and while they are often bold and strong, they are never dense and thick. As he said to Ian McCallum: 'Now, child, a colour can go muddy if you do not show the undercoat through.' When he did use dark colours, as on skirtings, he always broke the colour and the texture of the paint to prevent the effect looking solid.

He developed his approach for reasons of artistic decoration, and it was based initially on his close observation of old paint, particularly on furniture. Later he began to apply it in the decoration of country houses and for restoration, and then invariably he tried to discover past colour schemes through scrapes and to establish not only original colours of walls, but whether and how the enrichments were picked out and whether or not there had been any gilding. It would be interesting to know when people began to search for historical clues of that kind, but it was certainly starting in New England in the 1920s and Mrs Tree discovered the colour in the saloon at Ditchley in 1933. John Fowler's simple methods of scraping have been overtaken by technical advances, but even now it is rare for all the evidence to be discovered. However, he had such an extensive experience from working in architectural interiors that he had developed a remarkable sensitivity to the interpretation of evidence. On the other hand he was never a pedant, and, as John White has said to me: 'Evidence from scrapes of past work was always treated with great regard, but he strove for beauty, within the limits of that evidence, rather than a strict reproduction.'

Almost to the end of his life John would take up a brush when necessary, and he retained all his old dexterity as a marbler. He distinguished between two sorts of marbling: that done to imitate marble and that done to suggest it; and it was characteristic of him that he preferred the latter because it was livelier, looked simpler and gave more scope for imagination.

It was in rooms of strongly architectural character that John Fowler's real skill emerges and he loved to use colour to emphasize the form and punctuation of a room. Indeed he made a speciality of this, being possibly the first person to do so in England in this century. He looked very hard at the construction of a room and wanted the framing of a cornice, dado rail and skirting to make their proper statement and relate the chimneypiece to the doorcases and so on. In simple rooms he sometimes provided an architectural character through suggesting panelling by lining out the walls rather than through painting complete *trompe l'œil*

mouldings. Although he did not have a precise academic knowledge of the classical orders as an eighteenth-century architect might have had or as Raymond Erith had, he had an excellent working experience of them, so that he knew when to paint up and when down, when to pick out the flutes of a column and so on.

To quote John White again: 'He knew his architecture and his command of names of ornament was unequalled. I always felt a logic in his sequence of the colours and shades on various planes in the architecture of a room. He was not a purist, in the sense that his superb decorator's eye would not allow him to follow slavishly a scheme because it was authentic, although drab.' On the other hand he painted up more than was done in the eighteenth century.

His understanding of architecture is particularly apparent in his use of gilding and in his picking out of architecture. Such were the costs that he seldom was given the opportunity to gild an elaborate room from scratch, as he did at the Bank of England, and often he was restricted to adding a little to improve the balance in a room, as in the saloon at Sudbury [LXXV].

However, he was always fascinated by gilding and knew a great deal about techniques, although he himself was only able to oil-gild, the form usually found in architectural decoration; he could not water-gild. As in all his work his experience was based on very careful looking over a long period of time, and he had a remarkable understanding of how to plan its use, enjoying the flash and sparkle but liking to keep it light in effect, avoiding the heaviness of over-gilding. Again, as with tones of colour, he liked to use different colours of gold, having a particular penchant for lemon gold, which is light in colour and suits his whites and off-whites particularly well, as can be seen on the ceiling of the saloons at Haseley and Radburne [XXX, XXXI]. Similarly at times he liked to use silver leaf, which always has to be varnished to prevent tarnishing, but whose appearance can be varied through the tinting of the varnish. Also he understood the different effects created by black and white grounds as opposed to the more familiar red, and while he did not like gilding left too bright, he did not approve of antiquing it, preferring to tone it down with a wash that takes off the glare. When he was faced with a job of restoration, he would always insist on any old gilding being kept and the new being toned to match.

John Fowler made it all seem easy and natural, but many samples were made and tried in different parts of a room in different lights and he went on and on –

LVII. CHRIST CHURCH, OXFORD. THE LIBRARY VESTIBULE. This was decorated by John
Fowler in 1957.

LVIII. THE UPPER LIBRARY AT
CHRIST CHURCH. John Fowler
introduced the elaborate picking-out
in tones of white and the gilding
when the room was decorated in
1965.

LIX. HOUGHTON HALL,
NORFOLK. A BEDROOM. John
Fowler re-hung one of the original
beds, which had lost all trace of its
original treatment, with old silk
velvet and silver lace and fringe that
Lady Cholmondeley had inherited
from her brother, Sir Philip Sassoon.
The blue velvet had faded
considerably and unevenly, and so
ingenuity as well as skill was
required in planning its use and in
the placing of the galloon and lace.

LX. A DETAIL OF THE HEAD OF
THE BED AT HOUGHTON. This
shows the disposition of the galloon
and the lace.

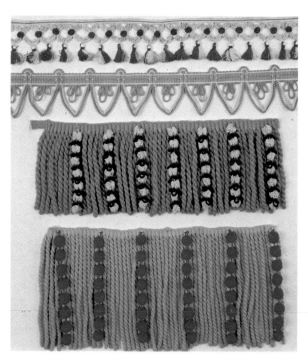

LXI. EXAMPLES OF CHARACTERISTIC FOWLER TRIMMINGS. In the top and fourth rows are bullion fringes decorated with bundles and bows; in the second row is a trellis fringe; in the third row is the gothick gimp; and at the bottom is a deep bullion fringe.

LXII. 'BOWOOD'. A floral chintz first copied either by Lady Colefax or John Fowler in the mid- or late-1930s from a piece presumably found at Bowood, Wiltshire. Later it was printed in a variety of colours.

LXIII. TRIMMINGS DEVISED BY JOHN FOWLER IN ABOUT 1935–6. The upper example is inspired by the detail on an eighteenth-century waistcoat and done in a copy of an old dot-and-cross lining chintz, which he had made, and a striped cotton. It was all hand-sewn. The lower, probably inspired by a trimming on an eighteenth-century dress, is in the same chintz combined with yellow slipper satin; the edges are scalloped and pinked.

LXIV. EXAMPLES OF TIE-BACKS AND ROSETTES.

LXV. 'OLD ROSE WITH FANCY'. A favourite chintz design and background of John Fowler, seen also in the chair in illustration 174.

LXVI. DITCHLEY. An early-nineteenth-century chintz still in use in a bedroom in that house when acquired by the Trees, as can be seen from illustration 125. Subsequently it was copied by John Fowler.

LXVII and LXVIII. 'BERKELEY SPRIG'. A modest mid-eighteenth-century wallpaper found by John Fowler when working on the restoration of 44 Berkeley Square and copied for use there. Later he used it on numerous occasions, for example in the gallery at Chequers [XLIV].

LXIX and LXX. THE END OF THE TWO SETTEES WITH THEIR PAINTED CUSHIONS IN THE QUEEN'S AUDIENCE ROOM AT BUCKINGHAM PALACE. The frames of the two settees are painted a blue-white, and they are covered in two different shades of oyster, with the two pairs of silk cushions painted in complementary ways. The design of the two sprays forming a circle round a crown is adapted from motifs on the border of the curtains and is painted with the aid of stencils. At each corner of the cushions are tassels made by Clarkes in white, oyster colours and touches of blue.

LXXI. ONE OF THE CURTAINS IN THE QUEEN'S AUDIENCE ROOM AT BUCKINGHAM PALACE.
The design of the border with roses, thistles and shamrocks was enlarged from a mid-nineteenth-century ribbon by John Fowler and George Oakes.

and on – until he was satisfied. And if he wasn't satisfied, it would all be done all over again. That would mean nothing to him in terms of cost, whether the client was paying or his own firm.

Mrs Bilibin, who, as Gwen Jervis, first met him at Peter Jones, then ran the studio in Smith Street and returned after the war to Brook Street, running the studio there until 1963, has written to me of how he set about about choosing colour for a room.

Colour patterns on large boards would be made by me to go with whatever was decided by John, the client and sometimes myself. But always the wall colour was the first priority and the client was either cajoled, bullied or hypnotized into agreeing with whatever John considered best. Once the room in question was prepared and ready for the final coat of paint or glaze I would be despatched to mix in situ literally gallons of colour for the local painters to apply ... The painters were always asked to put on the walls large patterns or even a whole wall would be painted only to have a small variation made by John, which meant the whole surface being undercoated again.

To quote John White once more:

My overall memory of him is one of confidence in his ability to arrive at the finished scheme, or colour. This may seem trite, but increasingly does not happen. When John was in charge, by the end of the day, you knew exactly what was decided and what was to be done, until his next visit and that was adhered to. His colours were always subtle – 'judicious use of black, dear boy, will "smoke" the colour' as he used to say.

In assessing John as a colourist, it is not just his use of paint that has to be considered, but also his approach to colour in materials. Indeed he liked to choose colours from stuffs rather than from paint samples, and his palette in the shop consisted of a great bank of plain materials with an infinite variety of shades arranged by colour; at the end of his life the palette that he took with him on jobs consisted of samples of materials rather than paint colours. Earlier, when he and Nancy Lancaster went on jobs together, he had an old suitcase full of fragments of material picked up all over the place, some new, some old, some intended for furnishing and Nancy says there were bits of her petticoats and his vests; but one disastrous day he left the suitcase in a taxi, and, not surprisingly, he never got it back. The Duchess of Hamilton has described to me how when they were planning the colours of a room round an Adamesque carpet, he threw down a bundle of plain silks and worked from them.

An essential element in his approach, at least after the war, was his reliance on dyed materials. Imogen Taylor suggested to me that this may have started in days of rationing when he had to make use of damask table cloths, old blankets and so on. When she was his assistant she often took lengths of material to Pilgrim Payne, where dyeing was still done in a completely traditional way, with men stripped to the waist plunging the material into vats of colour; and often they were sent back more than once until he was completely satisfied. On one occasion he wanted material dyed sulphur-yellow and sent her to the chemist to buy sulphur powder and take it to the dyers as a guide. Unfortunately the dyed colours tended to fade and even fly, but in fact he rather liked that; also he liked the way that wool and silk often did not take the colour completely evenly. However, that approach is impossible now, because there are apparently no dyers left in England prepared to work in that kind of way.

It is worth considering four more of his jobs in greater detail: Syon, where he repainted the hall and the Circular Closet; Wilton, where he did a good deal of work in addition to repainting Wyatt's gothick cloisters; the library of Christ Church, Oxford; and, in special circumstances, at the Bank of England.

The hall at Syon [L–LII] is one of Adam's noblest Roman works, but on many days in the year it could look too coldly Roman when painted in a single dead white, and when the Duke of Northumberland asked John Fowler to paint it, he decided not only to give greater articulation to the architecture but to introduce a degree of warmth as well. He did that by balancing four basic tones, painting up the architecture to emphasize the elaboration of the concept and to tie in the marble statues and the grisailles. However, it is only when one looks hard and long that it becomes apparent what he was doing, and even then there is a sense of mystery because the play of light in the room leaves one uncertain about the variation in tone. For a start probably many people do not take in the careful differentiation between the warm white of the main storey, which often takes on a suggestion of colour changing from pink to lilac, and the cooler white of the upper storey; similarly the colour used for the ground in the main frieze, for the rings of the columns, the frieze to the upper windows and in the coffers looks a grey-blue in some lights rather than the blue-grey of the skirting colour. There are three whites in the apse and four blues in the ceiling; grey-white for the main border that echoes the dado; banded by a warm white, which is also used for the cross-ribs, and echoing the main wall colour; with a slightly darker tone for the grounds to the rosettes in the ribs and in the big roses. Thus there is a counterpoint going on between different parts of the room, and the pedestals to the statues play their part in this, being painted as microcosms of the room and at the same time bringing the main wall colour below the dado rail, just as it re-appears in the scrolling brackets that support the architraves to the windows and in the panels beneath the windows. The whole scheme is a virtuoso performance, and not the least remarkable part of it is that it is never assertive but all the time plays up to Adam's concept; and what is more it was carried out by the estate painters who had never done anything of the kind before.

John Fowler had a remarkable ability to work with whites and all the tones that are closely related, but it is a more difficult task to repaint a highly coloured Adam room, because it is hard for us to adjust to the intensity of the original colours, we do not really understand the reasons lying behind their selection and it is not at all easy to match the texture of eighteenth-century paints in modern materials. And it is even more difficult to do one room in a suite. Here Syon provides another example. The Long Gallery there is a wonderfully mellow room, but it is now discoloured and faded, and in recent years a great deal of thought has been given to the problem of cleaning and repainting it. At one end, in the turret, is an enchanting circular closet [LIII, LIV], a complex design with niches and a ring of slender columns supporting a dome, and correspondingly elaborately decorated with plasterwork painted in pink, blue, white and gold. To plan its repainting demanded a very sure eye, because the pink is a stronger colour than most people would use today and the blue has to stand up to it. In fact there are three blues, a pale blue for the columns and all the strip of decoration on the main walls and in the dome, a darker blue for the frieze, which is also used in the roundels on the ceiling, and below the dado rail what is really a grey-blue, also used for the blocks just over the dado rail supporting the vertical strips on the main walls. That is the kind of detail that very few people would notice, and John would not have intended that anyone should, but it means that the eye takes in the room as a whole. Again just as the eye picks up the change of blue in the frieze, it notices the pink in the flutes of the capitals, but only after a time the suggestion of pink in the egg-and-tongue above the frieze and in the gilding at the top of the entablature.

If, at Syon, John was working in pure Adam rooms,

at Wilton the challenges were more extensive and more various, because it was a long time since much decoration had been done in the house and a great deal of pulling together was needed in the private rooms as well as those open to the public. From his point of view it was a particularly appealing job, because not only was it a wonderful house, but the 16th Earl of Pembroke, who had inherited in 1960, had a deep love and scholarly understanding of it as well as an appreciation of John, whom, as we have seen, he nicknamed 'Quand-même' because of his use of French words and phrases. John Fowler's most important contribution to the house was his redecoration of James Wyatt's gothick cloisters [LV], which is one of his triumphs of architectural painting. The all-grey galleries were crowded with the classical marbles collected by the 7th Earl, and Lord Pembroke wanted to use them as picture galleries, particularly for the series of views of Wilton and other family properties, with some sculpture to pace them out.

Nothing could be done to make the north front or the North Hall successful architectural experiences, and so a visit to Wilton starts in an unexpectedly low key. But as soon as one enters the North Hall, the twin arches provide a first glimpse of the vaulted cloisters and their warm tones. The apricot terracotta was a favourite kind of colour with John, but here it was perhaps suggested by the warm tone of the stucco facing of the cloister court and by the sunset in Wilson's most famous painting of Wilton. After twenty years there is a good deal of fading, which John Fowler no doubt expected, and that makes the vault difficult to analyse, but then one is not meant to be aware of how the fields between the ribs are varied and how that variation contributes to the sense of light and shade. The scheme could not be called an authentic restoration, but it is a brilliant interpretation and enhancement of an architectural experience that captures the lightness of its spirit without making it too pretty. The warmth of the colour suits the pictures and the marbles, particularly those with coloured togas, and their Mazarin plinths; and there is a stimulating relationship with the strong blue in the roundels of stained glass, the blue and white chinese pots and black lacquer chests.

He did nothing in the state rooms, but working in the house gave him the chance to study very carefully the planning of the gilding and to enjoy the relationship between its flash and the old white of the wainscot, and the uses of different colours of gold, which is not often seen in an English house. And there is evidence of what he studied in the way he treated the terms of the library doorcases [LVI] so that they echo the standing figures on the chimneypiece in the Double Cube Room; similarly in the same room he repeated the pattern of the eighteenth-century flock paper in the Corner Room and Cabinet. In the Little Smoking Room, there would appear to have been four points that influenced his decoration: the strength of the seventeenth-century chimneypiece and the boldness of the entablature, the darkness of the series of pictures by Morier in which the red coats stand out, and the weight of the old green used for the woodwork in the adjoining Large Smoking Room. His red complements the coats in the Moriers and stands up to the room.

If the hall at Syon and the cloisters at Wilton show his response to Adam's classic and Wyatt's gothick when working for private clients, it is only right to show his response to Rococo decoration and to consider how he coped with a corporate body other than the National Trust. Here his work in the vestibule and Upper Library at Christ Church, Oxford, is a great success [LVII, LVIII]. But, before describing what he did, it is worth considering the special difficulties of working for corporate bodies, even those who can afford what they want to do; and of all such bodies an Oxford or Cambridge college surely must be the most difficult of all, because the system of committees and governing bodies means that a great many people, often vociferous and forceful even when without experience in a particular field, have the right to give their views; and so it takes an immense amount of time to reach any series of decisions. That may be inevitable, but in visual matters it does not necessarily lead to the best results, because it is a method of procedure that is intensely discouraging and frustrating to any kind of designer. For him it is difficult to keep the spirit of his design alive, and, as with any kind of painting or writing, even a good idea may well go dead simply through delays and hold-ups.

Anyone going to the library at Christ Church (designed by Dr George Clarke in 1717 but not completed until 1772) would presume that the present decoration of the vestibule, staircase and Upper Library was part of a single plan, but in fact nine years separate completion of the first and second phases, and the work was done as two distinct operations, John Fowler never being asked to do a total scheme or even knowing that eventually he would be asked to paint the Upper Library. In May 1957, his was one of two names considered for redecorating the vestibule and staircase. His proposals were quickly accepted and were carried

out in the second part of that year. Three years later the College began the enormous task of repairing the external stonework of the building, and as soon as that was complete, in the autumn of 1962, John Fowler was invited to return to give his advice on the decoration of the Upper Library. However, that work was not carried out until 1965.

When he first went to Christ Church, the library building was in dramatically black, Piranesian decay and much more romantically Italianate than it is today, with its crisp details and beautifully balanced combination of white and buff stones; and it was the Italianate element that he seized on when he suggested a scheme of tangerine-apricot with grey-white and gold for the vestibule and staircase. There is little direct daylight in the vestibule, but ahead lies the arch leading through to the staircase and disguising the flood of south light through its tall window and also the unexpected height of the staircase hall and its curved ends. It is a dramatic, Baroque, conception, and even if painted in stone whites the effect would be impressive, but no doubt he felt that that would be cold and uninviting, and that the effect could be made much more exciting by the use of strong colour, even if it was neither broadly historical nor in the tradition of an academic institution. I am sure his reasoning was purely architectural, but equally he would have enjoyed doing something so bold within such hallowed and disputatious walls. If some of the Fellows looked askance at going to someone they, no doubt, dismissed as a Mayfair decorator, he could have been equally sharp over what he would have regarded as their lack of visual understanding.

Even after twenty-five years it is a surprise to open the door into the vestibule and suddenly find the glowing colour that not only defines the space so well but provides an excellent background for the eighteenth-century marble busts that line the walls, bringing out their individual qualities. John always knocked down his whites, but seldom as much as here, where the doorcases are painted a grey-white and then given a lift though lining out in gold, again an unhistorical embellishment but adding sparkle in the dull light.

The colour works particularly well on the staircase, because first it throws up the pattern of George Cooper's ironwork on the half pace and then seems to enfold one in constantly changing light, setting off first the statue of Locke, then the richly carved but unpainted and ungilded doorcase at the head of the staircase, and finally the deep coved ceiling, elaborately decorated by Thomas Roberts, the Oxford stuccadore.

Again John introduced a little gilding, and also he painted the cove of the ceiling a pale yellow.

It is now twenty-six years since he did this work, so naturally there has been some fading, and a few cracks and scuffs have appeared, but like so much of his best work it mellows gracefully and does not look shabby or dated; and it is to be hoped that it will survive for a long time to come, so that it is seen as a historical scheme of value in its own right.

When he devised that scheme, he must have thought of it as a preparation for the library, but that there was any unofficial understanding that he would be called back to it cannot be presumed. However, his scheme added immensely to the difficulty of anyone else devising any scheme for the library that would stand up to his own. Naturally there was a considerable body of opinion in the College against the use of any strong colour and against the introduction of gilding, but, with the exception of a little gilding omitted from the leaves of the capitals of the east and west windows, it was John Fowler's proposals that were executed. What photographs do not suggest is that the library is often rather dark, because there are only three windows in the centre of the north wall and windows at each end, and the splendid woodwork is sombrely masculine. So the colour has to stand up to the staircase, to the woodwork and to the superb plasterwork of the upper walls; and to tie the walls and ceiling together paler versions of the colour are carried into the cove and then into the bed of the ceiling, but the eye cannot work out how many different whites are used for the enrichment; and the final element is the gilding. It would be quite wrong to claim this as a historical scheme, and probably no eighteenth-century room was decorated up quite like that, certainly not in an Oxford college. On the other hand it is a marvellous virtuoso performance by someone with an understanding of how classical architecture and Rococo decoration respond to colour and gilding. And writing about it in the mid-1980s one has certain doubts that relate to attitudes of the 1970s and 1980s rather than to those of the 1950s and 1960s: academic attitudes to restoration have strengthened and private confidence has ebbed; and anyway there is no one who could bring off such a scheme today. So probably the right way to regard it is as one of the triumphs of the neo-Georgian enthusiasm that spanned the war years.

In the late 1960s John Fowler worked on the principal rooms at the Bank of England, the Court Room and the related Ante-Room, the Committee Room and the Directors' Dining Room. It was a flat-tering commission, not least because the recommendation came from Sir John Summerson, and John Fowler took it as a great compliment that his approach to decoration was receiving serious recognition. But it was also an exceedingly challenging commission, because there was a natural desire to make the Court Room and Committee Room look like historic rooms; yet Herbert Baker, when he reconstructed the Bank, had recast them with a disconcerting combination of arrogance and insensitivity. Although C.R. Cockerell had made certain changes, the Court Room and Committee Room had survived into the 1930s as noble interiors by Sir Robert Taylor. But Baker only respected their idea: he omitted a great deal of the neo-classical ornament, and he also altered much of it, introducing free Beaux Arts motifs for which there was no excuse; also, as in most of his work, the detail is unsharp and lifeless. The result is a room that is still noble in conception but does not stand up to close scrutiny. However, it was not reasonable to paint the room down, which in other circumstances would have been a way out, because then it would have gone flat and ended up looking like a hotel dining room. John Fowler took the other, braver, route, decorating it up so as to emphasize the basic form and, by infusing a sense of life into the plasterwork, giving the room a sparkle. His scheme, based on years of looking at genuine eighteenth-century rooms, is worked out with great skill, and the longer one looks at it the more one marvels at it; but even so he is not really able to triumph over Baker's weaknesses.

It is important to see the rooms in the right order and not when lit by their chandeliers. The first sign of John Fowler's involvement is at the head of the stairs, where the single window has a typical Fowler draped valance and curtains. Then follows the Ante-Room, an essay in the sort of inter-war simplified classicism that he particularly disliked, but it has an interesting chimneypiece and a good, probably English, Savonnerie carpet with a brown ground, which he took as the key to the colouring and texture of the room. He reversed the usual balance of tone almost certainly to disguise the architectural weaknesses: the fields of the panels are hung with a single and double pile striped flock paper in browns, so making the fields darker than the dado.

Off the Ante-Room is the Committee Room, which, like the Court Room, is a Baker recasting of a Taylor interior. The walls are painted in different tones and textures of pale yellow, dragged very thinly on the main fields and ragged on the framing, with a little pale blue in the grounds of the reliefs, and very full picking-out in gold of the cornice. Walls and ceiling are tied together through a more extensive use of blue on the surround to the central oval of the ceiling.

After the preparation of the strong Ante-Room and the light Committee Room, finally the double doors open to reveal all stops pulled out in the Court Room. Very quickly one's eye picks out the apricot terracotta colour used as the ground for the reliefs standing out against the basic scheme of greens, whites and a great deal of gilding: they create a sense of slight shock, which was surely intentional, because John must have wanted to distract the eye and at the same time stimulate it by using a colour that stands up to the yellow marble of the chimneypieces; and again he varies not only tones but textures. The idea of the screens at either end continues into the chimneypiece wall, with its shallow blind arcade, and so the wall is painted with the recesses paler and smoother than the framing, which is stronger and dragged, as is the dado; and the grounds of the reliefs are ragged. The ceiling is in three whites, one of the off-whites being warm and one cool, and two greens. Part of the shock comes from the gilding, because we are not used to seeing rooms fully picked out in new gold; but, as is usual with John, the balance is excellent. The room is not exactly as he envisaged it, because he had counted on a new carpet as part of his scheme, but in the end the Adamesque Wilton carpet laid in 1939 was retained.

How the room was originally painted is not recorded, but old photographs suggest considerable variation in tone and also a good deal of gilding, though, of course, that could have been a Cockerell scheme rather than an original one planned by Taylor.

John Fowler's work at the Bank is in my view not a complete success, but then that was impossible. However, I think it is most instructive, because it reveals both his strengths and his limitations and shows so clearly how he responded to the challenge of architecture; also it shows that he was not wholly at ease in the public and commercial spheres, and explains why he never sought commissions in that direction.

CHAPTER NINE

JOHN FOWLER'S APPROACH TO PATTERN AND UPHOLSTERY

After the Second World War, John Fowler's most significant work was as an architectural decorator and reviver of country houses, but long before that he had developed his interest in the textures and patterns of materials and wallpapers and in all aspects of upholstery. That was an essential part of the synthesis of his style and as distinctive as his use of colour. Indeed it played a much more important part in his work than is usual with an architectural decorator.

In the mid-1930s he began to acquire a reputation for his skill in drapery and for making curtains and bed hangings in light, simple materials and finishing them in an unusual, romantic way. But it was only in the early 1950s, after rationing ended, that the opportunities came to make regular use of richer, more formal materials and elaborate gimps, braids and tassels and to devise elaborate, even fantastic, curtains for fine rooms.

What is remarkable about John Fowler's upholstery and his use of materials and wallpapers, however, is that he never lost his love of simplicity; and even on the grandest occasions he would work in unexpectedly simple materials to play up the richer ones and give a sense of humanity and life to the rooms in which he used them. He appreciated palaces and saw the point of complete formality, but he was not really happy decorating in a completely formal way, which he found visually monotonous, unsubtle and unpainterly, and unsuited to mid-twentieth-century life. Thus it was natural to him to mix silks with linens and cot-

tons, to use matting instead of carpets, to introduce comfortable sofas and chairs upholstered in simple weaves or chintzes into rooms with gilt furniture, and to upholster a set of formal furniture in two or three materials of different weights and characters. It has become a commonplace of decoration to use simple materials in that kind of way, but John Fowler was one of the people – it would be rash to say he was the first person – to develop a definite style out of the traditional practice in English houses of using slip covers for practical purposes and combining the characteristics of a drawing room with those of a library or smoking room. No one else, however, has done the mixing so successfully.

In the early nineteenth century case covers were often made of chintz, and John's insatiable curiosity meant that he was always on the lookout for old fragments that might provide him with a design to copy or adapt. So over the years he built up at Colefax & Fowler a remarkable repertory of fabrics, which often started as a special order for a client in whose house he had found it; but he was never interested in marketing them in a fully commercial manner or selling them with a history. For convenience he would name a material after the house where the original came from, but why a material was called 'Bowood' or 'Sudbury' or a carpet called 'Rocksavage' was seldom explained in the shop; and now it is difficult to find out when some of them were first produced.

He was not, however, a true designer of textiles, but

he had a marvellous eye for a pattern that he felt could be faithfully reproduced or else be adapted; and sometimes the sources of adapted designs were not obvious. For instance one of the last chintzes he introduced, under the name of 'Angoulême', was taken from a fruit bowl of that china given him by a friend who knew its French version of 'humble elegance' would appeal to him; and he used the bowl all the time at the cottage. He could also see how a pattern could be developed: the 'Chevron Stripe', for instance, he devised from a gimp on moreen curtains at Sudbury. He had a feeling for the scale of patterns, for possibilities of recolouring them and their translation from one medium into another, as was the case with the splendid large repeat 'Double Damask' wallpaper, which he used at Holyrood [XL] and Sudbury and which came from a length of early-eighteenth-century damask that he owned. The paper called 'Berkeley Sprig' [LXVII, LXVIII] was copied from a mid-eighteenth-century fragment of a modest paper that he found at 44 Berkeley Square and printed for use there; later it was made in a variety of colours and as a cotton for general sale. With Brussels carpets the situation was much the same: the 'Tatton' design came from a battered foot-warmer he found in a carriage at Tatton Park, Cheshire. Thus the keenness of his feeling for scale, for colour and for detail more than compensated for his avoidance of drawing. But, as someone who knew him well said, he was not disciplined enough to be a manufacturer's designer.

Although his main interest lay in the eighteenth century and particularly in materials and wallpapers, he did not confine himself to that period when it came to patterns. Indeed, most of his chintzes and later his Brussels carpets were taken from early-nineteenth-century designs. In the 1920s and 1930s there was a growing historical interest in chintzes, as there was in wallpaper, not only in this country but also in America, and there was a growing demand for them, so that already by the time John Fowler joined Lady Colefax she had some chintzes that were exclusive to her firm. As far as the floral designs were concerned they were a natural choice for John, given his love of flowers and gardens and his feeling for a country style in London, but what strikes me as more original was his liking in the 1950s for certain Willement-like patterns such as 'Gothic Tracery' to which he may have been introduced by Nancy Lancaster, who had kept it in use at Ditchley after finding it there on a polonaise bed [125]. At the Ashburnham sale in 1953 they bought widely, and just as Lord and Lady Iliffe bought a William IV

bed [89], Nancy Lancaster bought a contemporary bed and carpet that she placed in the Tobacco Bedroom at Haseley [133], the carpet being copied by John Fowler as 'Rose and Ribbon'. Many of his trimmings [LXI], particularly his elaborate bullion fringes and trellis fringes, were also taken from designs produced in the 1820s and 1830s.

His interest in printed and woven materials was paralleled by a related interest in eighteenth- and nineteenth-century wallpaper. Here his early training, his facility as a painter and his visual and historical curiosity led him to develop a considerable understanding of it. Like textiles, it is not an easy subject to learn about, because, despite the growth of literature, documentation is scanty, and it is largely a case of studying many fragments over a long period of time. That, however, came naturally to him, and through his work he built up a large hoard of fragments, almost all of which he gave to the Victoria and Albert Museum, so that he figures in the recent catalogue of wallpaper as one of the principal donors. Again, though he was not really a designer, after the war he did a great deal to revive and adapt designs, as was seen with 'Berkeley Sprig' and 'Double Damask'. In the same category is 'Sudbury', a simple late-eighteenth-century design he found in that house, together with its border; initially he had it copied for use in the library and subsequently sold it widely. Among other papers that come to mind are 'Haddon Hall', which was an old ceiling paper that he had recoloured for use as a wallpaper (and David Hicks used on some of his early jobs), and 'Stripe on Stripe', which he devised as an economical alternative to damask hangings that were out of the question in big rooms like the drawing room at Shugborough [188] and the hall at Holyrood [XXXIX] and had printed in different widths and colours; and those who think of him as an Anti-Victorian should remember that it was he who first asked for Coles's 'Owen Jones' design. He had started to go to Coles after the war, when he began to find fragments in country houses and wanted to get them copied for use in them. Before the war the papers that appealed most to him were those produced by Mauny and he used them on many occasions; afterwards, however, they were often too expensive for his clients, though he used them when he could, as at Lennoxlove and Holyrood [XXXVII, XXXVIII].

It is difficult to say why patterns of materials approved by one person should have such a distinctive look about them, but certainly those chosen by John Fowler are immediately recognizable; and when used

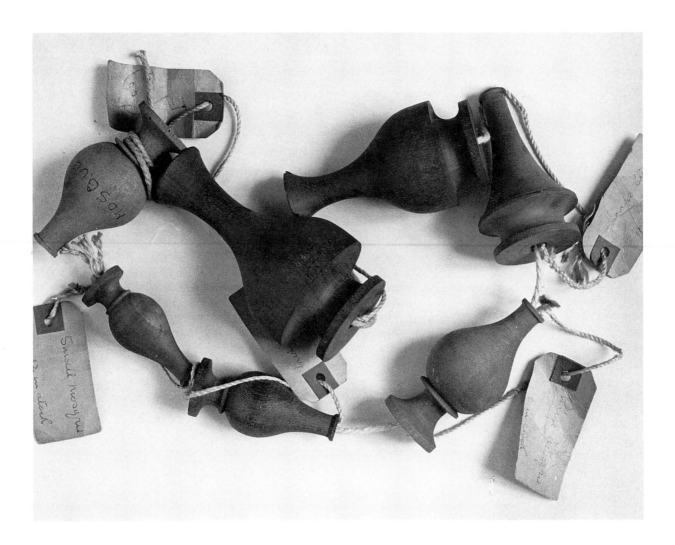

by him his control is apparent in the way they are finished, not only in the tones and weaves of piping but in the braids and gimps, fan edgings and fringes, cords, rosettes and tassels. As with chintzes and wallpapers, he was always on the look-out for old fragments, which he would squirrel away in his room at Brook Street or in an Aladdin's cave of a shed at the cottage, because he appreciated them not only as examples of a specialized art-cum-craft but as sources of ideas. He was always short-sighted, and, when he lifted his glasses to peer at a fragment of knotted fringe with hangers of bundles and bows that he was running through his fingers, the eighteenth century would come intensely alive in his imagination. Gimps, fringes and tassels had a particular fascination for him, and he knew exactly how every element was made: to a layman who takes such things for granted what seemed an extraordinary amount of thought was given to the silhouettes of the moulds of tassels [172] – back they would go to the turner if he was not completely satisfied – and there would be lengthy discussions not only about the colours of the threads to be used but the precise numbers of each colour and their distribution. With a two-colour block fringe, for instance, should the distribution be even or uneven or should the pace vary? Clients who were felt to be worthy of serious consideration were expected to take an intelligent interest in such things (while, of course, agreeing with his final decision); and even some husbands were expected to listen too, so that they understood the importance of detail and why it had to be absolutely right – and, of course, expensive.

For quite a long time all his best trimmings were made by B. A. Clarke in Little Britain in the City of London, an Edwardian firm that he kept in existence until their lease ran out in 1970. He used to love going

172. A SELECTION OF TASSEL
MOULDS. John Fowler devoted much
thought to the silhouettes as well as the size
of the turned wooden moulds used
for tassels.

173. A ROBE-POLONAISE OF ABOUT
1775–80 IN THE VICTORIA AND
ALBERT MUSEUM. It is of painted silk
trimmed with ribbon. Much of the
inspiration for the details of John Fowler's
upholstery were derived from costume.

there, and shortly before the firm closed he took me
with him so that I should understand some of the
processes and record them in an article for *Country
Life* (10 December 1970).

If a client could produce old gimps and tassels, John
Fowler always tried to use them, partly to save money,
but also because he liked the association of what was
genuine. Two examples are in the Duke of Hamilton's
apartment at Holyrood [XXXIX] and in Lady Haddington's sitting room at Tyninghame [XLI, XLII];
and in a class of its own is the bed done for Lady
Cholmondeley with old silk velvet and old silver lace
that she had inherited years before from her brother,
Sir Philip Sassoon [LIX, LX].

As an alternative to spun and woven trimmings
made by a trimmings maker like Clarkes, John Fowler
always liked to use ruffles and flounces, often scallop-
ing and pinking the edges and sometimes piercing

them. He first made them in the mid-1930s [LXIII],
when he could not afford spun and woven trimmings,
and he continued to use them for the rest of his life,
on cushions, on curtains and valances, and on bed
hangings. Much of the original inspiration for them
came from eighteenth- and nineteenth-century costume
seen at the Victoria and Albert Museum [173] and
possibly also from portraits. Later he probably found
historical confirmation for such fanciful details in fragments in undisturbed houses, but I do not remember
him talking about them. The only good example I
know is on an early nineteenth-century set of bed
hangings at Duivenvoorde near The Hague. He never
saw them, but Christopher Wall described them to him
and they copied them on curtains at Fenton House.

When it came to upholstering chairs, he was interested in every aspect, stuffing, line, tufting, nailing and
so on, his interest again going back to the mid-1930s.

174. A PAINTED CHAIR IN THE FRENCH TASTE. This chair, which belonged to John Fowler, was the epitome of the kind of elegant, understated eighteenth-century furniture that he liked best; and, typically, he upholstered it in one of his favourite chintzes, 'Old Rose with Fancy'. Great attention was devoted to the line of the upholstery, including the swell of the arms and the nailing.

At that time he occasionally used Victorian armchairs [xxi] that called for deep buttoning, which he would do in a theatrical way with bunches of silk ribbon; but such chairs were not really to his taste, and later only occasionally did he go in for deep buttoning. He much preferred the less exaggerated look of tufting, which he noticed on the backs of eighteenth-century chairs, and he enjoyed crisping up a pad in a chair with tufts and piping that often contrasted in a fresh and unexpected way with the main fabric. Similarly he liked planning out nailing, particularly space nailing, and

combining it with a looped fringe. His interest in the line of upholstery followed his visits to Paris in the late 1940s and early 1950s. Mary Duchess of Buccleuch, when she was re-opening and arranging Boughton after the war, remembers how much John helped them: 'He was so charming to *our* own work people, showing them how to paint and renew *and* how to *upholster* in the correct French way – he got the Louvre to send us the nails for the French stools and chairs, which were scattered all over the house . . .'

Given his love of stuffs and interest in fashion in

dress, it is not surprising that he specialized in drapery and curtains, but after the war the element of the dressmaker in him was fused with his feeling for architectural decoration and his growing historical sense. That is particularly apparent in his revival of the festoon curtain that originates in the saloon at Ramsbury [161] in about 1954: there the reasons were practical, visual and historical, as was explained. Later he frequently used them in a variety of materials in lofty rooms with sash windows and plenty of space for the material in the dead light above the window architrave, because he liked the contribution they made to the architectural balance of a classical room and the way the carving of window-architraves was left visible. He probably first encountered original, eighteenth-century, ones at Uppark or Osterley, but when he made the Ramsbury set it seems that he had never been able to take an old one to pieces to find out how it was made. Also he had to discover for himself how the pulley wheels worked in a pelmet board; but soon he found some old ones *in situ* and acquired some for himself, as well as pretty painted pelmet cornices and such details as cloak pins to wind the cords round.

If he wanted to achieve a more clothed effect, he liked to give draw curtains draped valances derived mainly from early-nineteenth-century patterns, and there came to be almost a Fowler formula of drapery and tails with contrasting cord and bullion fringe [175]. But within the formula there were many variations, often involving paning or bordering curtains, sometimes in toning colours and contrasting textures and sometimes contrasting colours and textures.

However, for a client who was prepared to give him his head the possibilities were infinite, as can be seen from the curtains that he did for Mrs Bruce, Lady Haddington and Mrs Lancaster. Perhaps the most elaborate of all were those made in 1960 for Lord Rothermere for the Saloon at Daylesford, which George Oakes has described to me. John Fowler had discovered that Warren Hastings had had curtains of periwinkle blue silk with painted and spangled stone velvet borders, and so he and George Oakes set about devising curtains that would reflect that idea. It was the kind of challenge that he enjoyed because it enabled him not only to draw on his historical knowledge but to produce something that was original yet subservient to an eighteenth-century spirit. He liked painted velvet and knew about spangles. As well as a band of white velvet painted with flowers, he gave me what I take to be an embroidered muslin valance of Indian origin decorated with sequins. I do not claim that he

used either as direct cribs for the Daylesford curtains, but the fact that he had acquired such things at some point in his life shows how he was able to make use of ideas derived from them. The design for the oyster velvet borders was based on an Indian chintz and was painted with the aid of specially cut stencils. John's sketches were in charcoal, and, while they were expressive, they needed George Oakes's drawing out. Then, when it came to the painting of the velvet, they did it together. The finished borders, a foot deep, were applied by hand to the blue-grey strié satin.

One of his favourite devices was to give draw curtains false draped valances sewn on to them, so that when the curtains were closed, the valances appeared complete, so changing the proportions of the window and therefore of the room. That idea, which he used in the library at Haseley, was one that came from Nancy Lancaster, who in turn had learned it from Edward Knoblock. Before she knew John, she had built up a scrapbook of curtain designs which she took to Brook Street; and since she had had curtains made by a great many people before the war, including Mrs Bethell, some of her valances became part of John's vocabulary. So again there is evidence of her contribution to his style that makes their partnership so hard to disentangle.

John Fowler's drapery always has a sense of life and movement about it that no one else ever seems quite able to match, but the results did not come easily. Peter Atkins has described to me the very special relationship that developed between John and those who executed his ideas. The process towards the perfection that he demanded was in a sense an evolutionary one, in that he produced an idea but the executants really had to understand what was in his mind in order to be able to realize it to his satisfaction; and that invariably involved alterations all along the line. John Fowler, for his part, was always pressing for perfection and, because of his inspiring personality, others were prepared to strive for it too, making alterations because they did not want to let him down, often not charging for them even though it meant they lost money on what they were doing for him. But that world and that attitude to business has gone: costs simply do not allow it. Nor are there the same number of skilled people to do the work: whereas a firm might have had a staff of thirty-two in the mid-1950s and early 1960s, since 1970 the number has declined to about eight or ten.

The upholsterers who did most of his work were Chamberlain & Mason. In 1947 John Mason Snr joined

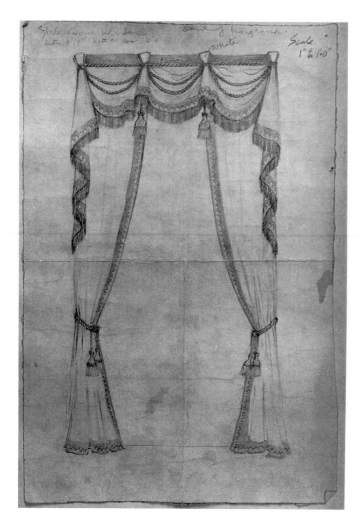

175 (left). A TYPICAL SKETCH FOR
CURTAINS BY JOHN FOWLER.

176 (right). SEZINCOTE,
GLOUCESTERSHIRE. THE
DRAWING ROOM. When John Fowler
worked on the room he took infinite
care with the replacement of the
Regency curtains, particularly in the
copying of the elaborate trimmings on
the drapery.

Joseph Chamberlain, who was already working for John Fowler, and, fortunately, John Mason Jnr, who continues the business, has kept most of the files relating to that work. There is a great deal of correspondence between the two Masons and Colefax & Fowler, with John Fowler himself appearing as the remote master, communicating directly only when he wished to pay one of his rare compliments or to criticize something that had been done or was behind schedule. All the same, what comes through is a sense not only of his passion for detail but of highly skilled people responding to a unique kind of direction in a very complicated field. The files put the work done in the 1950s into an economic context that already seems closer to the eighteenth century than to today. No doubt Lord Wilton thought his festoon curtains were quite expensive at the time, but in fact Colefax & Fowler were charged only £58 for making the three of them and

they were lined, interlined and fringed; and they were charged £70 for hanging the Small Drawing Room at Ramsbury. At that time the girls who did the sewing earned about 1s 9d. an hour; by 1962 this had risen to 5s. 4d.

The relationship between upholstery, artistic imagination and architectural decoration in John Fowler's work is perhaps best shown in the Queen's Audience Room at Buckingham Palace [LXIX–LXXI], which he decorated in the early 1960s. It was his only royal commission and came about on the recommendation of the late Lord Plunket. The room must have received its elaborate Anglo-French Rococo plasterwork in the early years of this century, and the idea of the room has continued to be Anglo-French and eighteenth-century, with pictures by Canaletto and Zuccarelli and portraits by Gainsborough, a Savonnerie-style carpet with a lot of light brown in it, and a set of chairs and

settees in the French taste by Linnell. John Fowler treated it as a semi-state room, avoiding all architectural gilding but at the same time not introducing any informal chairs as he would have done in a private drawing room; his aim was to make it light and feminine for the Queen by decorating it in blues and oyster colours but still strong enough to stand up to the formal effect of the pictures and furniture. The walls have had to be repainted and, although his colours appear to have been repeated, the results are not the same. However, his curtains survive and so does some of his upholstery; and he kept a sheet with the samples of material so that it is possible to see how he planned the close tones and also envisage him working in the way described by the Duchess of Hamilton (see page 185).

The most remarkable contribution to the room is the set of four big cushions for the two settees and his upholstering of the latter [LXIX, LXX]. The frames of the settees are painted a blue-white with gilding and are covered in two different shades of oyster, no doubt to prevent the room becoming stiff; and the two pairs of cushions are treated in complementary ways, like buhl and contre-buhl. Nothing else I have seen by John Fowler illustrates so well his artistry, his sense of detail, his feeling for understatement and his sense of fantasy. It is hard to believe that he did not wonder what Marie Antoinette would have liked to have had.

Very few clients were prepared to let John Fowler have his head with curtains, but in 1968-9, when Mr and Mrs David Bruce asked him to decorate their London flat, he had a marvellous opportunity. Mr Bruce was an old friend of Nancy Lancaster from Virginia days, and she had introduced John to them while they were *en poste* in France in the early 1950s; and later, when Mr Bruce was Ambassador in London, John

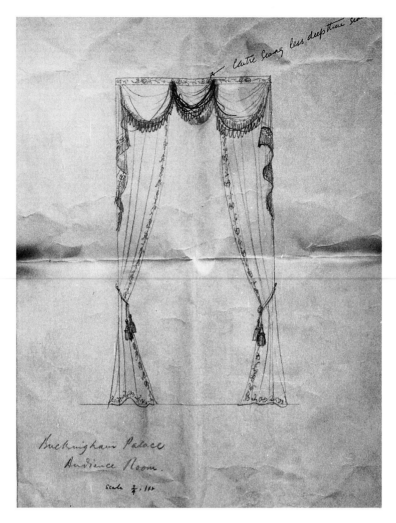

177. JOHN FOWLER'S SKETCH DESIGN FOR THE CURTAINS IN THE QUEEN'S AUDIENCE
ROOM AT BUCKINGHAM PALACE.

helped them at Winfield House. After Mr Bruce retired, they wanted to have a *pied-à-terre* in London and they took a set of rooms in a fine Georgian building. However, little of the internal detail is original, and much of it has a slightly off, Lenygonish, air. So John concentrated on colour and curtains. In the drawing room [LXXII] they are an amazing fantasy, having little to do with upholstery as it is normally understood – the ruffles were copied from a wedding dress in the Victoria and Albert Museum.

Since there is a double door between the drawing room and the dining room, and the view back and forth is important, the two rooms are tied together through the picking-up of colours: in the dining room the window seat is apricot-coloured like the draw curtains in the drawing room, and there is a little brown upholstery in the drawing room to answer the dining room curtains.

John Fowler intended the rooms to be glamorous and sparkling, not too serious, and that is what they are; and there is a sense of wit in his decoration that is apparent in the treatment of the jib door to the left of the chimneypiece, which is given a *trompe l'œil* portrait of Princess Caraboo painted by Christopher Hobbs in 1971 to balance a portrait to the right of the chimneypiece.

Over the years John Fowler dressed or redressed many beds, and on several occasions he restored eighteenth-century state beds. One of his last fine beds was for Lady Cholmondeley at Houghton in Norfolk [LIX, LX]. Besides the celebrated green velvet state bed and the embroidered bed in the state rooms on the first floor, there are on the second floor two contemporary beds, one with hangings of painted taffeta, which Lord and Lady Cholmondeley restored just before the Second World War, and a second one that

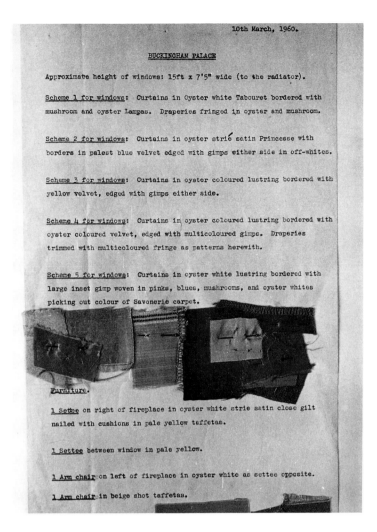

10th March, 1960.

BUCKINGHAM PALACE

Approximate height of windows: 15ft x 7'5" wide (to the radiator).

Scheme 1 for windows: Curtains in Oyster white Tabouret bordered with
mushroom and oyster Lampas. Draperies fringed in oyster and mushroom.

Scheme 2 for windows: Curtains in oyster strié satin Princesse with
borders in palest blue velvet edged with gimps either side in off-whites.

Scheme 3 for windows: Curtains in oyster coloured lustring bordered with
yellow velvet, edged with gimps either side.

Scheme 4 for windows: Curtains in oyster coloured lustring bordered with
oyster coloured velvet, edged with multicoloured gimps. Draperies
trimmed with multicoloured fringe as patterns herewith.

Scheme 5 for windows: Curtains in oyster white lustring bordered with
large inset gimp woven in pinks, blues, mushrooms, and oyster whites
picking out colour of Savonerie carpet.

Furniture.

1 Settee on right of fireplace in oyster white strie satin close gilt
nailed with cushions in pale yellow taffetas.

1 Settee between window in pale yellow.

1 Arm chair on left of fireplace in oyster white as settee opposite.

1 Arm chair in beige shot taffetas.

178. Samples of materials proposed for the Queen's Audience Room. It was
unusual for John Fowler to present a scheme in such a formal way.

was re-covered in an unsuitable chintz when the house was let at the end of the last century. For years Lady Cholmondeley had wanted to revive its original character. Fortunately she had saved from the Park Lane house of her brother, Sir Philip Sassoon, a set of wall hangings and curtains of pale blue silk velvet; also she had inherited from him quantities of old *passementerie*, including a good deal of silver lace, galloon and fringe that he had never used. The combination of blue and silver was well suited to Houghton, bearing in mind the existence in the state rooms of so much original plain green velvet and the gold lace on the green bed; and the fact that the pale blue had faded considerably and unevenly in places to tones of almost green and brown made it more at home than any new material would have done. However, there was scarcely enough velvet for the job, and it required ingenuity in planning and cutting to match up the dif-

ferent degrees of fading; and even then there was only enough for dress curtains for the windows, so there had to be draw curtains of another stuff; and the bed head and back board are in a slightly different colour and texture of blue. There was only just enough of the silver lace and fringing of different periods to pick out the design, and the narrowest braid used for outlining the back board had to be specially made.

It was not easy to find an upholsterer with the skill for that kind of work or with premises lofty enough to take the bed, and once it reached the workshop of John Mason, Lady Cholmondeley went with John Fowler on several occasions to discuss the planning of the lace, braid and fringing. It was just the kind of job that he liked, because it was testing and rewarding; it was very detailed and architectural; and it was for a stimulating client who was mistress of the finest eighteenth-century house in England.

CHAPTER TEN

JOHN FOWLER'S CONTRIBUTION TO THE NATIONAL TRUST

Posterity will learn of John Fowler's work largely through what he did for the National Trust in the last twenty years of his life, because it is likely that the rooms he restored and decorated in the Trust's houses will be valued at least in part for his interpretation of them and will be preserved partly because of that. But inevitably they will give an unbalanced view of his approach to interiors. Indeed, having discussed some of his Trust work with him in connection with articles for *Country Life*, it has come as a surprise to me to discover later how much his private and Trust work differed.

Between 1956 and his death in 1977 he was involved at an astonishing number of houses belonging to the Trust all over England, Wales, and Northern Ireland: Claydon in 1956-7 and again in 1976; Petworth in 1962 and 1972; West Wycombe in 1963; Shugborough in 1965 and 1969; Clandon in 1968-9; Wallington in 1968-9; Uppark, over a long period; Sudbury, 1968-70; Castle Ward, 1969-70; Blickling, 1969-70; Attingham, 1971; the Temple of the Winds at Mount Stewart, 1971; Peckover House, 1971-2; Tatton, 1972-3; Lyme, 1972-4; Montacute, 1972-5; Lacock, 1973; Treasurer's House, 1973-4; Erdigg, 1973-7; Felbrigg, 1974; Ormesby, 1974; Fenton House, 1974; Bath Assembly Room, 1974-5; Cliveden, 1975; Dyrham, 1976-7; Juniper Hall, 1976-7.

For a young, physically fit man, that list would have been evidence of remarkable activity - and a great deal of travelling was involved as well - but John had re-

tired in 1969 and it was a period of almost constant ill health and strain; it took immense courage and determination to carry on. He never complained, but it is worth quoting from a letter written by him about Erdigg to Merlin Waterson, the Representative responsible for the house, on 18 July 1976, just over a year before he died: 'I felt so sorry I had to back out on Tuesday & go home. I was in acute pain in my insides & tomorrow have to go through some humiliating experiences to find out what exactly it is. After 2 days (?) I feel much better - I don't fear the worst too much. I'm sure I'll be all right within a month ...' The strain on him also meant a strain on the much younger members of the staff whose responsibility the houses were and who had the difficult task of getting what they wanted from him while looking after him in cold, dismantled houses and usually uncongenial hotels.

His connection with the Trust started in the mid-1950s through a desire on his part to help friends who worked for it, but the formal arrangement came about only in 1969, when he wanted to retire from full-time involvement with his firm. It was the firm's agreement to retain John that enabled him to work for the Trust for a token fee of £1,000 a year: the Trust could never have afforded to pay him a proper salary.

From his point of view his formal association with the Trust was a marvellous challenge that he could never have expected in the mid-1950s, because it gave him opportunities to work in many more worthwhile and challenging rooms than he could have hoped would come his way through private clients, since most of his old friends and clients were no longer bent on decoration. Also I think that he realized there was little future for his kind of decorating in private houses, and he saw the Trust as having the need as well as the duty to maintain traditional skills and foster them for the future. The Trust also enabled him to give of his best to houses he loved and also serve an organization he much admired. In addition it brought him into regular touch for the first time with a circle of people with professional responsibility for notable houses, who were developing a much deeper interest and understanding of historic interiors, partly through his teaching and influence, and who could contribute to his own knowledge about houses, even if they did not stimulate him in the same way as people like Lady Haddington or Mrs Willis.

It would be wrong to make out that all his work for the Trust was equally successful, and some of it I regret. Also he particularly disliked having to work with committees. So it is interesting to have two accounts, written from differing points of view, of how he handled various kinds of Trust committees. The first is written by the Duchess of Devonshire, who got to know him well through serving on the special committee for Sudbury:

John was the prince of decorators, a scholar with a wonderful memory for whole rooms and the smallest details, and the best appreciator of beautiful places and things I have ever known. He had a clever way of making sure the right stuff or the right colour was chosen for covering furniture and making curtains for a National Trust house where a committee was meant to do the choosing. Knowing that he was the one who knew, he was determined, rightly, to make the decision, and he bowed to the committee like this: he produced several patterns and laid them out side by side. Picking up the first he said, 'I expect you think that blue is too pale,' the second, 'I'm sure you think that blue is not right for the date,' and the third, which he had already chosen, he would grasp in his hand and say with a note of triumph in his voice, 'And you, darling you, with your unerring eye, will say this one is perfect.'

On big jobs, particularly in the north of England, he liked to work with Bellerbys, the painters from York, and John White has written for me his account of John Fowler's approach to another committee:

He was a showman too, God bless him. I well remember a high-powered meeting bringing assorted aristocracy and upper echelons of the Trust together for mutual overawing.

As the wagon train of Rolls and vehicles of that ilk that were bringing them from a distant marshalling point swung into the drive way, John, who was talking to me in the room being decorated, disappeared.

The huge room filled with ten or twelve attending the meeting. Large voices were expressing excitement at the work so far, and mock petulance that John was not there to receive them. As if by magic or looking through the keyhole, at the right moment when the party was far enough down the room, the doors opened and John ... was standing there in profile ... almost a fencing pose. Then as the cries of 'John' echoed round the room, he sailed, still silent towards them, in that fragile walk of his, to dispense largesse to left and right and kiss strictly in the order of their coming.

If he had a deep distrust of all committees, and not just those of the Trust, it is also worth recording that he took great care to establish friendly relations with the Administrators of the houses where he was working. A client could be bullied, stampeded or even dropped, but he had a keen sense of the potentially difficult position of Administrators, who have day-to-day responsibility for the running and opening of houses but none for their appearance, a situation that on occasion can lead to friction and even bedevil the progress of work, whether restoration, decoration or simply rearrangement. He understood how easily their feelings could be bruised, and one of the then very young Representatives said it was an object lesson in sensitivity and tact to watch John establish cordial relations; needless to say he reaped the benefit in enthusiastic cooperation.

Private commissions gave him opportunities for the physical examination of houses but seldom for documentary research. He had neither the time nor the training for that; nor was there anyone at 39 Brook Street who could help him over it. An owner might show him designs for a house, but very few would have thought of showing him documents such as inventories or accounts. On only one occasion that I have come across was he shown an inventory and that was at Radburne. And it is only fair to remember the state of architectural history in England in the 1950s and early 1960s. Here the way *Country Life*'s articles on country houses have developed since the war is revealing. Before the war I doubt whether Christopher Hussey would have hunted for papers, and it was only when county record offices began to put private archives in order and catalogue them that it became possible to do detailed research; only in John Fowler's later years had interest extended beyond the building of a house to its furniture, and even then little work was being done on inventories and bills covering decoration. However, if someone in the Trust showed John a document he was invariably fascinated. When, for instance, he was working at Clandon, the inventory of 1778 became favourite reading at weekends: hours were spent going through it, puzzling over terms and the identification of rooms, wondering how servants coped with keeping fires going and details of that kind. It brought the house to life for him.

On the other hand the Trust's houses presented him with an exceedingly difficult challenge. To start with he was working in rooms that would be seldom if ever used either as they were intended to be in the past or in the present by people living in them, which was what interested him most. They were to be looked at only from certain angles and very briefly by visitors walking through them. Also it is very seldom that houses come to the Trust complete, and there is no way in which it is able to buy suitable pictures, furniture or fine carpets to fill gaps, so that he had to make the best of what he had got, a situation which did not occur in much of his private work. The small decorative objects and signs of daily living are often missing, and that makes it very difficult to give a sense of completeness or life to a room. Here flowers and plants can play an important part, and John Fowler, who had a great feeling for them and set considerable store by them both in his own cottage and in his work, devoted a great deal of thought to the types of plant that were suitable in scale and character. That might sound a simple matter, but, in fact, even the simplest plan proves difficult to maintain; and it is not at all easy to prevent rooms being spoiled by tortured arrangements of cut flowers or tight, bright pot plants in wretched containers.

Also, although I have only come to realize it quite recently, John Fowler was unable to achieve in the Trust's houses the kind of elaborate counterpoint that is so important in his private work, the counterpoint of colours and materials that ties rooms together and gives them that special but unexplained lift.

Of course, this rather negative picture is not the complete one. John Fowler's achievement lay in his ability not only to consider the work in hand but to see a house as a whole and to combine careful repair and restoration with new decoration based on or inspired by historical precedents; he was able to create a sense of unity and yet also variety of pace within a set of rooms; and he was able to see what was significant about a room and place pictures and furniture to advantage so that visitors would be able to direct

and concentrate their attention. The result was something mid-way between a true house and a museum, but that was inevitable when only two thirds of a room were available as showing space. St John Gore, who worked with John on numerous occasions, pointed out to me that at times in grand rooms for which there was little or no historical evidence available the Trust situation encouraged John to play up their architectural character almost too much to suit past occupants and certainly more than he would have done for a private client. In his private work a few clients egged him on so that he went too far in his decoration: with the Trust the reverse is true, and perhaps he became too abstract in his classicism.

There is a development between Shugborough and Clandon [LXXIV, LXXVII, LXXVIII, 186-188, 192], as will be explained, which derives in part from his strengthening position in the Trust and in part from his responses to outside influences and pressures. But he was never asked by the Trust to do a complete academic or archaeological restoration – that approach was not yet fully developed. However, the realist in him would have recognized that only on the rarest occasions is there both sufficient historical evidence as well as all the components to make it work. Virtually all Trust houses are reflections of the changes of history rather than complete statements of one owner preserved unaltered by succeeding generations.

If the work was difficult from John Fowler's point of view, and more difficult than anyone in the Trust probably appreciated, it is only right to consider the Trust's position too; and here it is important to realize how different was the situation in the late 1950s from that of the late 1960s and then the mid-1970s. House-opening had been established as part of the pattern of tourism and leisure by the late 1950s, but far fewer houses were then open to the public, the amount of access was more limited, as was the number of visitors, and their expectations were more modest. Government grant aid for repairs, which originated in 1953, was only just starting to make an impression, and the system of accepting houses and contents by the Treasury and handing them on to the Trust was also a novelty. The Trust itself was a small organization: in 1945 it had 93 buildings, 112,000 acres and 7,850 members; by 1965 the membership had increased to 157,000. In 1983 it had approximately 250 country houses, 486,000 acres, and 1,140,000 members.

However, in the late 1950s the pressure on the Trust was increasing, and Robin Fedden, who was then Historic Buildings Secretary, realized that he and his small

179. CLAYDON HOUSE, BUCKINGHAMSHIRE. THE NORTH HALL. The rococo decoration as photographed by *Country Life* in 1912 and painted with John Fowler's advice (but not supervision) in 1956-7. John Fowler repainted the room in 1976.

handful of Historic Buildings Representatives needed not only help with the interiors of some of the most important houses but help of a different kind as well. Also it was needed in houses where other agencies were involved, and there were special circumstances relating to funding.

That in turn introduces the broader subject of attitudes to interiors and to luxury trades in England. Positive preservation has been moulded by the Ancient Monuments approach, with its concentration on skilful repair of fabric, and there is really no tradition of looking after the interiors of major public buildings. The Court has only intermittently taken an interest in such things, and there is no tradition of royal or national support for the decorative arts and all the specialized trades involved with weaving, painting and gilding and metal working, as there has always been in France. Consequently interiors are invariably much less carefully and skilfully handled than structures. There is an almost puritanical reluctance to spend proper amounts of money on them. Gilding, for instance, is seen as not only an extravagance but even rather sinful. This basic attitude continues to run through all conservation funding. That in turn has made the Trust's task infinitely more difficult, because it has not only had to overcome the widespread opinion that decoration is by its very nature wasteful, but it has had to try to develop both a positive approach to it and also practical methods of getting work done.

John Fowler first helped the Trust at Claydon [179-81], which was given to the Trust in 1956 by the Verney family at the same time as the Historic Buildings

180. A DETAIL OF THE NORTH HALL AT CLAYDON. This shows it after it was painted, with
John Fowlers advice, in 1956–7.

181 (right). THE SALOON AT CLAYDON. John Fowler hung the walls with a copy of the Lydiard
Tregoze flock wallpaper.

182. PETWORTH HOUSE, SUSSEX. THE GRAND STAIRCASE. John Fowler painted the Victorian
balustrade and the dado of the staircase and the doors so that they would live more happily with
Laguerre's painting of the walls.

183. UPPARK, SUSSEX. THE SALOON. This early twentieth-century photograph shows the room
before it was first re-arranged by Lady Meade-Fetherstonhaugh in the early 1930s.

Council recommended what then seemed a very considerable grant towards its repair. The conjunction of
the gift and the grant aid led to the opening of the
house, and it was to make it suitable for opening that
John Fowler was asked to help. There was very little
furniture for the huge rooms on the ground floor, and
so it was a case of using colour to play up the architecture and make up for the sparseness of the rooms,
a situation he was to encounter on several occasions
in the future with the Trust. In addition, the work had
to be done on a shoestring.

It was five years before John Fowler was involved
with the Trust again. This time his job was to paint
the Victorian balustrade of the Grand Staircase at Petworth and the dado, so that they lived more happily
with the painting of the walls by Laguerre [182]. It

was the kind of task that he did with supreme skill,
while at the same time managing to disguise his own
part in it. Indeed, if one asked anyone what had John
Fowler done there, even those who knew his work well
would probably be defeated.

The same is true of Uppark, which of all the Trust's
houses is the one that had always meant most to him.
Somehow he saw it in 1930, or thereabouts, and it
made a deep and lasting impression on him; but how
that visit came about I cannot discover unless, as Mrs
Bilibin suggested to me, he was taken there by Ann
Talbot, one of the girls at Peter Jones, who was well
connected; nor do I know whether he went there in
the years immediately after the war. In the years after
it was given to the Trust in 1954 there was no money
and no inclination to do anything to the interior, but

184. THE STONE HALL AT UPPARK AS IT WAS IN 1940. By 1960 its decoration had become shabby, and so the walls were washed and the ceiling repainted under John Fowler's direction.

185 (right). THE LITTLE PARLOUR AT UPPARK IN 1940. One of the festoon curtains restored in the 1930s by Lady Meade-Fetherstonhaugh. By 1969, after Lady Meade-Fetherstonhaugh had left the house, John Fowler accepted that this room had to be repainted.

186. SHUGBOROUGH, STAFFORDSHIRE. THE ENTRANCE HALL BEFORE RESTORATION.
John Fowler was first consulted about how to remove the paint from the columns here and in the
saloon, which can be seen through the door, to reveal the original scagliola underneath. The results can
be seen in LXXIV.

187 (below) and 188 (right). THE RED DRAWING ROOM AT SHUGBOROUGH BEFORE AND
AFTER REDECORATION. It was here that John Fowler proposed the broad-striped wallpaper, which
he devised as an economical alternative to damask hangings. The colour was suggested by the curtains.
Not only does it help pull the room together but it gives it a vertical emphasis.

in 1960 the Trust received the offer of a grant of £2,000 towards redecoration, and, as a result, some re-painting was done under his direction, including the ceiling of the Stone Hall, while its walls and those of the staircase were washed. It is quite clear from the correspondence that the Historic Buildings staff always wished to do the minimum, and it was only in 1969 as a result of criticisms of the shabby state of the house after Lady Meade-Fetherstonhaugh's departure, the removal of pictures and furniture and the consequent dilution of the special spirit of the house that they were forced to review the position. Again John Fowler was consulted, and the record of his observations on the state of the rooms shows how cautiously he wished to proceed, with a strong emphasis on the washing of paint and retouching rather than repainting. Of the saloon, for instance, he said 'at all costs the grey and gold decoration of this room should be preserved. Walls and ceiling, however, should be retouched ...' And later he did more than he first intended in both the dining room and tapestry room, but that was forced on him by circumstances and was beyond his control. It seems that the only change he recommended was the restoration of the glazing bars in the windows. If Uppark was to him the *beau idéal* of the country house, it is the best example of his conservative approach: nowhere else did he have so much old decoration to hang on to.

After Claydon what became the next big job was at Shugborough, where there was a complicated administrative and financial situation. The house had been offered to the Treasury by the Trustees of the Earl of Lichfield in satisfaction of estate duty, but with only a small endowment, and the Trust was only able to accept it provided the Staffordshire County Council took a repairing lease and also financial responsibility for the showing; and the HBC recommended a grant for repair that was also to cover the redecoration of some of the main rooms. It was a case of the Trust having to redecorate virtually the whole house all at once while there was some money available and get it ready for opening. The house had been painted a uniform cream between the wars and so was flat-looking as well as tired; and while the Trustees handed over virtually all the contents, there was only just enough for the principal rooms, because too much had been sold in the course of the previous twenty or thirty years.

Christopher Wall, who had taken over as Historic Buildings Representative for that region in 1952 and was in charge of the operation, asked Robin Fedden whether he could consult John Fowler about how to clean paint off the columns in the entrance hall and saloon, which Christopher Hussey in his *Country Life* articles said had been scagliola. It was on that basis that John visited the house, and that led him to produce a choice of wallpapers for the drawing room and Bust Parlour and to direct George Oakes and Christopher Wall over the colours of other rooms, in particular the dining room. The limited nature of his initial involvement is important to remember, because while the ante-room and the library were quite deliberately left at the time and he was not responsible for the arrangement of the pictures or the furniture, it is the stamp of his colours and wallpapers that gives unity to what is a rather disjointed eighteenth-century house. The scagliola of the columns was revealed and the painting of the dining room and the papering of the drawing room were particularly successful. For the latter he devised a very broad self-striped paper in reds that he used again a good deal in other colours and Coles continue to make to special order.

Fairly soon after Shugborough was completed, similar negotiations began between Lord Vernon, the Treasury, the National Trust and Derbyshire County Council over Sudbury Hall [LXXV, LXXVI, 49, 50], near Derby, which was also in Christopher Wall's region; and again there was a great deal to do to the interior of the house, because virtually no decoration had been done for forty years, since Lord Vernon's parents had gone to live there and had sought the advice of Lenygon or a firm of that calibre over what was already a rather bare house. Here John Fowler was involved right from the start and there was a special committee to guide and help him, consisting of James Lees-Milne and the Duchess of Devonshire as well as Christopher Wall. James Lees-Milne and the Duchess provided some of the stimulus, discipline and interplay that John liked to have with private clients, but John's was the driving force both in the planning of colours, patterns and textures and in the arrangement of furniture and pictures.

It was a challenging job, because the scale of the house is as big as it is bold in character, and there were shortages of pictures other than portraits, furniture and smaller objects. So on the one hand John had to use colour and pattern to create a sense of progression in the house and make up for the bareness of most of the rooms, without being able to call on the support of much upholstery; and yet at the same time he wanted to keep existing schemes of decoration in several rooms. Thus on the entrance front, which faces north, he painted the walls of the Great Hall Italian pink and the walls of the staircase hall strong yellow to go with the staircase, which he stripped and painted white. However, he started quietly in the entrance hall, which is, in fact, the descendant of a screens passage, keeping the tones low by using the same wallpaper as he used in the dining room of the Duke of Hamilton's apartment at Holyrood but printing it in stone colours.

When he painted the staircase white instead of re-graining it as might have been expected, there was an outcry led by the late Ralph Edwards, who was no friend of his, but unfortunately the Trust had not left visible the evidence of white that had been found and on which the historical case was based. That was a serious mistake, because the white had come as a surprise to all who were interested and there were genuine doubts about it. Subsequently more historical information emerged that tended to confirm the evidence. Coupled with the trouble over the staircase there was considerable displeasure at the way John Fowler had painted the plasterwork in different tones of colour, which was an eighteenth-century idea but for which there was no evidence in the seventeenth century. Twelve years on, the rows are largely forgotten, and the results strike me as visually successful as I thought them in 1971.

To the south of the staircase hall lies the saloon, where John Fowler retained the existing, presumably nineteenth-century, decoration of the panelling; he merely washed it and added a little extra gilding to give more definition. The room had not been furnished in living memory and he did not attempt to soften it or make it look lived-in. Indeed he removed a pair of console tables. His only introduction was the rush matting, as much to give visitors a change of texture to walk on as for visual reasons. Sometimes his work is criticized for fussiness, but here, and, as will be seen, in some of the rooms at Clandon, he did nothing that would distract attention from the architectural decoration of the room.

In the nineteenth century the two adjoining rooms on the south front had been joined to form one more useful drawing room, but not only did that break the rhythm of the plan but there was an uncomfortable clash between the two ceilings, as can be seen [49]. So the rebuilding of the dividing wall was an important piece of restoration. However, the treatment of the rooms is decoration rather than restoration, and, since there was a shortage of contents, there was always a sense of stretch about this room, even when first done; and the decorative devices, which would

seem quite acceptable in a private house, do not convince visitors of the reality of the room's character. It does not work as a lived-in room, and, although such an effect is actually desirable at this point in the tour, there were neither the funds nor the things to achieve it. The library next door works rather better, but it lacks a proper focus. However, in both rooms it is the plasterwork and the form that matter most; the furnishing is of secondary importance.

Upstairs John Fowler restored the Queen's Bedroom, restoration in this case meaning having the damask wall hangings rewoven and cleaning the coats of paint off the top members of the overmantel to reveal the full height of the alabaster. The hangings of the bed were conserved and the existing undistinguished nineteenth-century damask window curtains were retained rather than replaced by new damask matching the wall hangings. In the gallery, after a great deal of discussion, it was decided to remove the nineteenth-century book shelving, which was not well made, and the seventeenth-century room was allowed to make its full statement, with a wave pattern of contemporary portraits on the long wall. The nineteenth-century colour scheme of the wainscot was retained and the cove and the ceiling were painted to tone with it.

To some people the house seems unlived-in and so lacking appeal, and purists, particularly rather literal-minded American students, find the freedom of treatment unacceptable and unintelligible; but while all involved with the house wish that it had survived more fully and richly furnished, it is surely better to accept it as it is rather than attempt to refurnish it with extraneous gifts and loans. Going to see it again, it struck me how skilfully John had pulled the house together and provided a series of marvellous experiences while also emphasizing the principal points about the building. A more academic approach might well have led to a flatter and deader feeling, and the stripped-down character of the house might have made it a disappointment. Certainly the house still feels fresh and undated: only a few minor details now seem 'decoratory' and irritating.

It was a big step for the Trust to turn to a decorator, and it was only the unique position that John Fowler had carved for himself and the respect that he had won from people like James Lees-Milne and Christopher Hussey that made it seem the right decision. In the winter of 1967/8 he started work at Clandon [LXXVII, LXXVIII, 189-192]. It was his most important job for the Trust, not only from the point of view of what he did to the house but for the impact it made

189. CLANDON PARK, SURREY. THE GREEN DRAWING ROOM AS IT WAS. The restoration
and rearrangement of the house in 1968-9 involved the removal of the state bed to its earlier situation,
recorded in the 1778 inventory, and the restoration of this room as the Green Drawing Room, again
recorded in the inventory. Its appearance after the completion of the work can be seen in
illustration LXXVII.

190. THE SALOON AT CLANDON IN THE EARLY 1960S. Before the restoration, the room was furnished rather half-heartedly and unsuccessfully as a drawing room.

191. THE SALOON AT CLANDON AFTER RESTORATION. It was possible to reveal the original colours on the ceiling and the entablature, and the walls were painted in three tones of blue on the basis of scrapes, while the overmantel was marbled to match the chimneypiece. The post-war curtains, made by Green and Abbott out of American army blankets dyed orange-red and violet, were retained.

192. THE PALLADIO ROOM AT CLANDON. John Fowler used colour to tie the original ceiling and the Louis Seize wallpaper together, and two different materials for the settees and chairs that survived from two different sets, yellow for the white and gold settees and red for the gilded chairs. The solution is not a historical one, but it makes visitors look at what matters most in the room.

LXXII. MRS DAVID BRUCE'S LONDON DRAWING ROOM. The draw curtains are of apricot silk with fan edges; the dress curtains of oyster-coloured faille trimmed with double ruffles scalloped and pinked; over them are draped valances with tails, also trimmed with double flounces, and they are caught by pairs of bows with choux in the middle. The pelmet boxes are painted in pale green and lilac stripes to reflect the clothes of the page in the centre of the picture between the windows.

LXXIII. UPPARK, SUSSEX. THE SALOON. John Fowler greatly admired the mellowness of this room and the way it had been redecorated in grey-white with elaborate gilding, presumably at the end of the eighteenth century. He insisted that it should be carefully cleaned, not repainted, and he restored only a little of the gilding, where it had worn completely away.

LXXIV. SHUGBOROUGH, STAFFORDSHIRE. THE ENTRANCE HALL AFTER RESTORATION. John Fowler was first consulted here about the way to remove the paint that had been put on the scagliola columns.

LXXV. SUDBURY, DERBYSHIRE. THE SALOON. The existing decoration of the panelling was merely washed and a little new gilding added to give the room greater definition. The room had not been completely furnished in living memory, and John Fowler did not attempt to do so.

LXXVI. THE LONG GALLERY AT SUDBURY. The nineteenth-century bookshelves [50] were removed, but the old colour scheme of the wainscot was washed and touched up; the cove and the ceiling were painted to tone with it.

LXXVII. CLANDON PARK, SURREY. THE GREEN DRAWING ROOM. A comparison with illustration 189 shows the extent of work in this room. The original green wallpaper found behind the damask was carefully cleaned piece by piece, re-backed and re-hung. This was the only room to have a good deal of old architectural gilding in it, and that was carefully retained; the fillet was re-gilded, and a little more gilding was added to improve the balance, particularly on the doors and the window architraves. The room lacked a set of suitable seat furniture, and so the furniture is a combination of Onslow and Gubbay pieces with a formal pattern of Onslow portraits built up to clothe the walls.

LXXVIII. THE HUNTING ROOM AT CLANDON. To support the shallow tapestries already in the room, John Fowler hung the walls with his diamond cloth; on the floor he used a Brussels carpet. On the walls he arranged some of Mrs Gubbay's collection of Chinese birds.

LXXIX. 117 EAST 62 STREET, NEW YORK, ABOUT 1970. Mario Buatta's drawing room, done under the influence of and in imitation of John Fowler.

on the staff and members of the Committee; also it brought him into a central position within the Trust, and that in turn gave him the opportunity to be such a powerful advocate on occasions, as with Erdigg, which we shall come to later.

Clandon had been a continuing worry to the Trust, because, despite considerable expenditure on structural repairs, the house struck people as gaunt, and there seemed to be no way of coping with that. Then in 1969 Mrs David Gubbay left the Trust her collection, together with a substantial endowment, on condition that it was placed in a country house near London. Clandon was obviously the most appropriate place for this bequest, but there was a problem of scale because Mrs Gubbay had lived in a small house since the early days of the war, when Sir Philip Sassoon, from whom she inherited many things, had given up Trent; and there she had to concentrate on objects of high quality but intimate size.

It is a most interesting experience to go back to Clandon almost fifteen years after it was completed, to see how John Fowler's work looks now, to see to what extent it has mellowed or dated and to consider how the house should be treated in the future. As at Sudbury, it is immediately striking how well the house has been looked after and how good is the condition of the decoration: it does not look tired or dated, and few things strike me as mistakes. Indeed what is so impressive is the way in which John directed the emphasis in each room, sometimes playing up the architecture, sometimes the contents, and how he strove to create a sense of visual unity out of a not altogether harmonious set of components.

His painting of the hall still seems a triumph of architectural painting, of subtle variations in the tones and textures of whites that not only gives added life to the whole concept and the ornamentation but makes up for the deliberate austerity of the furnishing. Italianate halls, particularly if they have such chilling marble floors, must always have been challenges to English owners, and different generations have responded to them in different ways, but there is no clue as to how the Clandon hall was furnished originally: the few things that used to be in it were much later arrivals. So, since there was no possibility of re-creating a balance of architecture, decoration and furniture, he concentrated on the architecture.

Then, as a contrast, he tried to make the neo-classical morning room deliberately different in mood as well as in style, combining Onslow family portraits and some of the furniture that Mrs Gubbay left the

Trust. After that comes a relatively bare and entirely Onslow room, the Palladio Room, with a fine bold original ceiling, an equally fine complete Louis Seize wallpaper that does not really relate to it, good neo-classical pier glasses but no tables to go with them, and the remains of two sets of contemporary seat furniture; and apparently late-eighteenth-century French curtains that must have been originally somewhere else. There was no obvious right way to go here, and he decided to use colour to tie ceiling and wallpaper together and two different materials for the settees and chairs, with the intention of preventing a too-empty room looking stiff. His solution is not a historical one, but it makes visitors look at what matters in the room, the plasterwork and the wallpaper.

The morning room, at the south-west corner of the house, is balanced by the Hunting Room at the south-east corner, and, although it is only apparent if it is thought about, he not only created a balance in the weight of contents in the two rooms but also a balance between the Onslow and Gubbay elements. The Hunting Room takes its name from a set of tapestries always in the house: they are fairly low in general tone and also rather shallow, and to cope with both John hung the walls with his cotton diamond cloth dyed brown and a green braid for a fillet, partly for reasons of cost but also no doubt because another line of gold would surely have emphasized the spread of the cotton. For the windows he made festoon curtains, an authentic eighteenth-century idea and even in the late 1960s still seldom seen in houses open to the public; and again for reasons of appearance as well as cost they are of printed cotton, in the brown and white seaweed, rather than in a formal silk material.

The axis changes in that room and next comes the Green Drawing Room, which had become the state bedroom. Here the balance of restoration and decoration was rather different. The first major decision was to remove the splendid early-eighteenth-century bed with its velvet chairs and place them once more in the original bedroom on the other side of the saloon, which had become a dull book room. When the wall hangings were taken down, it was discovered that the original green wallpaper survived more or less intact behind it, and John had an excellent job of restoration done on it. For the curtains festoons were made, but because they are against the light and seldom noticed they are of plain green cotton rather than silk. However, the room obviously lacked a set of suitable seat furniture, and so the furniture is a combination of Onslow and Gubbay pieces, with Onslow Regency chairs upholstered in green self stripes to run in with the walls.

The pace then changes once more in the saloon, where there is now virtually no furniture: it is an architectural space balancing the hall, with all attention concentrated on its plasterwork and on its remarkable colour scheme, which John discovered. Looking at the room now and also at the hall, my only regret is that he painted the doors in light tones rather than dark, which would surely have been correct. On the other hand the doors were made of a Victorian fiery red mahogany that was out of tone.

The last of the state rooms on which he did a lot of work (little was done in the dining room) is the state bedroom. Here the main structural alteration was to remove the too small chimneypiece and overmantel, which was a later insertion, and in terms of decoration the main contribution was to have the flock paper copied from a late-eighteenth-century fragment found in the room. John's interest in housekeeping led him to follow the 1778 inventory that listed case curtains for the state bed, and this became the first such bed in an English house to be properly protected once more.

It is all too easy to take John Fowler's control of tone for granted, but there is an interesting example of this at Clandon in the library, which the Trust was able to open to the public only several years after the main programme of the work. The room was re-painted *au Fowler* and the materials were from his shop, but the execution is not by him and the results fail to convince one visually, because the tones do not quite balance, the paint has not the right texture and the subtlety is lost. It is like the saleroom differentiation between a picture by Sir Peter Lely and one by Lely.

Clandon was only half an hour from John's cottage, and he was able to spend more time in it than in any house he ever worked in. He was often there much of both Friday and Monday, and hours were spent pottering in the attics sifting through piles of junk, while friends got frozen and exasperated waiting for him to be finally ready to leave. But I think that he grew to love what many people find a distinctly unlovable house. Certainly it became a stage on which he was able to explain his ideas and quite naturally consolidate his position in the Trust, although I am sure that he did not do that consciously. However, that was to be of great importance when it came to Erdigg, as I mentioned a little earlier.

Very soon after Mr Philip Yorke inherited Erdigg from his brother in 1966, he started to have discussions with the National Trust, but the negotiations were unbelievably difficult because of the physical and financial problems. By the time the Trust felt sufficiently confident to make a financial report, in early 1970, there were real doubts as to whether it was actually possible to save the house – was it possible, was it practical and where was the money going to come from? – and there was an understandable mood of despondency in the Trust about it. In fact the negotiations dragged on for three years more, and it was only during the course of 1973 that it was finally possible to start repair work.

In 1971, however, Merlin Waterson had taken over as Representative from Christopher Wall, who had nursed the problem for five years, and it fell to him to take John Fowler to see the house that year. By that time John had heard a great deal about Erdigg and he realized that it was full of things that would fascinate him, so he insisted on being taken to have a look.

His visit proved to be a crucial one, because he was so overwhelmed by the house that he sat in the car park outside Shrewsbury station and dictated impassioned letters to Lord Rosse, the chairman of the Properties Committee, and to Robin Fedden. These letters are worth quoting at length not only because they are so revealing of John but also because it was his pleas for Erdigg that finally persuaded the Trust to carry on negotiating against what still seemed insurmountable odds.

My dear Michael, I was taken yesterday by Merlin Waterson to see Erdigg. I have written at some length to R.[obin Fedden] about my reaction, which he may pass on to you. This is just to add my own fervent conviction that if Erdigg can be saved for the Nation I know of no other comparable house and its contents surviving since the tragically sad disintegration of Uppark. Forgive me, Michael, for butting in, but I must voice my own opinion, knowing full well that you of all people would get the point. I do assure you, I know it can be brought back in an utterly convincing way to its true magic.

To Robin Fedden he wrote:

Never since I first saw Uppark in 1930 have I been more moved by so much atmosphere. Of course the quantity and quality of the extraordinarily varied sets of gesso and lacquer furniture in particular dazzle one. The straightforward simplicity and superb joinery of the late seventeenth century panelling acts as a perfect foil to the furniture – but I could go on and on. It is unique. If the Trust could feel sure of the stability of the fabric, I am convinced one could create out of the sad chaos of neglect and discouragement something of

193. ERDIGG, CLWYDD. THE STATE BEDROOM. The bed was restored at the Victoria and Albert
Museum. The Chinese wallpaper, originally hung in 1771 and peeling off the walls as well as flaking
badly by 1970, was carefully removed, relined, remounted and put back by Graham Carr with advice
from John Fowler.

the rarest beauty. Its resurrection would, I am sure you
would agree, have to be handled most sensitively and an
emphasis on unapparent restoration, both of furniture, surfaces and fabrics, should be the aim. I do hope, dear Robin,
you and your Committee will make a supreme effort to do
everything possible to save Erdigg ...

In the end John was not able to go to Erdigg as
much as he would have liked, but even so his advice
was invaluable in many ways, particularly with regard
to the repair of the two chinese wallpapers [193, 194],
which was done by Graham Carr under his direction.
It was John's practical experience that enabled him to
realize what the Trust wanted and how to achieve it,
even if this was not always what he would have done

for a client. His appreciation of the atmosphere of a
house and his understanding of the importance of
practical as well as aesthetic details comes out in a
letter to Merlin Waterson written in the early stages
of planning work at Erdigg:

There are one or two things apart from what we all discussed which have struck me since and are nagging at me as
I feel *in part* responsible for the look of the final result. For
instance what about *the electric switches and plugs & points*
– all this if not v carefully done can enormously impair the
atmosphere of a place and I imagine you don't especially
want to continue the inept procedures of the former owner.
Are not minimal unnoticeable additions in the way of
switches etc the keynote of a tactful & sympathetic restoration? ...

194. A SECTION OF THE CHINESE WALLPAPER IN THE BEDROOM AT ERDIGG. The Chinese
painted scenes with English painted borders had to be removed from the old backing, relined and
reapplied to a new ground by Graham Carr.

What John and the National Trust were striving to do in the late 1960s and early 1970s, however, cannot be seen in isolation, because not only had architectural history come a long way in the previous twenty years and furniture history was developing at quite a pace, but the Department of Furniture and Woodwork at the Victoria and Albert Museum was coming to life again after the rule of Ralph Edwards, first under Delves Molesworth, who was its Keeper from 1954 to 1966 and came in from the Department of Sculpture,

and then until 1984 under Peter Thornton, formerly in the Department of Textiles. Also it was to be assisted by two inventions, the photocopier, which made it easier to gather together copies of country house accounts and inventories, and the polaroid camera, which made it much easier to do *aide-mémoire* photography. Together they made it possible to build up a research archive in the Department. That in turn encouraged members of the Department to ask much more direct questions about how houses were used and how they were arranged. One of the first such places was Spencer House in 1966-7, when a visit to the late Earl Spencer at Althorp prompted a whole range of questions about it which led to articles on the house in *Apollo* in 1968. About the same time the Department began to ask itself similar questions about Osterley and Ham, which had come to be regarded as extensions of the Museum galleries rather than as self-contained entities; and by June 1970 their plans for Osterley were sufficiently far advanced for a member of the Department to explain what was being done there in a couple of articles in *Country Life*.

Naturally the Trust and the Department have close contact both officially and unofficially, and its staff are often asked questions on matters of fact as well as points of view. Here Erdigg was to prove as significant, because both John and members of the Department made valuable contributions, and the Representative had to weigh up their different attitudes. The Department had first got involved there in 1968, when it persuaded Mr Yorke to allow the Museum to remove the state bed before any further damage occurred and carry out at its own expense what proved to be a most remarkable job of conservation on the understanding that if the circumstances were ever right the bed would go back to the house. In fact the Department would have liked to have seen a more far-reaching restoration, indeed reconstruction on the main floor, so that the state bedroom would have been restored to its original position. That, however, was contrary to the Trust's thinking, and the final result was on the one hand less archaeological and on the other hand less artistic, in that the existing character of the house was thought more significant and special and also more authentic than complete visual balance. On the other hand the formality of the furniture arrangement owes a good deal to Museum thinking.

It was a coincidence that John Fowler should have been very active on the Trust's behalf just at the moment when the Woodwork Department was anxious to explore new avenues and, being full of enthusiasm, keen to get its interpretation across; but again it has to be remembered how slender was the literature at that stage. Indeed one reason why John and I wrote *English Decoration in the Eighteenth Century* was that there was so little. By 1968, when I stayed with him for the first time, I had been a member of the Trust's Historic Buildings Committee for about three years, and, largely through getting to know Christopher Wall, at that time Representative in the Midlands, and working with him a little at Shugbor-

ough and rather more at Sudbury, I became aware of the need for a basic book on the history of decoration for Representatives. Then, as a result of getting to know John, came the idea of collaborating with him so that his experience would be set down on paper before it was too late – he and I were both aware that he might not live to complete the book – and naturally my thinking was considerably influenced by the work of the Woodwork Department, as is apparent in several sections of the book.

Since Erdigg the Department has played a constructive role in several National Trust houses where work has being going on, particularly at Charlecote and Cragside, but it would be wrong to disguise the fact that there have often been differences of view about both what the Trust has done and what the Department has done; and that is healthy. However, for a time that made it more difficult to appreciate the nature of John Fowler's contribution. On the one hand the growth of academic interest naturally influenced the younger members of the Trust's historic buildings staff, which had the result of strengthening their resolve that he should not go too far, and on the other it strengthened the Trust's resolve to strike its own balance between archaeological and painterly approaches and between restoration and decoration in its handling of interiors.

It was largely through what John Fowler did for the Trust in the late 1960s and 1970s and his influence that the Trust has achieved such a high standard of presentation in its houses and continues to set a high standard in what it intends to achieve. At times this causes a certain envious resentment among private owners and among those involved with government funding, who feel that the Trust is too ambitious and spends too much. The standard, however, is not just to do with restoration and decoration but is bound up with conservation and housekeeping too, and here John's long-standing fascination with housekeeping and how houses had been run became a positive influence on the Trust at a crucial moment.

John Fowler's contribution to the Trust, however, cannot be seen just in terms of the work that he did for it. What is just as important is his broader influence. That was admirably put to me by St John Gore:

What John had done for all of us was to arrest our interest and clarify our understanding of the past, of a house, the use of rooms, their colours, how they were cared for, the furniture and how surfaces and upholstery should be treated. The step to the archives only added a further element to a principle already established.

CHAPTER ELEVEN

ASPECTS OF JOHN FOWLER'S INFLUENCE IN ENGLAND AND AMERICA

It is always fascinating to trace the influence of any important artist or designer and to consider not only why he fits into his own time and his ideas strike a chord, but also to notice how others pick up, imitate and develop those ideas. In the case of John Fowler his influence is particularly interesting, because unlike most other successful designers in the third quarter of the twentieth century he never sought publicity. For most of his life he worked for a narrow circle of clients, whose privacy he respected; he seldom asked permission to have what he had done for them photographed; and he was even cautious about whom he allowed to have certain special designs. He was, of course, aware of the strong appeal of the exclusive and of the air of mystery that built up round him; and he was not averse to encouraging that. However, his attitude was also partly defensive, and that fused with an innate nervousness and a fearful disdain for all kinds of business, including the commercializing of his designs.

Nevertheless, his post-war work has proved to be the basis of virtually all traditional decoration carried out in England over a period of over thirty years, in terms not only of the overall look but of much of the detail as well. There has been an enormous amount of conscious copying of his decoration and probably just as much unconscious, and both continue. Moreover his influence has not been confined to England: it has become significant in America too.

He was almost certainly the first decorator in Eng-

land to have what can only be called an intellectual approach to the relationship of decoration to life and to be seriously interested in the whys and wherefores of historic interiors. He became a link figure between a private circle and a public world: the private circle of clients who saw their houses as a frame for their lives, with restoration playing a secondary role to that of decoration, and the public world which now sees that kind of life as having come virtually to an end and the roles of restoration and decoration reversed. More elusive but also important was his influence on his friends who were not decorators, but who have made or are making contributions in other fields. He was not only excellent company and a marvellous talker, but he wanted his friends to share whatever he had or whatever he knew, and he was a natural teacher, not least because he helped people to think about and analyse what they were looking at. There are a remarkable number of people who recognize their debt to him for having broadened their minds in visual and historical matters. Alan Gore, who met him in 1949, has written of how John began 'the laborious task of opening my eyes and teaching me that there are other things than the works of Le Corbusier and Mies van der Rohe'. And Miss Rosemary Amies said to me: 'He was someone that one could not have contact with without being influenced by him.'

However, in considering *how* John Fowler's influence came about, it is also necessary to try to work out *why*. He was not only a bridge figure in a period of rapid social and economic change, but he saw him-self as the last representative of *haute couture* in de-coration in England; and, while some might see that as a comment on other decorators, it is more signifi-cant as a comment on clients and their attitudes to and expectations of life. The post-war situation, with a declining number of domestic servants and gardeners, forced people to rethink their way of life and work out what they wanted to retain and what discard; and the process made them much more aware of their physical surroundings. Kitchens and heating systems had to be revolutionized, but at the same time tradi-tional appearances became infinitely more precious. In food there was one revolution that started with Eliza-beth David's *A Book of Mediterranean Food*, first pub-lished in 1950. And what she did for her readers, John Fowler did for decoration; but, of course, with him the process took much longer to work through, and the influence has been indirect. However, because 'humble elegance' was always the basis of his approach, it con-tinues to be relevant half a century after he began to develop it. People who did not know him often think of him now just in terms of his grander decoration. They misunderstand the fundamental point that, while he played up to splendid rooms, it was not a case of watering down in simple rooms; and what was origin-ally a post-Slump style can be adapted for use today, as is shown by Laura Ashley.

John Fowler was the right man for his time, but his influence came about in different ways. For forty years there has been the shop at 39 Brook Street and for most of that time its window. When he found the building in 1943, he took a gamble on it not being bombed, because he realized it was a perfect combi-nation of sophistication and modesty: a series of charming rooms [195] led off a Georgian staircase hall reminiscent of a modest country house, but there was one grand room at the back, designed by Wyat-ville [196]. The house has none of the grandeur of, let us say, Lenygon's house in Old Burlington Street, yet that suited the firm, because it never had the capital to invest in 'important' furniture; and anyway that was not what John Fowler liked best. It was architectural enough, however, to show off English and French painted furniture and pretty objects to advantage. And in days gone by the understated character of the place was apparently reflected in the prices of many of the objects. A great many people must have improved their eye through going there or just gazing in through the windows.

It would be interesting to know how many people went to John Fowler, as opposed to the shop, as a result of seeing photographs of his work in magazines and whether any of his important commissions came about in that way. *Vogue* published occasional articles, but it was *House and Garden* that was his most regular supporter. Some of the houses where he worked in the 1950s and 1960s were illustrated in *Country Life*, but the references to decoration were invariably brief, and often his name was not even mentioned. That practice at *Country Life* reflected the still widespread suspicion of decoration. Even as late as 1971 it was regarded as an unsuitable subject for extended comment in the magazine and gave rise to complaints to the editor.

Many of the clients of the shop and generations of pretty girls who have worked there have picked up part of the message, but it was the succession of assist-ants after the war who were in the best position to learn from him; and one way his influence has fanned out is through what they have done in the years after they left him. 'Best position', however, is really a mis-nomer, because it was an impossible job to be John Fowler's assistant. While he loved instructing and in-forming, he was unconscious of the fact that he re-sented rivalry close at hand; and there was a great deal of bullying and putting down of assistants, while at the same time he demanded total attention from them. Some submitted, and some stood up to him; but none could be regarded as his heir in matters of style or understanding. Indeed the story of John and his assist-ants seems to me almost the saddest part of his work-ing life.

On the other hand those with him in the 1950s whom I have talked to recognize how much they learned from him and remember with gratitude the good times as well as the horror of the bad. Keith Irvine was one of those who stood up to him and in 1959 he left to make his own career in America. He recalls how John would train his eye and memory: if, on a visit to a client, John spotted anything of interest on the way, the car would be stopped and Keith Irvine would be made to do a sketch and then later a draw-ing; and on the next visit the drawing would be checked against the subject. Similarly if John had im-parted some nugget of information that he thought ought to be remembered, later in the day he would check that it had been absorbed correctly.

Young assistants, however, could not provide all the back-up he needed, and he was always dependent on a handful of people. In the days of 292 it had been Joyce Shears and Gwen Jervis, and later he depended more than he realized on Imogen Taylor and George

195. SYBIL COLEFAX AND JOHN FOWLER'S SHOP AT 39 BROOK STREET IN 1947.

Oakes. Imogen Taylor joined the firm in 1949 after coming back to London from Paris, and in 1954 she was promoted to being John's assistant, a mission she fulfilled until 1966, when she became a partner in the firm. How she coped with him is a matter of wonder, and perhaps it was only because she is a generous, calm and balanced person who was fond of him and appreciative of his gifts but not possessive that she was able to ride out the rough water and laugh afterwards. From early days she in her turn was appreciated by his clients, and in the end she inherited a number of them, but she never allowed herself to appear as any kind of rival. Indeed he must have valued her calming influence on many a potentially explosive situation.

George Oakes's role was equally difficult but essential in a different way. In the mid-1950s John Fowler was looking for a decorative artist to assist him on certain jobs, and having in 1956 met George Oakes, who had been trained at the St Martin's School of Art, he asked him to collaborate with him on the wallpaper for the Palladian Room and the *trompe l'œil* decoration of the Gothick Room at Haseley for Mrs Lancaster [XIII–XV]. Stylistically and temperamentally Oakes was the right person. Not only did he love the same kind of light, understated painting, but he was able to understand what John had in mind and develop his sketches into full schemes of painted decoration and also work out designs for materials and carpets if

196. WYATVILLE'S RECEPTION ROOM AT THE BACK OF 39 BROOK STREET IN 1947. The room was used as the main showroom for the shop until it was given to Mrs Lancaster in 1958 and transformed by her and John Fowler into the Yellow Room seen in illustration XVI.

they were not straight copies. Also he did most of the mixing of colours on big jobs, unless painters like Bellerbys were involved.

John Fowler's influence on people, however, was much broader than it was on the people working in the firm. There are all those whom he came into contact with over his jobs, architects, specialist painters, specialist suppliers. Among architects, Philip Jebb, whom he first met in 1958 and with whom he worked on numerous occasions, often on his recommendation, is perhaps the outstanding example. Relations between decorators and architects tend to be fraught, because an architect, invariably, resents a decorator, feeling (usually quite wrongly) that he has equally good

colour sense, but Philip Jebb, the most generous of characters, saw the point of John's work right from their first meeting and at the same time was able to satisfy his sense of detail.

Among specialist painters there are not only the friends from Peter Jones and 292 days, such as Jean Hornak, but a number of younger people, among them Christopher Hobbs. He had been making props for the theatre and films when he was introduced to John by Lady Rosse in 1965/6. He has an original talent as a decorative painter and modeller, but also an unusual ability to find original solutions to all kinds of problems that occur in decoration. When, for instance, John needed light-weight busts or vases for brackets in the Bruces' London drawing room, Christopher Hobbs modelled vases in fibre glass and painted them in a delft style. And in the dining room of the same apartment it was he who painted a *trompe l'œil* portrait on a jib door to balance an existing picture.

Artistic influence is always a complex matter, and, whereas there are many aspects of decoration that are obviously indebted to John Fowler and many decorators are strongly influenced by him, David Hicks is not the one who would immediately spring to mind. So his acknowledgement of his debt is of particular interest, because he has been the most influential British interior designer in the generation after John Fowler and has approached the challenge of interiors and design in a different way. He remembers being enchanted by the windows of the shop in Brook Street when he was a seventeen-year-old art student in 1946, by the combination of understatement, prettiness and attention to detail; and then he was bowled over again two years later when he met Mrs Lancaster at Kelmarsh and saw that way of decorating for the first time. That made him want to meet John Fowler all the more, an ambition he realized about two years later. Soon afterwards he became one of John's lodgers at 292, and he tried to persuade John to take him on; but John would not agree, and he even tried to dissuade him from decorating and stick to painting. David Hicks, however, was determined; and also he knew that he had to be different from John and establish his own style. At the same time he recognizes that he learned much about the basic principles from talking to him and studying his work, about scale and proportion, about strength and boldness of line and about quality of detail, and about comfort.

Another, perhaps unexpected, figure is Terence Conran. In 1958 he and John Fowler discussed the production of a line of furniture. In the end nothing came of it, but the idea is worth recording, because it is revealing of John's approach both to people and the role of design. The proposal came from Michael Astor, Mrs Lancaster's cousin, for whom John had already worked in his two houses, as had Terence Conran to a lesser extent. It was observant of Mr Astor to see how their talents might be combined to commercial advantage, with Terence Conran providing the main thrust of the design and business skill while benefiting from John Fowler's acuteness of eye for both line and finish and his general experience. They discussed the scheme for about a year, with John organizing visits to the Victoria and Albert Museum and to Uppark as well as rounds of antique shops so as to develop

thoughts about design. Terence Conran still looks back on the experience with gratitude and regrets that nothing came of it, remembering in particular how surprising it was that John was so interested in life below stairs and in simple things.

Not only did John teach and influence people, but he often put work in their way when they needed it most, and he had a way of looking out for receptive people who might have a talent that he could release and encourage while remaining very economical with praise. The result was that many people started successful careers of their own, with special skills that are still much in demand. He had a remarkable ability to stimulate those working for him. As John White has written to me: 'Of the decorators I have worked with, I have never known one with ... [such an] ability to involve and stimulate the men actually doing the work.'

His clients too learned a great deal from him, not only about decoration but about gardening and about the eighteenth century. Lady Annan, for whom he worked when her husband was Provost of King's College, Cambridge, wrote: 'His clients could learn almost as much as his staff if they were prepared to put up with almost the same amount of bullying. To be Fowlerized just once was an education for a lifetime of doing up houses.'

Often the dividing line between friends and clients was completely blurred, because virtually all the good clients became friends, and that is particularly so in the case of Mrs Paul Mellon. Over the years she bought a good deal from John and in a roundabout way he decorated their house in New York, but the help he gave Mrs Mellon was more important to her than what he actually decorated for her: what she valued, and still values, is their conversations, mainly about houses and gardens. Mrs Mellon first met John in 1948, having been told of him by Mrs Maugham's daughter, Liza, now Lady Glendevon; also she knew Nancy Lancaster, who had only recently bought the business. Her old school friend, Mrs Henry Parish, had arranged to sail on the same boat, going over to discuss a business tie-up with Nancy and so meet John. Thus they got to know him at the same time. Although Mrs Mellon continued to see John when she was in England afterwards, he did not do any decoration for her until they rebuilt their house in New York, and it was Mrs Mellon's hope that she would be able to persuade him to cross the Atlantic. But she was unable to do so. The work had therefore to be done in London and the painters were sent over to take instruction from him. Like the young architect, what she values was his influence on her understanding, and even now when confronted by a problem, her natural reaction is to wonder what John would have suggested. Naturally in talking to her what comes out is his influence on her, but I have no doubt that the traffic was not just one-way: he would have appreciated her understanding and in turn been stimulated by her.

It was a pity that John never went to America, because he would have found there confirmation of what he liked best, in simple houses and furniture, materials and use of colour; but if he had gone it would not have been a voyage into the completely unknown, because he was aware of eighteenth-century American design and liked its cleanness and purity. Keith Irvine remembers John showing him details of American things in books. Also, of course, Nancy Lancaster had told him much about the houses of Virginia.

In considering John Fowler's influence both in England and in America it is, of course, essential to bear in mind his partnership with Nancy Lancaster, because quite apart from their influence on and stimulation of each other, a good deal of John's influence was tied up with her own, what he did for her and so through her. After all it was admiration for her houses, both before and after the war, that brought many clients to the shop, and ultimately it is her role in the business that explains his influence in America.

What is extraordinary about his influence in America is the involved personal way in which it has come about. Here, apart from Nancy Lancaster, the key person has been Mrs Henry Parish, now almost the senior figure in American traditional decoration. Mrs Parish's family had a summer house in Maine close to that of Mrs Lancaster's aunt, Mrs Charles Dana Gibson, and although the two families did not quite match in generation, it was there that Mrs Parish and Mrs Lancaster first met. Mrs Parish, whose approach to decoration has been based on her family's houses in New York and New Jersey, started to decorate before the Depression, and, during the war she moved her business from New Jersey to New York. It was there that Nancy Lancaster contacted her afterwards, proposing a link up with Colefax & Fowler. What Nancy had in mind was a clever business idea, but it proved not to be legal because of currency restrictions, and so it petered out. However, it was as a result of discussing the business with John Fowler, who at the time was only a name on a piece of paper to her, that Mrs Parish immediately appreciated that he was a unique figure who shared many of her enthusiasms and got to know him as a friend; and she readily acknowledges

the extent of his influence on her. She used to come to London every year, and not only was the Brook Street shop one of her main ports of call for furniture and materials, but she invariably spent a weekend with John at his cottage; he always was willing to share his knowledge and tell her how anything was done or what was its special point. As she said to me, 'John was a student. None of the rest of us are.'

However, the pattern of John's influence does not stop there, because Mrs Parish's business has had its own considerable direct and indirect influence in America. But it is difficult for me to write of that, because I have not seen enough American decoration.

On the other hand John Fowler's own work was little known in America in the late 1950s and early 1960s, and a young would-be decorator like Mario Buatta, as a student at the Parson School of Decoration in 1961, did not yet know his name. However, a little later he saw photographs of Mrs Lancaster's rooms in Avery Row and then coincidentally he went to work for Keith Irvine, John's former assistant who had moved to New York. It was while Mario Buatta was with Keith Irvine in 1962–3 that he heard about Colefax & Fowler and about Nancy Lancaster and John Fowler, and so when he came to England to look at country houses in 1964 he went to call on John. After that he came over two or three times every year, to shop, to see country houses and to see John, becoming a regular visitor to the cottage. Indeed on about ten occasions he was a substitute for Father Christmas there, flying in with absurd jokes and making the house rock with laughter. Gradually he absorbed every detail of the Fowler look, but what might strike some people as shame-faced copying was based not only on admiration but on affection. As with so many people who fell under John's spell, Mario Buatta used to discuss his own work, particularly in his own apartment, with John, who took on the role of academic supervisor; when in 1968 he was doing what he describes as 'a real copy-cat room' in yellow for himself at 117 East 62nd Street, John gave him a chip of the Avery Row yellow paint to copy, and later a piece of cornice to get copied in America for a job in New Jersey.

Mario Buatta's first work appeared in *House and Garden* in 1969 and the East 62nd Street room was illustrated in January 1970. Subsequently that room was illustrated a great deal, in *The New York Times* on 27 September 1970, in *Colliers Year Book* in 1971 and the *Architectural Digest* in 1974. At the time it first appeared the English country house look was little known in America except to those who had direct experience of English houses; nor was it widely fashionable. But that first article and all subsequent ones picked up that aspect, and helped to establish the look in America. Quite deliberately Mario Buatta stuck to what was readily identifiable as his decoration in what he allowed to be illustrated, and so most of the published photographs are of his own apartments – he moved in 1976 – or what he did, usually with his own possessions, in decorators' show houses at exhibitions. Other decorators used to laugh at him coming with all his ruffles and bows, but he established them and soon others were copying them.

I do not suppose that it is realized in America that almost every aspect of the English look actually derives from John Fowler's own work. It has become fashionable for its sense of ease and comfort and for its associations; and also because it is known to have received the blessing of people who are regarded in America as oracles of taste, even if it is forgotten how long ago those people first got to know John and established their friendships with him.

It is surely an extraordinary story and not only a fascinating illustration of how influences and fashions work but also of how English and American threads intertwine.

ILLUSTRATION ACKNOWLEDGEMENTS

Black and white

The author would like to thank the following owners for allowing objects to be photographed or for supplying photographs: 11: The Duke of Rutland; 18, 39, 80: The National Trust; 86: Trustees of the Chatsworth Settlement; 87: Private Collection; 102: The Duke of Wellington; 172, 176, 178: Colefax & Fowler Ltd; 173: Trustees of the Victoria and Albert Museum; 174: Mr Hardy Amies; 175

All photographs were supplied by *Country Life* except the following: 16, 17: Trustees of the British Museum; 172, 175-8 Timothy Beddow; 86: Trustees of the Chatsworth Settlement; 87: A. C. Cooper; 101: Courtauld Institute (by courtesy of the Duke of Wellington, Stratfield Saye, Reading, Berkshire); 174: Mark Fiennes; 41: Greater London Council; 25, 40: Mrs Christopher Hussey; 85, 91, 188, 190: A. F. Kersting; 76, 107, 129, 132, 133, 145-52, 195-6; Millar and Harris; 18, 19, 39, 183: The National Trust; 167-8, 170-71: Mr Eddie Ryle-Hodges; 144, 157: Paul Tanqueray; 173: Trustees of the Victoria and Albert Museum; 118, 124-6: Mr Michael Tree;

155-6: H. M. Tennant; 112-14: The Hon. Desmond Guinness; 180: Edwin Smith; 93: Mrs Alan Palmer; 182, 191-2: Jeremy Whitaker

Colour

The author would like to thank the following owners for allowing objects to be photographed or for supplying transparencies: LXIX, LXX, LXXI: Reproduced by gracious permission of Her Majesty the Queen; LXXIX: Mario Buatta; I: Dowager Marchioness of Cholmondeley; LXI, LXII, LXIV, LXV, LXVI, LXVII, LXVIII: Colefax & Fowler; XLVII: Stanley Falconer; XVII, XVIII: The Hon. Desmond Guinness; IV, V, XLVIII, XLIX: Mrs Christopher Hussey; XXII, XXIII, XXV, LXIII: Mrs Hourigan; XII: Mr Michael Tree; VI, VII: Mrs P. A. Tritton.

All photographs were taken by Tim Beddow except the following: LXXIX: Authenticolour; IV, V, VIII, IX, XI, XX, LXXV, LXXVI: *Country Life*; XLIV: Her Majesty's Stationery Office; XVI: Interiors (James Mortimer); X: Fritz von der Schulenberg; LXXIII, LXXIV, LXXXVIII: Jeremy Whitaker.

INDEX

References to illustrations are in square brackets